Form-Analysis and Exegesis: A Fresh Approach to the Interpretation of Mishnah

with special reference
to Mishnah-tractate
Makhshirin

JACOB NEUSNER
University Professor
Professor of Religious Studies
The Ungerleider Distinguished
    Scholar of Judaic Studies
Brown University

University of Minnesota Press
Minneapolis

Copyright © 1980 by the University of Minnesota.
All rights reserved.
Published by the University of Minnesota Press,
2037 University Avenue Southeast,
Minneapolis, Minnesota 55414

Library of Congress Cataloging in Publication Data

Neusner, Jacob, 1932-
    Form-analysis and exegesis.
    Includes bibliographical references and index.
    1. Mishnah. Makhshirin—Commentaries. I. Title.
BM506.M23N48   296.1'2306   80-17616.
ISBN 0-8166-0984-5
ISBN 0-8166-0985-3 (pbk.)

The University of Minnesota
is an equal-opportunity
educator and employer.

Form-Analysis and Exegesis:
A Fresh Approach
to the Interpretation of Mishnah

For
Milton and Lisa Gwirtzman

Transliterations

Hebrew		Latin
א	=	ʾ
ב	=	B
ג	=	G
ד	=	D
ה	=	H
ו	=	W
ז	=	Z
ח	=	Ḥ
ט	=	Ṭ
י	=	Y
כ ך	=	K
ל	=	L

Hebrew		Latin
מ ם	=	M
נ ן	=	N
ס	=	S
ע	=	ʿ
פ ף	=	P
צ ץ	=	Ṣ
ק	=	Q
ר	=	R
שׁ	=	Š
שׂ	=	Ś
ת	=	T

Preface

Mishnah, the basic law code of Judaism, produced ca. 200, is an exceedingly difficult text; this book, in the nature of things, is not easy either. What I try to do here is to explain and extensively exemplify my approach to Mishnah, specifically, my methods of reading and explaining the document. The issues of this ancient Judaic holy book are subtle, and its modes of expression exceedingly tight and elusive. The approaches I have devised, for their part, flow from my adaptation of contemporary conceptions of form-critical and historical-critical interpretation. These conceptions are not accessible without a good measure of reflection and patient thought.

The importance of investing intellectual effort in Mishnah derives from Mishnah's centrality in the formation of that kind of Judaism paramount from the Mishnah's time to ours. Whether the effort required to follow what I have to contribute to the interpretation of Mishnah, and to the solution of certain long-standing problems, is commensurate with the result will be settled by the reader, I expect, only when the work is done. Then, in comparing what is proposed here with what is available in other commentaries to the same text, the reader will judge. I may only express the hope that the reward will be in accord with the effort. But at the outset I state that the effort required to grasp what is offered here is not going to be negligible.

The organization and purpose of the book should be explained briefly. After stating what I believe to be many of the problems that anyone proposing to study Mishnah will confront (Chapter 1), I set forth the solutions I have devised for some of those problems. The solutions, which focus upon exegetical method, are presented in two ways. First, at the beginning and end of each chapter of Parts I, II, and III, I explain in general and theoretical terms the methods to be followed for the several purposes of study. Second, in the shank of each chapter, I illustrate these methods through the study of a particular tractate. The beginnings and endings are entirely fresh. The shank is generally drawn from my *History of the Mishnaic Law of Purities* XVII, which material has been thoroughly reorganized, revised, and reworked, particularly in Parts II and III.

The sequence of problems is clear from the foregoing statement of the contents; we proceed systematically to examine the Mishnah-tractate at its smallest complete units of thought, (Part I) the individual pericopae. After an important digression (Part, II) we go on to see how these are formed into groups (Part III) and made to relate to, and respond to, one another. Finally, we seek to discover how the tractate as a whole fits together (also Part III), thus; to resort to a common metaphor, trees, thickets, groves and forest.

The digression, Part II, deals with problems of Mishnah-study as they are presented to us not by the logic and structure of the document and its literary and conceptual problems, but by the history of their prior study. Students must master a sizable corpus of Mishnah-commentary if they wish to understand the document in all of its rich potentialities. I have therefore to relate what is presented in this book to those other, established approaches awaiting careful and reverent attention. This is done in Part II.

First, all earlier commentators to Mishnah who knew Tosefta made ample use of that document. (Likewise, for tractates to which there is a Talmud, all commentators regard what the Talmud has to say about a pericope as definitive, indeed nearly exhaustive, of its meaning.) So I introduce an example of how Tosefta treats the most difficult problem of the tractate, the interpretation of M. Makshirin Chapter One. This allows me to treat the chapter as a whole.

Second, having presented my own view of how the chapter is to be read, at great length I treat the problems and their solutions as proposed by the great commentators of the established exegesis of Mishnah. My purpose is not to criticize what they have to say, let alone systematically to "refute" their ideas. The opening chapter of this book explains what is new in my approach. Whether or not the specific explanations of given pericopae converge with, or differ from, what has been said earlier about the same matter is immaterial, indeed, uninteresting. My purpose is only to make sure that students of this book have a decent appreciation for the accomplishments of the great masters of Mishnah-study, and for this purpose an account of the problems and how they are solved seems to me ample treatment.

As I shall explain in a moment, what is done in this book for Makhshirin already has been done by myself and my students for the entirety of Mishnah-Tosefta. I should not have written this book, if I did not expect that what I already have done is going to be redone, not once but many times, by successive generations, who will take up my methods and refine them, reconsider my results and criticize and improve them. Thus I think it important not only to present the results, but to explain the methods by which results are attained. It is especially important to do so in a way conveniently accessible to the students, some of whom, I hope, soon will make my work obsolete by doing not only different, but better, things.

Written at the suggestion of Richard Abel, Editor of the University of Minnesota Press, this book presents a systematic, exemplification and a brief exposition of some of the methods I have created, or borrowed and adapted from the study of other ancient literature, for the critical exegesis of Mishnah. My purpose is to spell out, through a protracted example, the form-analytical approach, results, and methods, of my *History of the Mishnaic Law of Purities* (Leiden, 1974-1977) I-XXII, *Holy Things* (Leiden, 1978-1979), I-VI, *Women* (Leiden, 1979-1980), I-V, *Appointed Times* (Leiden, 1980-   ) I-V, and *Damages* (Leiden, 1981-   ), I-V, and my students' parallel studies on *Agriculture*.[1] In those works are pro-

[1] At this writing, only one of these commentaries has reached print: Richard S. Sarason, *A History of the Mishnaic Law of Agriculture*. Section Three. *A Study of Tractate Demai*. Part One. *Commentary* (Leiden, 1979: E. J. Brill). Work on the other tractates is well advanced. In manuscript at this time are the following: Tzvee Zahavy, *Berakhot*; Irving R. Mandelbaum, *Kilayim*; Leonard Gordon, *Shebiit*; Alan Peck, *Terumot*; Martin Jaffee, *Maaserot*; Peter Haas, *Maaser Sheni*; Abraham Havivi, *Hallah* Chapters One and Two; David Eisenman, *Hallah* Chapters Three and Four; Howard Essner, *Orlah*; Margaret Wenig Rubenstein, *Bikkurim* Chapters One and Two. (Peah will receive its commentator in 1980). It is expected that the monographs of Essner, Rubenstein, Havivi, and Eisenman will be

vided analyses and results for both the exegesis and interpretation of the whole of Mishnah. There too are presented new methods for the reconstruction of the world-view of the framers of Mishnah, in its historical unfolding over nearly two centuries. But here I deal only with the exegetical side of the work.

In this textbook my intention is to explain how the exegesis is carried out. By explaining and exemplifying some of the methods of the larger work, I shall make it possible for others to develop their own approaches to Mishnah's concrete problems of interpretation and their solution. Of still greater potential·value, the same sorts of approaches, with obvious adaptations, may prove useful in the exegetical form-analysis of other rabbinic documents of late antiquity. For Mishnah is only the first in a long line of those numerous anonymous, public compilations awaiting a genuinely historical exegesis in the study of the Judaism of the ancient rabbis.

The book explains the methods of exegesis applied, specifically, to Mishnah-tractate Makhshirin in my *History of the Mishnaic Law of Purities.* XVII. *Makhshirin* (Leiden, 1977); that tractate is brief and provides a good occasion for the illustration and demonstration of some of the critical methods I have devised for dissecting and reconstructing a Mishnah-tractate. By reviewing some of the results originally presented elsewhere, but now revised in the context of explaining precisely how they are achieved, I believe I can best provide a full statement of method and show how other texts of the same sort may be subjected to a fresh reading.

To assist the reader in working through the discussions as well as the texts, I have provided a glossary at the end, defining uncommon words or terms used throughout the book. Without reference to it, many items may not be accessible.

The Hebrew text is that of H. Albeck, with the pointing by H. Yalon, *Shishah sidré Mishnah. Seder Tohorot* (Jerusalem and Tel Aviv, 1958: Bialik Institute and the Dvir Publishing House) © 1958

published in due course in William Scott Green, ed., *Approaches to Ancient Judaism* III and IV (Missoula, 1980 and 1981, respectively), with Essner and Rubenstein in III and Havivi and Eisenman in IV. The dissertations by Mandelbaum, Gordon, Peck, Jaffee, and Haas will be published in book form, as will Zahavy's book on Berakhot. But none of the work on the history of the law for the division of Agriculture has been systematically accomplished, nor have we a clear picture of the relationship of Mishnah to Scripture for the tractates of that division. Still, I expect that the whole work will be complete by 1983.

by The Bialik Institute and Dvir Co., reproduced by permission. I wish to thank both publishers for generously allowing me to reproduce this text. Variant readings are cited only when they affect the exegesis of a passage, principally in M. Makhshirin Chapter One.

It remains to thank.those who have read this book in manuscript and helped me to clarify my meaning. Mr. Alan Peck, Professors Richard S. Sarason, Hebrew Union College. Jewish Institute of Religion, and William Scott Green, University of Rochester, reviewed the entire book for that purpose and made important suggestions for its improvement.

This book explains and exemplifies half, the exegetical half, of my two methodological initiatives in the historical study of Mishnah and its time. A correct understanding of what the text of Mishnah meant to the people who made it up makes possible the other half of those initiatives, the religious-historical half. That half encompasses three closely related disciplines, history, history of ideas, and history of religions. The work of describing and interpreting the system of Mishnah as a whole in the context of its times and the methods used in doing that work are laid forth in other books of mine. These are, first, *Method and Meaning in Ancient Judaism* and *Method and Meaning in Ancient Judaism. Second Series* (Missoula, 1979 and 1980, respectively: Scholars Press for Brown Judaic Studies), and, second, the *summa* of the whole, *Judaism: The Evidence of the Mishnah* (in progress for The University of Chicago Press). In those books I have given the results of form-analytical exegesis for description and interpretation of the system of Mishnah and its social and historical setting. There are various facets to this other half of the methodological contribution but I have not been able to identify and spell out the reconstructive methods for history of ideas and religions as clearly and concisely as I have the exegetical methods explained here. Once the final work of reconstruction is complete, I plan to turn to the problems presented by the Talmuds for form-analytical interpretation, alongside the historical issues presented in consequence of what, I hope, will yield fresh approaches to long-standing problems of exegesis. For the real problem of Mishnah, to which this book too must be addressed, is what people would ever want to do with such a document, and how they might survive its promulgation as the foundation of their social and imaginative life. For Mishnah is mostly fantasy, of a curious sort, as the reader soon will discover—as did the Talmuds' founders and philosophers.

The book is dedicated to a college classmate and friend of thirty years and to his wife. I admire and take pride in the careers and achievements in public service of Milton and Lisa Gwirtzman and through this dedication express my joy in the enduring friendship between ourselves and our families.

J. N.

Providence, Rhode Island
15 Shevat 5740
February 2, 1980
*A tree for Danny and
Matthew Gwirtzman.*

Contents

Form-Analysis and Exegesis:
A Fresh Approach
to the Interpretation of Mishnah

CHAPTER 1

Introduction

Answers without questions do not inform: First I have to ask the question, then answer it. Learning new ways to ask questions to find answers, without a clear picture of the fundamental problem solved by the exercise of learning, teaches us nothing we can use, nothing worth knowing. That is why, at the very beginning, we have to take a detour, a trip in our imagination, and try to construct, in terms familiar to us, the sort of intellectual problem presented by Mishnah-Tosefta (see glossary). Mishnah (with Tosefta) is one-half of the constitution of Judaism. The other half is Scripture, which is mediated by Mishnah. When we study Mishnah and examine Mishnah and Scripture as a whole, therefore, we analyze the bedrock of that kind of Judaism known as Talmudic, or Rabbinic, or Classical that has predominated among the Jews from the second century to our own day, and that in its classical as well as its modernized forms, continues to constitute and define the only Judaism the world now knows. So if we wish to study the origins and structure of Judaism, we must approach Mishnah, asking questions about how it came into being and was put together, and what it meant in its own day, just as we should approach any other document of a definitive and fundamental character.

Questions worth asking about Mishnah are many. In order of priority, the first are these: What is Mishnah? How did it come into being? and, especially, What did it mean to the people who made it up? The second set concerns the place of Mishnah in the world-view of those people: what they meant to say in creating Mishnah, and whether and how Mishnah solved their problems and answered their deepest human questions.

The first group of questions, in general, are those of literary analysis: the study first, of redaction, that is, how a document is put together, and second of exegesis, the explanation of the meaning of a document, sentence by sentence, paragraph by paragraph, chapter by chapter, tractate by tractate, division by division, and, finally, as a whole (in the context of Mishnah, "Judaism"). The work of exegesis is a work of interpretation of language and of how people use language to say what they mean. This is the set of questions answered in this book.

The second group of questions, in general, are those of the history of ideas and religions, and, given the character and concerns of Mishnah-Tosefta and of Judaism, they illuminate the history of a religion, Judaism, in its principal and generative intellectual expression. In questions addressed to the history of religious ideas, we want to know not only what people were thinking but the meaning of their thought.

In the first instance, this matter of meaning is worked out against the background of the times of the people behind the document. For whatever else people intend, they always address their ideas to problems of their own age and place. This is why we have to begin with to establish the time in which the Mishnah was made up and spell out the problems confronting the people who made it up. We have to ask whether we are able to take what people had to say and relate it to the world that, without choice or possibility of evasion, they had to explain. For the study of ideas is the description and interpretation of how thinking people make sense of their own world.

So before us in this book is a task of finding methods for the exegesis of Mishnah. Later on I hope to present an account of methods for the historical reconstruction and interpretation of Mishnah's ideas. That is, we need to find means of discovering what people were saying in their own day and why they were saying it at the time, in the place in which they did their work, and to the particular people to whom they were speaking. What did they say? To whom did they say it? What did they mean when they said it?

These are the sorts of questions before us. Answering them is not so easy as one might imagine. For the document, Mishnah, presents special problems. To the description and specification of these special problems we must now turn.

i. The Problem of Mishnah

To understand why Mishnah presents a sizable problem for both exegesis and history of ideas, one has to be aware of two facts.

First, Mishnah is not written by a person who identifies himself. Furthermore, there is no one author; Mishnah is a collective 'document. It speaks for and to a community, the people who believe in its authority and who sponsor it. Mishnah does not want to be identified with the opinions of some one person. It speaks anonymously. Whoever is cited in it uses a single, highly formulaic, therefore public language. Mishnah's sages do not resort to language of idiosyncrasy and, in fact, eliminate signs of personal linguistic preference. This public and collective statement is a kind of constitution that does not want to be identified with one person or one viewpoint; therefore we cannot be entirely certain who in particular speaks to us through this document.

Second, and to the contrary, Mishnah assigns a great many of its sayings to named authorities, who in general are assumed to have lived over a long period of time—approximately two hundred years. So we are faced with a document that is both anonymous and full of attributed sayings. Furthermore, as we will see later on, the style of Mishnah is uniform. What individual authorities are made to say is phrased without regard to distinctions and differences of individual style. Everything is woven together into a single, uniform fabric of style.

Now to that set of problems of a historical character—problems of finding out who said what, to whom, when, under what circumstances, for what purpose—are added yet a second set, this one linguistic. The Hebrew of Mishnah is not broken up into sentences or paragraphs. In its earlier manuscripts Mishnah is transmitted in long columns, at best divided into chapters. So we have to find a way to determine where a unit of thought begins and where it ends.

We have to find out which sentence belongs in one unit of thought, which in some other. We must discover a way of asking Mishnah to tell us, on the basis of its own internal evidence, not only on the basis of what much later printers or editors decided. So we have the problem of defining a unit of thought.

In addition to the historical and linguistic problems awaiting attention, there is a difficulty so overwhelming as to make the very doing of the work exceedingly tentative and taxing. Mishnah and Tosefta have been studied for nearly sixteen hundred years. The way in which those documents are supposed to be read is already established, in the minds of nearly everyone who studies Mishnah-Tosefta. For the larger number of tractates of Mishnah, first of all, there are the two Talmuds, one created in Babylonia from about 200 to about 600, the other created in the Land of Israel ("Palestine") from about 200 to about 450. These Talmuds purport to explain what Mishnah means. They carry forward and develop the discussion of Mishnah's problems.

The intent of the Talmuds is to treat Mishnah not as a document by itself, but as a statement in an ongoing discussion. What is subject to discussion is "Jewish law" in general. Mishnah is therefore broken up into small units of thought on "the law," each one of them treated as authoritative to be sure, but none of them addressed in terms of the larger, particularly and distinctively Mishnaic, setting in which it originally occurs. Now this approach to the study of the Mishnah, which seeks to unite Mishnah's law to later discussions of the law and to give Mishnah the pride of place in the formation of Jewish law in general, is necessary and right for the purpose of creating and applying the law. It takes seriously precisely what Mishnah takes seriously, which is to say, those many specific allegations about the law that Mishnah makes.

In only one aspect is such an approach to the interpretation of Mishnah not going to serve. The approach to Mishnah as foundation of the Talmuds, as the beginning of Jewish law, does not permit Mishnah to address its own times. This legal approach does not consider Mishnah as a single, totally coherent document, important in its own context. It will not allow Mishnah to be read systematically and whole, in context, as the statement of people who lived at some one period, people who faced some distinctive set of problems, and who through Mishnah proposed to deal with the world in which they lived. But Mishnah *began* as a whole and in context.

So there are these three problems—(1) the anonymity of the document, its lack of a specific author, (2) the linguistic uniformity and absence of all punctuation of Mishnah's language, and (3) the established, atomistic and ahistorical, anticontextual tradition of how Mishnah is to be studied. Before proceeding to spell out methods for solving these problems, let me now conduct an experiment of imagination. We must try to translate the work of studying Mishnah into terms more readily accessible to people in our contemporary setting.

Let us imagine that we are students of American history and culture, living a thousand years hence. We want to know about the beginnings of American institutions and ideals, the problems faced by the people who laid the foundations for the sort of society and culture in which we live so much later. Naturally, we hope that, in understanding the documents that tell us who we are and what we are supposed to do and to be, we shall better understand the world in which we live. For this world of ours is made by these documents. We have the notion that, to reach that understanding, we must see where it all began. We wish to unpack those lasting structures of law and public policy that made and now define this world in which we live. So we are going to attempt to explain and interpret the formative documents of American civilization.

Now when we determine what they are, that is, the Declaration of Independence, the Constitution, the Bill of Rights, the Federalist Papers, and the like, and then imagine that they are, in form, similar to Mishnah-Tosefta, we come across a curious problem.

First of all, these documents (in our imagination) have been subjected to a very long process of transmission, over many centuries.

Second, they come down to us not all by themselves. They are laden with the gifts of many minds, the contributions of great thinkers who lived for hundreds of years after the Revolution and the Federalist age. Instead of writing their own books and signing their own names, these great thinkers simply added what they had to say to the original documents. This they did by cutting up the Constitution into little bits and commenting on one bit or another. Or they divided up the Declaration of Independence, and so amplified and augmented its parts that it is difficult to read it whole.

But that is not the only problem. The documents themselves are not so accessible as we might hope. For they were, to begin with, written in a different way from what we might expect. They were not written by a single person, nor on the basis of what various people agreed to say. They do not contain only generally accepted statements. On the contrary, they represent a great many viewpoints, and these viewpoints are given in various ways. Throughout this imaginary Constitution are general statements followed by specific points of difference, in the names of one or another of the members of the Constitutional convention on 1787. Consequently the Constitution is more like an epitome of the debates of the Convention, than a single, cogent document. It hardly is an agreed-upon, single account of things as they should be. One section of the Constitution contains points of disagreement with some other section of the same document, yet lacking the names of the people who hold those divergent views.

So in the long history of American civilization, the Constitution, the Declaration of Independence, the Bill of Rights, the Federalist papers, and other basic documents of our government and politics turn out to have been made into the carriers of the intellectual history of our country. They never were closed, treated as complete: Whatever people later came to believe, they would add to these original documents, so that the Constitution and Bill of Rights reach us heavily burdened with later opinions, in response to problems of thought or conditions of life unimagined by the original authors. Further, as is clear, the documents themselves are so framed as to present a single, cogent view of what were, in fact, widely divergent opinions. Yet these differing opinions are preserved within the documents themselves.

Now let us ask of this imaginary Constitution those questions with which we began: What does the document mean to the people who first made it up? How shall we isolate their ideas from those imputed to them in later times? What modes of interpretation may we formulate in order to make sense of what these people were saying to one another, in their own day? Finally, having made some sense of the original, historical meaning of what is before us, how can we then begin the work of reconstruction? How shall we relate *content* to *context?*

These and similar problems are the ones that we must now begin to solve for the Mishnah.

ii. Prevailing Solutions to the Problem of Mishnah

If we may now move onward from this statement of the inescapable problems facing anyone who wishes to undertake the exegetical and historical study of Mishnah, our first task is to summarize the prevailing mode of reading the text before us. The simple fact is that the problems I have outlined are not generally deemed to be problems at all. The fundamental historical question plays no role in the reading of the document. Mishnah is not read in the context of its own times, and is not read as a *singular* document at all. So the two points of critical importance—When does this document come into being? What at that particular time does this document wish to say?—are simply not addressed in most schools in which this critical document is read. All the rabbinic sources thus are treated as representatives of a single, seamless world-view. They are taken to be expressions of a simple, essentially united group, either the Jews as a whole or *the* rabbis as a group. Although some more critical people concede that distinctions may have existed between the first-century rabbis' thought and that of the fourth, the distinctions make no material difference in accounts of "the rabbis" and their thought. *The* rabbis are represented in their views on God, world, and redemption, as though all rabbis for seven hundred years had the same thing to say as all others. Mishnah is not a differentiated stage or sector but part of something larger than itself.

Now this prevailing representation of the rabbis is subject to an important, commonplace qualification. Mishnah and the Talmuds abound in the recognition of differences between the teachings of various rabbis in different periods. This occurs in discussions of which tradition or source was followed by the proponent of this or that opinion. But the recorded differences are about particular, trivial points. The Talmudic discussion of a Mishnaic passage, moreover, is normally directed towards reconciling them. What is particularly lacking in available accounts of "the rabbinic mind" is a recognition and delineation of different general positions on basic attitudes, of the characteristics, make-up, and backgrounds of different schools. No one but myself has emphasized the change of teachings in the course of time and in relation to historical changes. Obviously, there is plenty of speculation on how an individual or a group reacted to a particular historical situation or event. But these random speculations are unsystematic, and appear to be made up for the occasion. These apparent exceptions to what I say have to be recognized; they prove the accuracy of my description of the prevailing consensus.

Second, as to the sources, since Mishnah and the documents of earlier rabbinic Judaism exhibit an internally uniform quality of style, the scholars who represent a seamless world accurately replicate the literary traits of the sources of the protrait. It is exceedingly difficult to differentiate on formal or stylistic grounds among the layers of the Mishnah, which is the document of rabbinic Judaism first brought to redaction. The two Talmuds then so lay matters out as to represent themselves as the logical continuity from the Mishnah. They do so by breaking up the Mishnah into minute units and then commenting on those discrete units of thought. Consequently, the Mishnah as a document, a document that presents its own world-view and aims to lay foundations for its own social system, is not preserved. It is normally printed as part of another document, the Talmud. And the Talmuds do not present themselves as successive layers, built upon, but essentially distinct from, the Mishnah; rather, the Talmuds attempt to completely harmonize their own materials both with the Mishnah and among themselves, despite the obviously contradictory character of the materials.

Once more we observe, what is suggestive is that there are limits to disagreement. The continuing contentiousness of the documents, their preservation of diverse viewpoints on single issues, underline the rigidly protected limits of permissible disagreement. Intense disagreement about trivialities powerfully reinforces basic unities and harmonies. That out there were Jews who decorated synagogues in ways the Talmuds cannot have led us to anticipate is mentioned only in passing, as if it is of no weight or concern. What matters to this literature is not how the Jews lived, nor even how they worshipped, but only the discussions of the rabbinical schools and courts. What the documents say is what we are supposed to think, within the range of allowed difference. Consequently, the intellectually unitary character of the sources is powerfully reinforced by the total success of the framers and redactors of the sources. Stylistic unity is secured within documents and, in some measure, even among them.

These considerations do not prevent scholars from writing about history, biography, and theology, on the basis of the unanalyzed and unchallenged allegations of the rabbinic sources. Just as before the rise of form-criticism people had arguments about what Jesus *really* said and did, so the rage and contentiousness of scholars of Mishnah and Talmud mask the uncertainty of their entire structure. It is as if, as in the Talmuds themselves, by arguing on essentially minor points, people may avoid paying attention to the epistemological abyss beneath them all. And those who—to shift the metaphor—ask where are the emperor's clothes are only rarely answered.

Finally, these assured and unquestioned results of a hundred years of critical scholarship following on fifteen hundred years of uncritical scholarship, which produced exactly the same results, enjoy the powerful support of the three great communities that read the Mishnah and the rest of rabbinical literature. I mean, Orthodox Jews in Yeshivas, scholarly Jews in rabbinical seminaries and Israeli universities, and the generality of Christian scholars of New Testament. To the Orthodox, the rabbinic sources are part of the whole Torah of Moses "our rabbi," the revealed word of God. For them, "our holy rabbis" cannot deceive. To the scholars in rabbinical schools and Israeli universities, the critical program of scholarship on early Christianity is perceived from a distance. In their books and articles they settle complex questions of literary analysis and historical epistemology with an array of two assumptions, three logical arguments, and four "probative" examples. They do not perceive the immense, detailed work that stands, for example, behind debates on Q and the Synoptic problem. Indeed, the work of analysis of sources bores them. Whether work is original or dull, the bulk of it simply dismisses as settled, questions that would be deemed urgent in biblical and patristic literature and in the history of early Christianity. As to the New Testament scholars, their view is that things go better when we read rabbinical literature as a set of facts that speak for themselves, rather than complex problems requiring solutions. For them, the rabbinic literature as it stands, unanalyzed and uncriticized, tells us about Jerusalem and Galilee in the time of Jesus.

In general, therefore, Mishnah presents no *special* problems, either of exegesis or of history, to the generality of scholars of the rabbinic literature. Their exegetical problems are constructed on a much larger scale, and, so far as they do history at all, it is credulous and gullible, believing everything the sources say as fact, therefore asking for nothing more than the facts.

Let us now turn to a preliminary account of that fresh approach to Mishnah promised in the title of this book. We do so in the knowledge that what is genuinely fresh in this book is its basic supposition that it is important to study Mishnah as a document distinct from all other documents produced later on, to approach it as a statement expressive of a viewpoint shaped for its own times. Here we try to read the Mishnah in the context of its age.

iii. Some Fresh Approaches to the Problem of Mishnah

Now that some of the basic problems of the document before us are clear, I shall rapidly outline the particular solutions that this book is meant to give through extensive illustration in Mishnah-tractate Makhshirin.

The approach of this book to the exegetical study of Mishnah has several facets, of which two are of widest general interest: exegesis and forms. Two others are of historical, not exegetical importance, and these should be introduced here, though only in a different context will they be spelled out and exemplified. In this way what we do with regard to exegesis of Mishnah may be kept in relationship to what is to be done with respect to historical study. These historical methods concern the use of attributions, and the issue of anonymous materials. Each problem and its solution may be briefly stated.

Exegesis: All earlier exegetes take as their problem the placing of Mishnah's laws into relationship with all other laws, of all documents and all periods, so forming a single construct: *the* law, *the halakhah.* An account of what Mishnah means when seen by itself and in its own context could not be expected under such conditions.

Forms: To determine Mishnah's meaning to its original authors, we must ask whether its language provides guidance. What we shall learn is that Mishnah provides its own first and best commentary. Recognition of that fact is my principal contribution. Mishnah explains its original meaning through its highly formalized rhetoric and syntax. My supposition in so stating is that from the way people formulate and frame their ideas, we may come to a reliable view of what they originally meant to say. It will follow that a document of such a highly stylized and formulaic character and persistently patterned language as Mishnah contains its own exegesis in these very forms, redactional patterns and contrasts, and formulary patterns. These forms thus constitute our evidence of what the document meant to the people who made it up.

Analysis of the large-scale formal traits—hence: form-analysis— shows, moreover, that forms as we have them are mostly imposed within the processes of redaction. There is little formulation anterior to redaction of the Mishnah itself. Redaction proves in the end to constitute the governing and commanding act of formulation, to define original meaning. It follows that Mishnah's highly distinctive forms themselves reveal little or no history. Form-history, strictly speaking, is not possible. These procedures, so far as they are indicated in the Mishnah, do not go back much before A.D. 200.

Now let us turn to historical problems, relevant only in a general way to the exegesis of the document.

Of what good are attributions? Let me define with some precision the problem of attributions. In fact two separate questions arise: One is the question of the reliability of the exact quotation— *ipsissima verba.* I know of no way to show that any rabbinic attribution contains *ipsissima verba* of the rabbi to whom the words are assigned. It is easy to show, on the contrary, that most of what is attributed takes the formal traits and adheres to the redactional requirements of the document in which the attribution appears. So it is uncommon to have anything like *ipsissima verba.*

The second question, which is much more important, is that of the reliability of an attribution of the essential content of a statement. If for example we could show that the gist, if not the exact wording, of what is attributed to Hillel actually was said by him, then we should have information on what one person, either in Hillel's time or afterward, sumed up of what Hillel had said, and we should be able to relate that person's thought to the ideas of others of roughly the same time and place. This is the important matter, not the wording of what is assigned. And here there has been some progress, if not enough.

I am able to show whether a fair number of statements belong *in the period* in which the men to whom these statements are attributed are believed to have flourished. Let me now explain. We can ask whether there are correlations among groups of sayings given in the names of authorities generally supposed to have lived in successive periods, intersecting sayings that deal with a single topic. If a saying is in the name of an earlier authority, is its principle or conception prior in logic, more primitive in principle or conception, than an intersecting saying given in the name of a later authority? If there is a correlation between temporal attribution and traits of logic or conception, so that what is attributed to an early authority is shown in the character of what is attributed to be relatively primitive, then that saying may be shown to be prior to another, with that other saying shown to be posterior.

This matter of testing the value of attributions for the study of history, biography, law, and theology brings us to the much vexed matter, of *what is not attributed.* In the case of Mishnah, we shall be unable to find the problem pressing. The reason is in two parts.

First, you will learn here (in Chapter 6) that a Mishnah-tractate is not merely a collection of information but a careful essay about a set of problems concerning a given topic. A ruling lacking an attribution nonetheless finds its place within the intellectual framework of the tractate that contains it. There are very few so totally out of context as to be insusceptible to location or situation within an established framework.

Second, when we work with the known, the pericopae that can be located and reliably situated, we normally are able to relate the unknown to the known. It follows that an anonymous ruling containing an idea otherwise first attested in named materials, let us say, after A.D. 140, is not apt to go back to a period a hundred or two hundred years earlier.

In fact, the really interesting thing is not what the tractates of the Mishnah contain but what they assume. We now are in a position to describe the ideas held by people ultimately represented in the Mishnah at various stages in the Mishnah's history. Since a history of Mishnah's law now is complete, we can proceed to give an account of two things.

First, we can say with a measure of accuracy what ideas come relatively early in the history of Mishnaic law, even in the period before A.D. 70.

Second and more compelling, we also are able to provide a catalogue of ideas taken for granted before Mishnah got underway. We know what the framers of Mishnah take for granted and treat as settled facts of life and law.

This opens a second route toward the description of one part of the world of Judaism before 70, even though we must use a document that came to closure about a century and a half later. We may even engage in controlled speculation on the origins of some ideas and facts that lie deep in the Mishnah's substructure, and that do not appear in Scripture. This controlled speculation is a method of hypothetical-exegetical reconstruction through a series of contrastive or analogical processes (see glossary).

The single most significant thing we shall accomplish in this book is to remove the exegesis of Mishnah from the context of a whole transtemporal legal system. Here we shall insist that the document be read as a statement of a single system, a single world-view, produced at a given moment by a group of people who addressed a distinct and distinctive set of problems. That is why Part I is so long. In this I correct what I believe to be the principal error in earlier work. As I said, this error has been to treat all sayings and all stories, whereever they occur, as part of a single "rabbinic" corpus of materials, of pretty much identical origin and provenance, all to be handled atomistically and out of documentary context.

Let me explain this point. When the Mishnah is read in a larger framework than Mishnah, we are prevented from seeing Mishnah's materials as a coherent corpus on their own. This approach to Mishnah is absolutely opposite to our purpose. For I propose to state and historically to account for the unfolding of the law of Mishnah *in particular.* If we assume that Mishnah constitutes a single document—and the internal harmonious formal and intellectual traits of Mishnah require that we make that assumption—then we have no choice but to honor the limits of the document when attempting to describe and interpret it.

The work done here therefore differs from that of all earlier exegetes. Others read and interpret Mishnah in a different context. Mishnah is read as part of a large, unitary corpus of law, *the halakhah.* It is the purpose of nearly all exegetes to relate each of the parts to the transcendent whole, and to force the whole to encompass all of the parts. It is not the ahistorical (or, antihistorical) and harmonistic purpose of the earlier exegetes that made their Mishnah-commentaries so intellectually prolix, indeed, indifferent and irrelevant to the text under discussion. That is a misunderstanding. It is, rather, that the earlier exegetes presuppose something much more profound, much less susceptible to articulation: This is the construct, "Jewish law," or *"halakhah."* To them Mishnah constitutes an important component of this construct. In their mind the correct approach to Mishnah's interpretation is to relate its *halakhah* to other *halakhah,* that is, to *"the* law."

This harmonistic, atomistic yet encompassing approach is natural for people who keep the law and who take for granted their audience wants to know *the* law, even though not all of the law of a given document is practical and practiced. But the point of interest is clear, and it explains to them what is relevant and what is not. Since social context and intellectual framework define what is relevant, their essays—to us, total chaos—to them are orderly and reliable. But the fact remains that in a different world, their language of exegesis is puzzling, just as is ours to them.

So what we shall do is to state clearly what Mishnah wishes to say, in *its* own setting, within the limits of *its* own redactional framework, on the subjects chosen by *it,* and for purposes defined within the mind of those specific people, its authors, who flourished in one concrete social setting. Reading the document by itself, in its historical context and therefore outside of its atemporal, *halakhic* context, requires a different approach.

No longer is it possible to treat the diverse corpus of rabbinical literature as a uniform whole. Once one document, Mishnah, the principal one, is shown to bear its distinctive formal and intellectual characteristics, then all others must be subjected to appropriate analysis, to determine the characteristics of each.

No longer are the anonymity and the collective character of documents to be allowed to prevent differentiation and discrimination within a document and between documents. The work of harmonization is in ruins.

In the Talmuds and midrashic compilations we have the result of centuries of harmonization and cogent construction. Understanding these documents and the world they portray requires us to unpack them and see how they function. For in the end, knowing what people thought, without understanding the world about which they reflected, does not help us either to understand the people who did the thinking or to interpret the result of their reflection. Although without such understanding we may take the results of their thinking—their theology, their exegesis of Scripture, and their law—and we may build on it for one purpose or another, we essentially know nothing of the inner structure of that building which we ourselves propose to construct. Not knowing the points of stress and places of tension in the building, not knowing the main lines of the foundation of the structure, not knowing the places at which the builder put the strongest joints and beams, we add to the building in total ignorance. This is not building: It is destruction,—making things up as we go along.

In front of us is a labor of description and interpretation, establishing context and providing exegesis. We have a sizable corpus of texts that clearly express a world-view and propose to create a society and a way of life for a distinctive group of people. To describe that world-view and to understand the society and way of life shaped by the ancient rabbis, we have to interpret texts. To interpret those texts, we have to establish context and setting. We have to describe the world in which the texts took shape and to offer a theory of the questions that seemed urgent and compelling to the people who made the texts as they are and not in some other way. So the work of exegesis depends on establishing the appropriate context of exegesis. At the same time, to describe the context, we have to read the texts.

And yet, beyond text and context lies yet another fact, the inner cogency and continuity of the texts beyond their original context. For Judaism as we know it emerges from the documents under study, and its claim from ancient times to the present is to constitute the logically necessary spinning out of the principles contained in the ancient Torah of Moses "our rabbi" and of the rabbis of olden times. In this regard the *halakhic* approach to a unitary law is sound. That inner logic that precipitates and governs the unfolding of the theology and law of the rabbis has itself to be discerned.

There is then this threefold task, a triple cord not to be separated: text, context, inner logic. When we have discerned the threads of the cord and shown how they are interwoven, we shall perceive what holds together and imparts meaning to an ancient world that yet is with us.

If we ask ourselves why people should want to know about these things, we need not fall back upon the bankrupt claim that they are intrinsically interesting. Nor yet, in this setting, do we have to offer historical salvation to scholars of early Christianity and say they cannot understand their subject without also knowing this one. The formation of Judaism by itself is a compelling social and intellectual phenomenon, for among other such phenomena, it teaches us how to describe and interpret the interplay between the historical situation of a distinct society, on the one side, and the world-view brought into being to explain and shape that historical situation, on the other. When we can relate the religious world-view and way of life of the ancient Talmudic rabbis to the society whose vision they chose to shape and whose conduct and institutions they wished to govern, we can report much about what it is that religion, as a mode of constructing reality and explaining the world, is and does.

Here, before our eyes, is the literature made by a particular group of men, in a particular time, for a particular society. That literature of antiquity defined what would happen for all time. In unpacking the end-product, in taking it apart to see how it works, we can tell our own times more than a little about this remarkable achievement. For this was a world-view capable of bringing order to the chaotic world of ancient times, and it remains capable of preserving a stable and enduring world from antiquity to the present. Given the world's potentialities for disorder and the difficulty of holding together any group of people subject to those ongoing disruptive forces affecting all continuing historical societies, we should find more than merely interesting the story of Judaism's formative centuries. In a world of disintegration and an age of disorder, we should find urgent that story, indeed any story, of restraint, order, balance, and continuity—all in the name of the sacred.

iv. Conclusion

This general discussion of problems of method in the study of Mishnah is meant to be a prologue. The real work is to study a text and digress—that is, to *do* the work, but then to explain to ourselves, to reflect upon what we have done. For this purpose we shall work through a tractate of Mishnah in the way in which I believe we should. I have selected Mishnah-tractate Makhshirin, both because of the intrinsic interest of the ideas of the tractate (if not of the subject-matter) and also because of the typical and therefore suggestive character of the exegetical problems to be solved. In this way we shall both learn a tractate in the way in which, in my and my students' *History of the Mishnaic Law,* I have carried out a complete commentary to Mishnah, and explain what we are doing *while* we are doing it. People who wish to approach other important documents of rabbinic literature and to adapt the methods worked out for Mishnah will then have a clear account of what has been done and why the work has been done in one way and not in some other. Of still greater hope, people who want to rework tractates that my students and I have studied and to propose alternative theories of explanation and interpretation will have a clear grasp of how our results have been attained and of suitable grounds for criticizing those results.

We are going to proceed systematically from the smallest units of Mishnaic discourse, the individual pericopae that contain a complete idea (Part I), to the intermediate units of Mishnaic discourse, the groupings of these individual pericopae into chapters (Part III,

Chapter 5, and, at the end, to the largest unit of Mishnaic discourse, a whole tractate (Part III, Chapter 6). This requires that we plough through one pericope after another, time and again to ask the same questions: What are the traits of language? What does language bearing these traits wish to tell us? What is the law? How does the analysis of the patterns and formularies and formal traits of language—once more: form-analysis—tell us about the original meanings of the people who made up these pericopae and who expressed their ideas in these patterns and in this formulaic language? There is no point in abstract speculation on such matters, in forming a theory of exegesis through analysis of forms.

The theory will emerge from the concrete work of explaining Mishnah's ideas, unit by unit, in this way and not in some other, in this context and not in the established one. Most striking in the following material is what we choose not to discuss, the topics we eliminate as unimportant, impertinent to the original meaning of the document. Form-analysis, as I have explained, asks all those questions of primary meaning that *halakhic* analysis—the implications of a pericope for the law in general, the implications of the law in general for a given pericope—neglects. And the contrary is also the case. So let us turn to a specific text.

PART I   The Trees
        Exegesis of Mishnah

CHAPTER 2

A Sample of Form-Analytical Exegesis of Mishnah

i. Introduction

As much as *what* people say, the *way* they say it conveys meaning. The supposition of the approach to the explanation of Mishnah's meaning in this book is that Mishnah's language and in particular its formalized and patterned way of expressing its ideas constitute the first and best explanation of Mishnah's meaning. When, therefore, we wish to know what the sentences of our document meant to the people who made them up, we have to concentrate to begin with upon the formal traits of its individual units of thought, its smallest building blocks of meaning. In this protracted exercise, covering Mishnah-tractate Makhshirin Chapters Two through Six, we shall undertake the explanation of the document through paying special attention to its language—syntax, morphology, recurrent grammatical arrangements, and the like. Rather than discuss at length the theory of form-analytical exegesis, we shall learn the approach (one among many, as I stress in the conclusion of this chapter) by actually following the things it does, and does not do, in solving a given problem of explanation.

The dominant stylistic trait of Mishnah is the acute formalization of its syntactical structure, and its carefully framed sequences of formalized language, so organized that the limits of a theme correspond to those of a formulary pattern. The smallest units of a complete thought resort to a remarkably limited repertoire of

23

formulary patterns. Mishnah manages to say whatever it wants in one of the following formal patterns:

1. the simple declarative sentence, in which the subject, verb, and predicate are syntactically tightly joined e.g., *he who does so and so to such and such is . . . ;*

2. the duplicated subject, in which the subject of the sentence is stated twice, e.g., *He who does so and so, lo, he is such and such;*

3. mild apocopation, in which the subject of the sentence is cut off from the verb, which refers to its own subject, and not the one with which the sentence commences, e.g., *He who does so and so . . . , it* [the thing he has done] *is such and such;*

4. extreme apocopation, in which a series of clauses is presented, none of them tightly joined to what precedes or follows, and all of them cut off from the predicate of the sentence, e.g., *he who does so and so . . . , it* [the thing he has done] *is such and such . . . , it is a matter of doubt whether . . . or whether . . . lo, it* [referring to nothing in the antecedent, apocopated clauses of the subject of the sentence] *is so and so. . . .*

In addition to these formulary patterns, in which the distinctive formulary traits are effected through variations in the relationship between the subject and the predicate of the sentence, or in which the subject itself is given a distinctive development, there is yet a fifth.

5. In this last one we have a contrastive complex predicate, in which case we may have two sentences, independent of one another, yet clearly formulated so as to stand in acute balance with one another in the predicate, thus, *He who does . . . is unclean, and he who does not . . . is clean.*

It naturally will be objected: Is it possible that a simple declarative sentence (1) may be asked to serve as a formulary pattern, alongside the rather distinctive and unusual constructions which follow? The answer is that while, by itself a tightly constructed sentence consisting of subject, verb, and complement, in which the verb refers to the subject, and the complement to the verb, hardly exhibits traits of particular formal interest, yet a sequence of such sentences, built along the same gross syntactical and grammatical lines, may well exhibit a clear-cut and distinctive pattern. The contrastive predicate is one such example, and Mishnah contains many more.

The important point of differentiation, particularly for the simple declarative sentence, appears in the intermediate unit, that is, a set of sentences on one distinct subject. It is there that we see a single pattern recurring in a long sequence of sentences, e.g., *the X that has lost its Y is unclean because of its Z. The Z that has lost its Y is unclean because of its X.* Another example will be a long sequence of highly developed sentences, laden with relative clauses and other explanatory matter, in which a single syntactical pattern will govern the articulation of three or six or nine exempla. That sequence will be followed by one repeated terse sentence pattern, e.g., *X is so and so. Y is such and such, Z is thus and so.* The former group will treat one principle or theme, the latter some other. There can be no doubt, therefore, that the declarative sentence in recurrent patterns is, in its way, just as carefully formalized as a sequence of severely apocopated sentences or of contrastive predicates or duplicated subjects.

The exercise of explanation ("exegesis") that follows does its work in two ways. First, I present a translation of the Hebrew pericope that highlights the formal traits of the Hebrew. The smallest whole units of meaning are set off in separate paragraphs; the use of letters simply helps in designating what is under discussion later on. This translation constitutes a commentary—an assertion of meaning. Second, I present a protracted discussion of what has just been translated. This discussion constitutes a second commentary to the whole. In the discussion I deal, in general, with four questions, though it must be stressed that all four sorts of questions are rarely asked of a single unit:

First, what is the plain-sense of the law?

Second, what are the literary traits of the pericope before us? Is the passage smooth or does it exhibit major structural, stylistic, or substantive difficulties?

Third, what are the formal and formulary aspects of the pericope? Does it conform in an established pattern of formulation, construction, and organization?

Fourth, what are the redactional characteristics of the pericope, both by itself and in relationship to others with which it is brought into relationship for the final redactor?

I make no effort whatsoever to contribute to the elucidation of the meaning of words, but rely upon the available dictionaries, translations, and other lexicographical resources, however unsatisfactory these may be to students of Mishnaic Hebrew.

In the commentaries that follow, I frequently cite the received exegetical essays listed in the abbreviations and bibliography. This is done simply by introducing the idea or approach of a given commentator and so signifying by adding the abbreviation for his name. Thus in square brackets I shall add the idea I believe required for the understanding of a given unit of thought, and, therein, add the source in parentheses, so [()]. A quick reference to the abbreviations will show who is cited. I make no effort at all to survey all of the antecedent opinions on each pericope and its problem, except, as indicated, in Chapter 4. I also do not undertake a systematic, historical account of the thousand-year sequence of comments, because this is not a book about the exegetical tradition of Mishnah, but about the exegesis of Mishnah. Within the logic of the law and its problems, the various commentators live on a single, timeless plane and talk with one another without regard to priority or posteriority. And so do I.

It is important to explain why so prominent a role is given to Maimonides in the exegesis that follows. Maimonides is the first and the greatest exegete of Mishnah as such. That is, he treats Mishnah in the terms and issues defined solely or principally within the framework of discourse of Mishnah itself. While the framers of the Talmuds also interpret Mishnah, it is not within the same highly disciplined program of explaining Mishnah wholly within its own program and issues. Maimonides approaches the document, moreover, in two ways. First, he provides a systematic exegesis of Mishnah in his commentary to Mishnah itself. Second, in his monumental law-code, *Mishneh Torah,* he goes back and restates what he understands of Mishnah, now as decided law. This latter work must stand as the greatest systematic legal commentary Mishnah has ever received or will ever receive. Throughout the following pages I cite Maimonides' version of a Mishnah-unit because what he has to say must stand as the single decisive interpretation of each difficult passage.

If I may now specify the one important, new thing I believe I contribute by my emphasis on the traits of patterned language and syntax, it is very simple. Trying to make sense of a unit of Mishnah requires us, to begin with, to focus on what is important in that unit, what is central and critical to its message. Even though we know the meaning of all the words, we do not grasp their sense and purpose, unless we can state, *This* is what the framer of the unit wants to say, to stress, to emphasize. Focusing on what is important to that person, we uncover the point and purpose—what I call, the exegetical fulcrum—of the whole. Not focusing on what clearly is at issue yields confusion. If we do not look for the main point, we learn nothing, even though, in the manner of the Talmudic exegetes of Mishnah, we are able to pick out points of repetition, contradiction, and other sorts of formalistic difficulty. If we do not search for the principal message of the unit, we learn nothing, even though, in the style of the later *halakhic* exegetes of Mishnah (to whom Mishnah never was a very critical document), we can link the law of the passage before us with some other law in any document, whether Talmudic or much later than that. In all, close analysis of syntactic patterns of stress and conflict leads us to the heart of the matter. And that is what the interpretation and explanation of the materials to follow intend to do.

The tractate under study in this book is Makhshirin, that is, "liquids that impart susceptibility to uncleanness." To understand the facts that the tractate takes for granted, we have to begin with the concern of the division of the Mishnah in which the tractate finds its place, *Tohorot,* or Purities. At issue here is how a person attains that state of cultic cleanness ("ritual purity") demanded by the Book of Leviticus of those priests who undertake to carry out the sacrificial rites of the cult of the Lord in Jerusalem. The basic principle of this division of the Mishnah is that an ordinary person at home is to eat meals in a state of cleanness analogous to that cultic cleanness demanded for service at the altar of Jerusalem. Hence when someone is unclean, he or she is not to eat ordinary food that has been preserved in a state of cleanness; but when someone is clean, then food in a state of cultic cleanness may be eaten. The division of Purities is about three things: (1) how one becomes unclean, that is, sources of uncleanness, especially those specified at Leviticus Chapters Twelve through Fifteen; (2) what becomes unclean, that is, persons or objects that are susceptible to uncleanness; and (3) how, having become unclean, an object or a person becomes clean, that is, rites of purification. Within that tripartite division, our tractate falls within the first of the three concerns, sources of uncleanness and how something or someone becomes unclean.

The tractate's basic fact derives from a fairly routine exegesis of Lev. 11:34, 37-8. These verses are understood to mean that dry food is not susceptible to uncleanness, and food that has been watered or wet down in some way is susceptible to uncleanness, so that, when brought into the sphere of influence of a source of uncleanness such as a dead creeping thing, said food in fact is deemed unclean. A person intended to preserve cultic cleanness and to eat food in the state of cleanness is not to eat that food. The verses are as follows:

Lev. 11:34: Any food in [an earthen vessel] which may be eaten, upon which water may come, shall be unclean. . . .
Lev. 11:37-8: And if any part of their carcass falls upon any seed for sowing that is to be sown, it is clean; but *if water be put on the seed* and any part of their carcass falls on it, it is unclean to you.

The italicized phrase, *If water be put,* is a recurrent formula in our tractate. That which falls "under the law, If water be put," is susceptible to uncleanness, or, simply, unclean; and that which does "not" fall "under the law, If water be put," is not susceptible to uncleanness, or, simply, clean. So at issue in our tractate is the matter of what is wet and dry, with specific reference to food.

But there is an important qualification, and it is what brings the tractate into being by generating all of its sustained discourse. Taken for granted throughout is a simple conception. Merely because food is wet does not mean that that produce automatically is susceptible to uncleanness. The law does not work *ex opere operato.* It depends, rather, on circumstance. The special circumstance, or context, which the law knows to be operative throughout, is the human will, purpose, or intention. If accidentally water merely

happens to fall upon a pile of barley, that means nothing. The barley—we all know—remains in a state of cultic cleanness, as if it were
completely dry. If, on the other hand, someone has deliberately
poured water on the barley, then, but only then, the barley is
deemed to have been made susceptible to uncleanness. So throughout the tractate before us we shall want to know about the circumstance or context in which water is put on produce.

Given this cutting edge of the inquiry, we shall in fact examine
a subtle and sophisticated essay on the character of human purpose
or intention, and on the interplay between what a human being
wants and the state of nature: the power of a human being through
his or her mere will to affect the state of nature and to effect a
change in that state. In the final chapter (Chapter 6) I shall specify
the several positions worked out on this profound and deeply
metaphysical·theme, expressed in extraordinarily trivial examples
and never specified and articulated at all. Yet at the end, when we
have seen the tractate three times, first in its bits and pieces, then,
second, in its conglomerations of units, finally, as a whole, you
will judge whether or not I have read into the matter what, in fact,
is not there at all. For I shall claim at the end that the tractate is
conceptually whole and intellectually deeply integrated. It is an
essay about a problem. It explores the full depths and dimensions
of that problem. And it does so in such a way that, once its peculiar mode of discourse is understood, we simply cannot miss the
point of what it wishes to tell us.

ii. Mishnah Makhshirin Chapter Two

זֵעַת בָּתִּים, בּוֹרוֹת, שִׁיחִין, וּמְעָרוֹת – טְהוֹרָה. זֵעַת הָאָדָם –
טְהוֹרָה. שָׁתָה מַיִם טְמֵאִים וְהִזִּיעַ – זֵעָתוֹ טְהוֹרָה. בָּא בְּמַיִם
שְׁאוּבִים וְהִזִּיעַ – זֵעָתוֹ טְמֵאָה. נִסְתַּפֵּג וְאַחַר כָּךְ הִזִּיעַ – זֵעָתוֹ
טְהוֹרָה.

A. The sweat [of damp walls] of houses, pits, cisterns, and
caves is clean [in respect to imparting susceptibility to un-
cleanness].

B. The sweat of man is clean.

C. [If] one drank unclean water and sweated, his sweat is clean.

D. [If] one entered drawn water and sweated, his sweat is unclean.

E. [If] he dried himself off and afterward sweated, his sweat is clean.

M. 2:1

The pericope is in two parts, a simple declarative sentence, A, and the little problem laid forth by B-E. B does not contrast with A but introduces a problem and unit of its own. The point of C is that the unclean water that has produced the sweat has been transformed in the man's body (along the lines of M. Miq. 10:6-8), and does not impart susceptibility to receive uncleanness. D then does contrast with C, and the pair concludes at E, a triplet expounding B.

The interpretation of D is diverse. Maimonides takes what to me is the logical route, which is to see the sweat as mingled with the drawn water on the body. This drawn water has the power to impart susceptibility, because a human being drew it. Therefore the sweat also is susceptible to uncleanness and imparts susceptibility to uncleanness, inasmuch as it is mingled with the water on the man's body. E surely invites this interpretation. But this poses two problems. First, the reference is to the *sweat,* and not to the mixture of sweat and water. Second and more compelling, the inclusion of the detail about drawn water does raise secondary issues not covered in Maimonides' simple explanation, for instance, the issue of the man's deliberation in taking up the water. This is an example of the limitations of form-analysis. Where Mishnah's patterned language yields no insight, we are unable to propose solutions to problems of exegesis. Later on we shall make this observation again. It is useful to notice even now that the approach exemplified in this interpretation of Mishnah solves some long-standing problems but in no way contributes to the solution of others.

מֵרָחָץ טְמֵאָה – זֵעָתָהּ טְמֵאָה; וּטְהוֹרָה – בְּכִי יִתֵּן. הַבְּרֵכָה
שֶׁבַּבַּיִת, הַבַּיִת מֵזִיעַ מֵחֲמָתָהּ: אִם טְמֵאָה – זֵעַת כָּל הַבַּיִת
שֶׁמֵּחֲמַת הַבְּרֵכָה, טְמֵאָה.

A. [If the water of] a bath-house is unclean, its sweat is unclean.

B. And [if the water of a bath-house] is clean, it[s sweat] is subject to the law, If water be put.

C. The pool that is in the house—

D. the [wall of the] house sweats on its account—

E. if it [the pool] was unclean, the sweat of [the walls of] the entire house that is [produced] on account of the pool is unclean.

M. 2:2

We resume the discussion left off at M. 2:1A. The rule is completed at A-B. C-E limit the foregoing. The sweat of the house is clean, but if the sweat is caused by the pool, and the pool was unclean, then the sweat of the house is unclean (M. 2:1A). Accordingly, the sequence is M. 2:1A, M. 2:2A-B, then M. 2:2C-E, a qualification built upon the foregoing. The point of A is clear. If the water of the bath is unclean, then the sweat which comes from the walls both imparts susceptibility to uncleanness and at the same time imparts uncleanness, as at M. 1:1. If the water is clean, however, then it nonetheless imparts susceptibility to uncleanness, and this is a clear limitation of M. 2:1A.

C-E follow from this rule. If there is a pool in the house, then the house falls into the category of the bath-house of A-B. What we have, therefore, is a considerable study of the implications of M. 2:1A. The sweat of houses is clean, that of bath-houses is unclean, and that which generates the latter rule may also apply in the former situation. The little pericope about the status of human sweat, M. 2:1B-E, is interpolated into this continuous construction. We shall now see that M. 2:3 depends upon M. 2:2C-E. But we shall first have to study M. 2:3 in its larger unit of tradition, M. 2:3-11. There is no way to break up this immense formal construction without violating its aesthetic and linguistic authenticity.

שְׁתֵּי בְרֵכוֹת, אַחַת טְהוֹרָה וְאַחַת טְמֵאָה, הַמַּזִּיעַ קָרוֹב
לַטְּמֵאָה – טָמֵא; קָרוֹב לַטְּהוֹרָה – טָהוֹר. מֶחֱצָה לְמֶחֱצָה –
טָמֵא. בַּרְזֶל טָמֵא שֶׁבְּלָלוֹ עִם בַּרְזֶל טָהוֹר: אִם רֹב מִן

הַטָּמֵא – טָמֵא; וְאִם רֹב מִן הַטָּהוֹר – טָהוֹר. מֶחֱצָה לְמֶחֱצָה –
טָמֵא. גִּסְטְרָיוֹת שֶׁיִּשְׂרָאֵל וְגוֹיִם מַטִּילִין לְתוֹכָן: אִם רֹב מִן
הַטָּמֵא – טָמֵא; וְאִם רֹב מִן הַטָּהוֹר – טָהוֹר. מֶחֱצָה לְמֶחֱצָה –
טָמֵא. מֵי שְׁפִיכוּת שֶׁיָּרְדוּ עֲלֵיהֶן מֵי גְשָׁמִים: אִם רֹב מִן
הַטָּמֵא – טָמֵא; וְאִם רֹב מִן הַטָּהוֹר – טָהוֹר. מֶחֱצָה לְמֶחֱצָה –
טָמֵא. אֵימָתַי? בִּזְמַן שֶׁקָּדְמוּ מֵי שְׁפִיכוּת, אֲבָל אִם קָדְמוּ מֵי
גְשָׁמִים, אֲפִלּוּ כָל שֶׁהֵן, לְמֵי שְׁפִיכוּת – טָמֵא.

הַטּוֹרֵף אֶת גַּגּוֹ, וְהַמְכַבֵּס אֶת כְּסוּתוֹ וְיָרְדוּ עֲלֵיהֶן גְּשָׁמִים: אִם
רֹב מִן הַטָּמֵא – טָמֵא; וְאִם רֹב מִן הַטָּהוֹר – טָהוֹר. מֶחֱצָה
לְמֶחֱצָה – טָמֵא. רַבִּי יְהוּדָה אוֹמֵר: אִם הוֹסִיפוּ לְנַטֵּף.

עִיר שֶׁיִּשְׂרָאֵל וְנָכְרִים דָּרִים בָּהּ, וְהָיָה בָהּ מֶרְחָץ מַרְחֶצֶת
בַּשַּׁבָּת: אִם רֹב נָכְרִים – רוֹחֵץ מִיָּד; וְאִם רֹב יִשְׂרָאֵל – יַמְתִּין
כְּדֵי שֶׁיֵּחַמּוּ הַחַמִּין. מֶחֱצָה לְמֶחֱצָה – יַמְתִּין כְּדֵי שֶׁיֵּחַמּוּ
הַחַמִּין. רַבִּי יְהוּדָה אוֹמֵר: בְּאַמְבָּטִי קְטַנָּה, אִם יֶשׁ בָּהּ
רָשׁוּת – רוֹחֵץ בָּהּ מִיָּד.

מָצָא בָהּ יָרָק נִמְכָּר: אִם רֹב גּוֹיִם – לוֹקֵחַ מִיָּד; וְאִם רֹב
יִשְׂרָאֵל – יַמְתִּין כְּדֵי שֶׁיָּבוֹא מִמָּקוֹם קָרוֹב. מֶחֱצָה לְמֶחֱצָה –
יַמְתִּין כְּדֵי שֶׁיָּבוֹא מִמָּקוֹם קָרוֹב. וְאִם יֶשׁ בָּהּ רָשׁוּת – לוֹקֵחַ
מִיָּד.

מָצָא בָהּ תִּינוֹק מֻשְׁלָךְ: אִם רֹב גּוֹיִם – גּוֹי; וְאִם רֹב יִשְׂרָאֵל –
יִשְׂרָאֵל. מֶחֱצָה לְמֶחֱצָה – יִשְׂרָאֵל. רַבִּי יְהוּדָה אוֹמֵר: הוֹלְכִין
אַחַר רֹב הַמַּשְׁלִיכִין.

מָצָא בָהּ מְצִיאָה: אִם רֹב גּוֹיִם – אֵינוֹ צָרִיךְ לְהַכְרִיז; וְאִם
רֹב יִשְׂרָאֵל – צָרִיךְ לְהַכְרִיז. מֶחֱצָה לְמֶחֱצָה – צָרִיךְ לְהַכְרִיז.
מָצָא בָהּ פַּת – הוֹלְכִין אַחַר רֹב הַנַּחְתּוֹמִין. וְאִם הָיְתָה פַת
עִיסָה – הוֹלְכִים אַחַר רֹב אוֹכְלֵי פַת עִיסָה. רַבִּי יְהוּדָה

אוֹמֵר: אִם הָיְתָה פַת קֵיבָר – הוֹלְכִין אַחַר רֹב אוֹכְלֵי פַת קֵיבָר.

מָצָא בָה בָּשָׂר – הוֹלְכִין אַחַר רֹב הַטַּבָּחִים. אִם הָיָה מְבֻשָּׁל – הוֹלְכִים אַחַר רֹב אוֹכְלֵי בָשָׂר מְבֻשָּׁל.

הַמּוֹצֵא פֵרוֹת בַּדֶּרֶךְ: אִם רֹב מַכְנִיסִין לְבָתֵּיהֶן – פָּטוּר; וְלִמְכּוֹר בַּשּׁוּק-חַיָּב. מֶחֱצָה לְמֶחֱצָה-דְּמַאי. אוֹצָר שֶׁיִּשְׂרָאֵל וְגוֹיִם מַטִּילִין לְתוֹכוֹ: אִם רֹב גּוֹיִם – וַדַּאי; וְאִם רֹב יִשְׂרָאֵל – דְּמַאי. מֶחֱצָה לְמֶחֱצָה – וַדַּאי; דִּבְרֵי רַבִּי מֵאִיר. וַחֲכָמִים אוֹמְרִים: אֲפִלּוּ כֻלָּם גּוֹיִם, וְיִשְׂרָאֵל אֶחָד מַטִּיל לְתוֹכוֹ – דְּמַאי.

פֵרוֹת שְׁנִיָּה שֶׁרַבּוּ עַל שֶׁלַּשְּׁלִישִׁית, וְשֶׁלַּשְּׁלִישִׁית עַל שֶׁלָּרְבִיעִית, וְשֶׁלָּרְבִיעִית עַל שֶׁלַּחֲמִישִׁית, וְשֶׁלַּחֲמִישִׁית עַל שֶׁלַּשִּׁשִּׁית, וְשֶׁלַּשִּׁשִּׁית עַל שֶׁלַּשְּׁבִיעִית, וְשֶׁלַּשְּׁבִיעִית עַל שֶׁלְּמוֹצָאֵי שְׁבִיעִית – הוֹלְכִין אַחַר הָרֹב. מֶחֱצָה לְמֶחֱצָה – לְהַחְמִיר.

I. A. Two pools—

   B. one clean and one unclean—

   C. that [wall which sweats] nearer to the unclean one is unclean, and that [which sweats] near the clean one is clean.

   D. Half and half [Danby: "Those that are midway"] —it is unclean.

II. E. Unclean iron that one smelted with clean iron—

   F. if the greater part is from the unclean, [the consequent metal] is unclean,

   G. and if the greater part is from the clean [ore], it is clean.

   H. Half and half—it is unclean.

III. I. Pots into which Israelites and gentiles urinate—

   J. if the greater part is from the unclean [gentile source], [the urine in the pot] is unclean,

K. and if the greater part is from the clean [Israelite source], [the urine in the pot] is clean.

L. Half and half—it is unclean.

IV. M. Dirty water on which rain-water fell—

N. if the greater part [of the consequent mixture of water] is from the unclean [water], it is unclean.

O. And if the greater part is from the clean, it is clean.

P. Half and half—it is clean.

Q. When [does the foregoing rule apply]? When the dirty water came first,

R. But if the rain-water,

S. in whatever volume,

T. preceded the dirty water, [the consequent mixture] is unclean.

M. 2:3

V. A. He who plasters his roof [with unclean water and clay] —

B. and he who launders his garment—

C. and rain fell on them—

D. if the greater part is from the unclean [water], it is unclean.

E. And if the greater part is from the clean [rain], it is clean.

F. Half and half—it is unclean.

G. R. Judah says, "If [the rains] continued dripping [at greater speed, the whole is clean]."

M. 2:4

I. A. A city in which Israelites and gentiles dwell—

B. and in which a bath-house [which was open and] heated on the Sabbath—

C. if the majority is gentiles, one washes in it forthwith [at the end of the Sabbath].

D. And if the majority was Israelite, one must wait a sufficient time for the water to be heated.

E. Half and half—one must wait a sufficient time for the water to be heated.

F. R. Judah says, "In the case of a small bath, if there is in [town] [a gentile] magistrate, one washes in it forthwith."

M. 2:5

II. A. [If] one found in [a town in which Israelites and gentiles dwell together] a vegetable [assumed to have been plucked on the Sabbath] which is sold [at the close of the Sabbath] —

B. if the majority is gentile, one purchases [it] forthwith.

C. And if the majority is Israelite, one must wait [at the end of the Sabbath] sufficient time for [others] to come from a nearby place.

D. Half and half—one must wait [at the end of the Sabbath] sufficient time for [others to] come from a nearby place.

E. And if there is in it [the town] [a gentile] magistrate, one purchases forthwith.

M. 2:6

III. A. [If] one found in it an abandoned child,

B. if the majority is gentile, it is deemed a gentile.

C. And if the majority is Israelite, it is deemed an Israelite.

D. Half and half—it is deemed an Israelite.

E. R. Judah says, "They follow the status of the majority of those who abandon babies [who are assumed to be gentile]."

M. 2:7

IV. A. [If] one found in it something that was lost,

B. if the majority is gentile, one does not have to proclaim [that fact].

C. And if the majority was Israelite, one has to proclaim [that fact, seeking the rightful owner].

D. Half and half—one has to proclaim [that fact].

V. E. [If] one found a piece of bread in it [the city in which were both Israelites and gentiles],

F. they follow the status of the majority of the bakers.

G. And if it was a piece of bread made out of pure flour, [with reference to tithing] they follow the status of the majority of those who eat bread made out of pure flour.

H. R. Judah says, "If it was a piece of bread made out of coarse meal, they follow the status of the majority of those who eat bread made out of coarse meal."

M. 2:8

VI. A. [If] one found in it meat,

B. they follow the status of the majority of the butchers,

C. If it was cooked, they follow the status of the majority of those who eat cooked meat.

M. 2:9

I. A. He who finds produce by the wayside—

B. if most people store up [their produce] in their house, it is clear [of the obligation to tithe].

C. And [if it is the practice of most people] to sell [their produce] in the market, it is liable [for tithes].

D. Half and half—it is deemed doubtfully tithed produce.

II. E. A storage bin into which Israelites and gentiles put their produce—

F. "if the majority is gentile, [produce found in the bin] is certainly [untithed].

G. "And if the majority is Israelite, it is doubtfully tithed produce.

H. "Half and half—it is certainly [untithed]," the words of R. Meir.

I. And sages say, "Even if all of them are gentile, but a single Israelite puts [his produce] into it [the storage bin], [the whole is deemed] doubtfully tithed produce."

M. 2:10

III. A. Produce of the second year that exceeded in quantity produce of the third year,

B. and produce of the third year that exceeded in quantity produce of the fourth year,

C. and produce of the fourth year that exceeded in quantity produce of the fifth year,

D. and produce of the fifth year that exceeded in quantity produce of the sixth year,

E. and produce of the sixth year that exceeded in quantity produce of the seventh year,

F. and produce of the seventh year that exceeded in quantity produce of the year after the seventh year—

G. they follow the status of the majority.

H. Half and half—to impose the most strict status [Danby: "If they were equal, they must apply the more stringent of the rules (governing the two years)."]

M. 2:11

Only the opening item of the large unit, M. 2:3-11, is relevant to our tractate. Its rule has already been introduced at M. 2:2C-E, upon which M. 2:3A-D depend for meaning. It follows, given the very careful weaving together of M. 2:1-2, that the entire chapter, exclusive of the interpolated unit on human sweat, is a unitary construction, with the introduction of M. 2:1A, 2A-3D followed by the spinning out of diverse cases along a single formal model. M. 2:3E-H are verbatim at M. Kel. 11:4.

The dirty water of M. 2:3M (translated by Segal as "slop-water") is assumed to be unclean, which accounts for the shift, N, to *unclean*. Rain-water does not impart susceptibility to uncleanness unless it falls with human approval. It annuls the slop-water (M. Miq. 1:4). Q's point is that the rain-water can clean the slop-water when the slop-water was diluted by the rain-water. But if the rain-water was present first and then the slop -water fell into it, the mixture is unclean. Why? The rain-water has been gathered in a utensil, therefore is wanted and is made unclean by the falling slops. The unclean slop-water makes the rain-water unclean and is not neutralized by the larger quantity of rain-water as it is in O.

M. 2:3 introduces a massive construction, put together because of common formal traits, with apocopation for the case, and the whole of each unit given in four stichs, as at M. 2:3A-D. There are three formal groups, five, six, and three, with the third clearly awry at M. 2:11, as I shall explain. The obvious point throughout is that what is nearer to what is unclean is deemed unclean, and what is nearer to what is clean is deemed clean, with appropriate variations. What is midway (or "half and half" in some other context) is unclean. In all there are fourteen exempla of the generative form, with some interesting variations. M. 2:3A-M give us four, glossed at Q-R for the fourth. M. 2:4B is an interpolation, C is required to set up the problem, and G glosses. Again at M. 2:5, F is a gloss; M. 2:6E, M. 2:7E, and M. 2:8H do the same. At M. 2:l0 we have a dispute, F-H versus I. But without the sages' view at I, Meir's saying would follow the established form. The construction ends at M. 2:ll, which deliberately breaks the pattern, specifically through the immense protasis, A-H. But G-H adhere closely to the form, and I am inclined to see the pericope as integral to the larger construction. It is common for the final item in a major unit to vary the form and so signify the conclusion of the construction as a whole.

M. 2:4B is an obvious interpolation. The rule otherwise follows the foregoing model. Judah's saying contains no conclusion, but by contrast to F should end, *clean,* as given. The point is that if the dripping increased in frequency, the rain-water is deemed to form the larger part over the dirty water.

At this point, the unit relevant to our tractate concludes, five items, with only II entirely out of place. The next two groups bear no relationship whatever to Makhshirin and its interests. The issue of M. 2:5-6 concerns the Sabbath. In the former case, we want to be sure that the water is not heated on the Sabbath for Israelite use. If that were to be done, Israelites could not benefit from it, even later on. In the latter, we want to be sure that the vegetable has not been harvested on the Sabbath for Israelite use. M. 2:7-9 are clear as given. The consideration important to M. 2:10 has to do with whether the produce has been tithed. If people store up food in their houses, then we assume the produce has been properly tithed. But people do not tithe what they sell. M. 2:ll, finally, introduces the diverse tithing requirements of the several years in the septennial cycle. In the first, second, fourth, and fifth years, produce is liable to First Tithe, given to the Levite, and Second Tithe, to be consumed in Jerusalem. In the third and sixth years, produce is liable to First Tithe, and Poor man's tithe (Third Tithe), which is given to the poor. Then we have a mixture, for example, first and second, second and third, third and fourth, and so on. The stringent alternative, H, is to give the tithes due in both years; e.g., in the case of a mixture of second and third year produce or of that of the fifth and sixth years, one gives First Tithe *and* Second Tithe,

which must be separated; its value is given to the poor to be consumed in Jerusalem. In the case of a mixture of produce of the sixth
and seventh year, First and poor man's tithes are given. In a mixture
of seventh and first year produce, First and Second Tithes must be
given, and also the regulations of seventh year produce must be
observed.

iii. Mishnah Makhshirin Chapter Three

שַׂק שֶׁהוּא מָלֵא פֵּרוֹת וּנְתָנוֹ עַל גַּב הַנָּהָר, אוֹ עַל פִּי הַבּוֹר,
אוֹ עַל מַעֲלוֹת הַמְּעָרָה, וְשָׁאֲבוּ: כָּל שֶׁשָּׁאֲבוּ – בְּכִי יֻתַּן. רַבִּי
יְהוּדָה אוֹמֵר: כָּל שֶׁהוּא כְּנֶגֶד הַמַּיִם – בְּכִי יֻתַּן, וְכָל שֶׁאֵינוֹ
כְּנֶגֶד הַמַּיִם – אֵינוֹ בְּכִי יֻתַּן.

A. A sack that is full of pieces of fruit and [which] one
placed on the side of the river,
   B. or over the mouth of the cistern,
   C. or over the steps of the cave,
   D. and [the pieces of fruit] absorbed [water] —
   E. All [the fruit that] absorbed [water] is under the law,
If water be put.
   F. R. Judah says, "Whatever is over against the water is
under the law, If water be put.
   G. "And whatever is not over against the water is not under
the law, If water be put."

M. 3:1

The dispute consists of A+D-E *versus* F-G, with Judah's saying
depending on the antecedent construction for context and meaning.
B-C are a gloss (M. Miq. 4:4). Whatever water is absorbed affects
the fruit. Judah wishes to distinguish between the fruit which lies
over against the water and that which does not. The latter fruit
does not absorb liquid; what is not directly affected by the water
therefore is deemed to be insusceptible (Albeck, p. 421, p. 594).
A-E maintain that even though the liquid absorbed by the fruit
not opposite the water is apt to be slight, the fruit nonetheless is

deemed susceptible. We take for granted that the owner wants the
fruit to absorb water to become heavier and fuller (Sens, Bert., MS,
Segal, p. 479, n. 2). Judah's view is that, if such were the case, the
owner would have spread out all the fruit in such a way as to bring
it within access of the water (GRA). That is, as we shall see at
M. 3:6-7, he would have done a deed to indicate his intention (MA).
As often, Judah maintains that what one does defines what he
originally wanted to do. Since one has not laid out the fruit so
that it would absorb water, the fruit has not been wet down with
the owner's approval, that is, at the owner's intention. Consequently,
the fruit is not susceptible to uncleanness, since the owner has not
deliberately watered it. Later on, we shall see other theories of the
role of one's will or intention in watering produce; on the one side,
the susceptibility of said produce to uncleanness, on the second
side, and the power of the water to impart susceptibility to uncleanness, on the third. All of this unfolds, so far as Mishnah is concerned,
in accord with Mishnah's theory of the topic, and not in accord
with the inner logical principles governing the law (e.g., Judah's
position, the opposite of Judah's position, and so on).

חָבִית שֶׁהִיא מְלֵאָה פֵרוֹת וּנְתוּנָה לְתוֹךְ הַמַּשְׁקִין, אוֹ מְלֵאָה
מַשְׁקִין וּנְתוּנָה לְתוֹךְ הַפֵּרוֹת, וְשָׁאֲבוּ: כָּל שֶׁשָּׁאֲבוּ – בְּכִי יֻתַּן.
בְּאֵלּוּ מַשְׁקִים אָמְרוּ? בַּמַּיִם, וּבַיַּיִן, וּבַחֹמֶץ. וּשְׁאָר כָּל
הַמַּשְׁקִין – טְהוֹרִין. רַבִּי נְחֶמְיָה מְטַהֵר בַּקִּטְנִית, שֶׁאֵין הַקִּטְנִית
שׁוֹאֶבֶת.

A. A jar [made of porous material] that is full of pieces of
fruit and placed into liquid,

B. or one that is full of liquid and placed among pieces of
fruit,

C. and [the pieces of fruit] absorbed [water] —

D. whatever they absorbed is under the law, If water be put.

E. About what sort of liquids did they rule?

F. [They ruled] about water, wine, and vinegar [which can
be absorbed].

G. But [in the case of] all other liquids [capable of imparting susceptibility to uncleanness, the pieces of fruit] are clean.

[Maimonides, *Uncleanness of Foodstuffs* 14:6: "Not enough
of them can be absorbed through the earthenware to render
susceptible the produce beside them."] [Maharam reads *unclean.*]

H. R. Nehemiah declares clean in the case of pulse [mois-
tened by water, wine, or vinegar], since pulse does not absorb
[moisture].

M. 3:2

Whatever water reaches the pieces of fruit is deemed absorbed
with approval; otherwise the owner would not have put the fruit
into the porous jar and the jar into the water. All of this accords
with Judah's theory of the matter. The liquids are those that can
be absorbed (E-G). The others are too thick to pass through the
porous jar (Rosh). Nehemiah glosses, adding a trivial point; he
does not reject the basic rule.

הָרוֹדֶה פַּת חַמָּה וּנְתָנָה עַל פִּי חָבִית שֶׁלַּיַּיִן – רַבִּי מֵאִיר
מְטַמֵּא; וְרַבִּי יְהוּדָה מְטַהֵר. רַבִּי יוֹסֵי מְטַהֵר בְּשֶׁלַּחִטִּים,
וּמְטַמֵּא בְּשֶׁלַּשְּׂעוֹרִים, מִפְּנֵי שֶׁהַשְּׂעוֹרִים שׁוֹאֲבוֹת.

A. He who took hot bread [from the side of the oven] and
put it over a jar of wine —
B. R. Meir declares it susceptible to uncleanness.
C. And R. Judah declares it insusceptible to cleanness.
D. R. Yosé declares clean in the case of bread made of wheat,
and declares unclean in the case of bread made of barley,
E. because barley absorbs [liquid].

M. 3:3

The point in dispute is registered at E: Do we deem the bread to
absorb the wine? Let us first consider the facts of the case. The
bread is kneaded with fruit juice and is therefore insusceptible to
uncleanness (Bert.). Then, when placed over the wine-jar, does it
absorb the wine-vapor and so become susceptible to uncleanness?
An alternative view (both are at Rosh) is that the bread is kneaded
with water and is susceptible. The wine is unclean. Does the bread

absorb the unclean vapor of the wine? Maimonides *(Uncleanness of Foodstuffs* 14:7) gives both versions:

> If a man takes hot bread off the side of an oven and puts it
> over the mouth of a jar of wine, if it is wheaten bread, it is
> not rendered susceptible, but if it is barley bread, it is suscep-
> tible, because barley absorbs moisture. So too if the wine is
> unclean, and the bread is wheaten bread, the bread remains
> clean, but if it is barley bread, it becomes unclean because it
> absorbs unclean liquid.

Self-evidently, on the surface Yosé agrees with Judah. That is, if
the bread can absorb liquid, it is assumed to do so. What is at issue,
however, between Meir and Judah? Meir's position is clear. The
hot bread is assumed to absorb the wine-fumes. Does Judah differ
on that point? I do not see how he can; the facts, after all, speak
for themselves. Yosé leaves no doubt that, if there is absorption,
then he deems that to be the decisive matter. But why should Judah
differ as to the facts? It seems more likely that he takes a position
governed by a different perspective or principle. *Even though* there
is absorption, contrary to Meir, the bread remains insusceptible
(and Yosé then cannot agree after all). Why is the bread insusceptible, in Judah's view? Perhaps Judah's position depends upon that
at M. 3:1F-G. If a man put the fruit against the water, it is going
to absorb water, but if he did not, it will not. Accordingly, we adjudge the matter in accord with the man's deed: If a man wanted
to put wine into the bread, he would not take the dubious course
of putting the hot bread over the wine-jug, but would have poured
wine into the bread. This he did not do, and, accordingly, he does
not want wine in the bread. He could and would have done exactly
what he wanted to indicate his intention, and, not having done
so, has not made the wine capable of imparting susceptibility to
uncleanness to the bread that happens to be subject to its fumes.
This radical position, stressing the primacy of deed over indicated
intention and treating deed as definitive of intention, recurs throughout Judah's rulings.

הַמְרַבֵּץ אֶת בֵּיתוֹ וְנָתַן בּוֹ חִטִּים, וְטָנָנוּ, אִם מֵחֲמַת הַמַּיִם –
בְּכִי יִתֵּן; וְאִם מֵחֲמַת הַסֶּלַע – אֵינָן בְּכִי יִתֵּן. הַמְכַבֵּס אֶת
כְּסוּתוֹ בָּעֲרֵבָה, נָתַן בָּהּ חִטִּים, וְטָנָנוּ, אִם מֵחֲמַת הַמַּיִם –
בְּכִי יִתֵּן; אִם מֵחֲמַת עַצְמָן – אֵינָן בְּכִי יִתֵּן. הַמְטַגֵּן בַּחוֹל,
הֲרֵי זֶה בְּכִי יִתֵּן. מַעֲשֶׂה בְאַנְשֵׁי הַמָּחוֹז שֶׁהָיוּ מְטַנִּין בַּחוֹל,
אָמְרוּ לָהֶם חֲכָמִים: אִם כָּךְ הֱיִיתֶם עוֹשִׂים, לֹא עֲשִׂיתֶם
טַהֲרָה מִימֵיכֶם.

I. A. He who sprinkles his house [with water] and [after-
ward] put wheat into it,

B. and [the grains of wheat] became damp—

C. if it is on account of the water, it is subject to the law,
If water be put.

D. And if it is on account of the rock-floor, it is not
under the law, If water be put.

II. E. He who washes his clothing in a trough and [afterward]
put into it grains of wheat, and they became damp,

F. if [the moisture] is on account of the water, it is subject to the law, If water be put.

G. And if [the moisture] is on account of itself, it is not
under the law, If water be put.

III. H. He who dampens [wheat] with sand, lo, this is under
the rule, If water be put.

I. M'SH B: The people of Maḥoz were dampening
[wheat] in sand.

J. Sages said to them, "If thus you have been doing, you
have never in your entire lives prepared [food] in accord with
the rules of cleanness."

M. 3:4

We have a triplet of the following units: A-D, E-G, H, and the
illustrative case serving H, I-J. In all cases we distinguish between
sources of moisture. If the water was sprinkled with approval and
thereafter affects the wheat, the wheat is deemed susceptible to

uncleanness (A-D). But if the wheat is moistened through the rock-
floor, then, in line with M. 2:1A, the wheat is deemed still insusceptible to uncleanness. The same point is made at the second case,
E-G. For the diverse readings of G, Albeck (p. 422) (= MS, Maimonides) prefers *on its account* ('SMH), that is, the moisture is on account of the wetness that is absorbed in the wooden sides of the
trough. At H we do not assume that the sand is utterly lacking in
moisture. Since the man has made use of the sand with the intention
to moisten the wheat, the wheat is deemed to be susceptible. The
people of Maḥoz wet down the wheat. Since they supposed it was
insusceptible, they may not have taken precautions to keep sources
of uncleanness away from the wheat, which therefore is assumed
to have been susceptible to uncleanness and made unclean.

Maimonides *(Uncleanness of Foodstuffs* 14:8) rephrases matters
only slightly:

If a man besprinkles his house with water and puts wheat
therein, and the wheat grows damp, if this is effected by the
water, it is rendered susceptible; but if it is effected by the
rock floor, it is not rendered susceptible. If a man washes his
garments in a trough and then puts wheat therein, and the
wheat grows damp, if this is by reason of the water, it is rendered susceptible; but if it is by reason of the moisture of the
trough, it is not rendered susceptible.

הַמְטַנֵּן בְּטִיט הַנָּגוּב – רַבִּי שִׁמְעוֹן אוֹמֵר: אִם יֶשׁ בּוֹ מַשְׁקֶה
טוֹפֵחַ – בְּכִי יֻתַּן; וְאִם לָאו – אֵינוֹ בְּכִי יֻתַּן. הַמְרַבֵּץ אֶת
גָּרְנוֹ, אֵינוֹ חוֹשֵׁשׁ שֶׁמָּא נָתַן בָּהּ חִטִּים וְטָנְגוּ. הַמְלַקֵּט עֲשָׂבִים
כְּשֶׁהַטַּל עֲלֵיהֶם, לְהָטֵן בָּהֶם חִטִּים–אֵינָן בְּכִי יֻתַּן. אִם נִתְכַּוֵּן
לְכָךְ, הֲרֵי זֶה בְּכִי יֻתַּן. הַמּוֹלִיךְ חִטִּין לִטְחוֹן וְיָרְדוּ עֲלֵיהֶן
גְּשָׁמִים: אִם שָׂמַח – בְּכִי יֻתַּן. רַבִּי יְהוּדָה אוֹמֵר: אִי אֶפְשָׁר
שֶׁלֹּא לִשְׂמוֹחַ, אֶלָּא – אִם עָמַד.

הָיוּ זֵיתָיו נְתוּנִים בַּגַּג וְיָרְדוּ עֲלֵיהֶן גְּשָׁמִים: אִם שָׂמַח – בְּכִי
יֻתַּן. רַבִּי יְהוּדָה אוֹמֵר: אִי אֶפְשָׁר שֶׁלֹּא לִשְׂמוֹחַ, אֶלָּא – אִם
פָּקַק אֶת הַצִּנּוֹר, אוֹ אִם חִלְחֵל לְתוֹכָן.

הַחַמָּרִי שֶׁהָיוּ עוֹבְרִים בַּנָּהָר וְנָפְלוּ שַׂקֵּיהֶם לַמַּיִם: אִם
שָׂמְחוּ – בְּכִי יֻתַּן. רַבִּי יְהוּדָה אוֹמֵר: אִי אֶפְשָׁר שֶׁלֹּא לִשְׂמוֹחַ,
אֶלָּא – אִם הָפְכוּ. הָיוּ רַגְלָיו מְלֵאוֹת טִיט, וְכֵן רַגְלֵי בְהֶמְתּוֹ,
עָבַר בַּנָּהָר: אִם שָׂמַח – בְּכִי יֻתַּן. רַבִּי יְהוּדָה אוֹמֵר: אִי
אֶפְשָׁר שֶׁלֹּא לִשְׂמוֹחַ, אֶלָּא–אִם עָמַד וְהֵדִיחַ בָּאָדָם..וּבַבְּהֵמָה
טְמֵאָה לְעוֹלָם טָמֵא.

A. He who dampens [wheat] with drying clay —

B. R. Simeon says, "If there is [still] dripping moisture [sufficient to dampen the hand] in it, it is under the law, If water be put.

C. "And if not, it is not under the law, If water be put."

D. He who sprinkles his threshing floor does not scruple lest he put in it grains of wheat and they grow damp.

E. He who gathers blades of grass when the dew is on them to dampen wheat in them — [the moisture] is not under the law, If water be put.

F. If, however, he intended thus, lo, this is under the law, If water be put.

I. G. He who brings his grain to the mill and rain fell on them —

H. if he was happy on that account, it is under the law, If water be put.

I. R. Judah says, "It is not possible not be be happy on that account. But: if he stood [still so that more rain should fall on the wheat, then the water that has fallen on the grain is under the law, If water be put] ."

M. 3:5

II. J. [If] his olives were located on the roof and rain fell on them —

K. if he was happy, it is under the law, If water be put. [And if not, it is not under the law, If water be put.]

L. R. Judah says, "It is not possible not to be happy on that account.

M. "But: if he stopped up the water-spout,

N. "or if he shook the olives in [the rain] , [then it is under the law, If water be put. And if not, it is not under the law, If water be put.] ."

M. 3:6

III. O. The ass-drivers who were crossing the river, and whose sacks fell into the water—

P. if they were happy, it is subject to the law, If water be put.

Q. R. Judah says, "It is not possible not to be happy. But if they turned over [the sacks] , [it is under the law, If water be put] ."

IV. R. [If one's feet were full of mud,

S. and so the hooves of his beast—

T. he crossed the river—

U. if he was happy, it is subject to the law, If water be put.

V. R. Judah says, "It is not possible not to be happy.

W. 1. "But: if he stood [the animal] still and rinsed off [its feet] —

2. "in the case of man—

X. "and in the case of an unclean beast, it is always unclean."

[Segal: "But in the case of man and an unclean beast, it is always unclean." Segal comments (p. 482, n. 5): One is particularly pleased when the feet of a man or of a riding animal are washed in the river, therefore even R. Judah admits that the water falling from their feet after crossing a river can render produce susceptible to uncleanness. TYT+Maharam: A beast for slaughter (= clean) need not have clean hooves, but hooves of one used for riding should be protected.]

M. 3:7

The set presents the following major segments: A-C, D, E-F, G-I, duplicated at J-N, O-Q, R-X, that is, four versions of Judah's item. A-C form a single declarative sentence, D a second, then E-F a third. The whole set begins with the participial substantive, *he who*, which produces apocopation, e.g., at E, in which the apodosis does not refer to the subject of the protasis. The model of I shows that N is secondary, so too X, which poses a further problem, as we shall note shortly.

The exegetical fulcrum for Simeon's group, A-F, is at E-F. If one gathers blades of grass in the morning, when dew is on them, the moisture does not impart susceptibility to uncleanness to the wheat. Why not? Because the man's primary intent was to gather not dew but grass. But if it were the man's intention to do exactly that—namely, to use the dew to dampen the wheat—then the wheat of course is rendered susceptible to uncleanness by the dew. Clearly, this lucid statement of the distinction between intention and lack of intention accords with Simeon's, A-C. (Judah will take a more extreme position.) Thus Simeon says that even if one dampens wheat with drying clay, the wheat is not necessarily rendered susceptible to uncleanness. That is only the case if there is enough moisture in the clay to wet the hand. Then, Simeon will have to concede, the man has done nothing other than to apply water to his grain. But if there is moisture merely inhering in the clay, that is of no effect. It is difficult to see how Simeon can agree with the rule on sand at M. 3:4. For what difference can there be between sand and drying clay? M. 3:4 has distinguished among the *sources* of water or moisture. M. 3:5, by contrast, will not make such a distinction, but is primarily interested in the attitude of the person, as at E-F. D follows the same line of reasoning; the presence of moisture by itself is of no account. Accordingly, M. 3:4 and M. 3:5A-F are primarily concerned, respectively, with the source of the water and with the man's attitude toward the water.

Judah, M. 3:5G-I, 3:6-7, then introduces a still further consideration, which produces remarkable leniency. Whereas Simeon will regard one's *attitude* toward the water as decisive, Judah says we assess one's attitude toward the situation solely in terms of what he actually *does*. Accordingly, if rain falls on the grain, one obviously will be glad to have the grain wet down. But, unless by some concrete action or gesture one is implicated in the wetting down, attitude alone is of no effect. Simeon's position vis à vis Judah surely accords with that of sages in the four disputes.

M. 3:6J-N pose no problem nor do M. 3:7/O-Q. There are two approaches to the parsing of W-X. Following GRA, Albeck inter-

prets *in the case of beast* to pertain both to W and to X. That is, if
a man or (clean) beast stood still and rinsed off the feet or hooves,
then the water that further drips off when the man or beast reaches
the shore is deemed to have been detached with approval and is
therefore capable of imparting susceptibility to uncleanness. In the
case of an unclean beast, whether or not the animal stood still and
rinsed off its hooves, the water always is deemed capable of imparting susceptibility. Albeck does not claim to know the reason
for this latter rule. Segal, following T. Mak. 2:4 and all commentaries, says that we move *in the case of man* from W to X, as shown.
Then he says man and the unclean beast—which is to say, the horse
or some other riding animal—always are glad to have the mud
washed from the feet. Accordingly, I should imagine, the reason is
that even Judah concedes that men and riding animals can be
assumed to have made the necessary movements to indicate approval
and make use of the water in connection with rinsing the feet.

הַמּוֹרִיד אֶת הַגַּלְגַּלִּים וְאֶת כְּלֵי הַבָּקָר בְּשָׁעַת הַקָּדִים לַמַּיִם,
בִּשְׁבִיל שֶׁיָּחוּצוּ, הֲרֵי זֶה בְּכִי יֻתַּן. הַמּוֹרִיד בְּהֵמָה לִשְׁתּוֹת:
הַמַּיִם הָעוֹלִים בְּפִיהָ – בְּכִי יֻתַּן; וּבְרַגְלֶיהָ – אֵינָן בְּכִי יֻתַּן.
אִם חָשַׁב שֶׁיְּדוֹחוּ רַגְלֶיהָ, אַף הָעוֹלִין בְּרַגְלֶיהָ – בְּכִי יֻתַּן.
בִּשְׁעַת הַיַּחַף וְהַדַּיִשׁ לְעוֹלָם טָמֵא. הוֹרִיד חֵרֵשׁ שׁוֹטֶה וְקָטָן,
אַף עַל פִּי שֶׁחוֹשֵׁב שֶׁיְּדוֹחוּ רַגְלֶיהָ – אֵינָן בְּכִי יֻתַּן, שֶׁיֵּשׁ לָהֶן
מַעֲשֶׂה, וְאֵין לָהֶן מַחֲשָׁבָה.

A. He who brings down wagon wheels and cattle yokes to
the water at the time of the east wind so that [the cracks]
may swell out—
    B. lo, this is under the law, If water be put.
    C. He who brings down a cow to drink—
    D. the water that comes up in her mouth is under the law,
If water be put.
    E. And that which comes up with her hooves is not subject
to the law, If water be put.
    F. If he gave thought that her hooves should be rinsed off,

then even the water that comes up with her hooves is under the law, If water be put.

G. In the time of hoof-disease or threshing, [the water dripping from the hooves] is invariably unclean.

H. [If] a deaf-mute, an imbecile, or a minor brought down [the beast], even though he gave thought that her hooves should be rinsed off, it is not subject to the law, If water be put.

I. For they have the power of deed and do not have the power of intention.

M. 3:8

The pericope is composed of the following units: A-B, C-E + F, G, and H-I. D-G do not suggest knowledge of the foregoing and, as indicated, go over the ground of M. 3:7V-X in particular. The opening rule requires little comment. We intentionally wet down the wagon wheels and cattle yokes. Since, C-E, we want the water that the cow drinks, that water, when it drips, is able to impart susceptibility to uncleanness. But we did not intend to rinse the hooves, E, and so that water which drips off the hooves is not capable of imparting susceptibility to uncleanness. F states the obvious. G then adds that if conditions are such as to necessitate rinsing off the feet, we take for granted that the owner approves the use of that water, and it invariably is deemed subject to the law, If water be put. H-I go over familiar ground, as indicated.

Maimonides (Mishnah-commentary) here introduces an interesting conception of a two-stage process in imparting susceptibility. If (1) the utensil is wet down with approval, and (2) afterward produce touched that utensil, also with approval, then the produce is rendered susceptible to uncleanness. At *Uncleanness of Foodstuffs* 13:3-4, he states the pericope as follows:

If a man takes wagon wheels or cattle yokes down to the water at the time of the east wind to fill out the cracks in the wood, any water that comes up on them is deemed to be detached with approval.

It is the stress on "detaching with approval" that shows the two-stage view of the process most clearly. Maimonides does not then introduce the matter of the detached water's touching produce. It is not necessary for his picture of the matter. He continues:

> If a man takes his beast down to drink, water that comes up
> on its mouth is deemed to be detached with approval, but
> that on its legs is not deemed to be detached with approval.
> But if his purpose was that its legs should be rinsed, or if it is
> the season of the autumn or of threshing, that which is on its
> legs is also deemed to be detached with approval. If a deaf-
> mute, an imbecile, or a minor has taken it down, even though
> their purpose was that its legs should be rinsed, water that
> comes up on its legs is not deemed to be detached with ap-
> proval, because with them the act alone is of consequence,
> while the intention is of no consequence.

iv. Mishnah Makhshirin Chapter Four

הַשּׁוֹחֶה לִשְׁתּוֹת, הַמַּיִם הָעוֹלִים בְּפִיו וּבִשְׂפָמוֹ – בְּכִי יֻתַּן.
בְּחָטְמוֹ, וּבְרֹאשׁוֹ, וּבִזְקָנוֹ – אֵינָן בְּכִי יֻתַּן. הַמְמַלֵּא בֶחָבִית,
הַמַּיִם הָעוֹלִים אַחֲרֶיהָ, וּבַחֶבֶל שֶׁהוּא מְכֻנָּן עַל צַוָּארָהּ,
וּבַחֶבֶל שֶׁהוּא לְצָרְכָּהּ – הֲרֵי זֶה בְּכִי יֻתַּן. כַּמָּה הוּא צָרְכָּהּ?
רַבִּי שִׁמְעוֹן בֶּן אֶלְעָזָר אוֹמֵר: טֶפַח. נְתָנָהּ תַּחַת הַצִּנּוֹר – אֵינָן
בְּכִי יֻתַּן.

A. He who kneels down to drink—

B. the water that comes up on his mouth and on his mous-
tache is under the law, If water be put.

C. [The water that comes up] on his nose and on [the hair
of] his head and on his beard is not under the law, If water
be put.

D. He who draws [water] with a jug—

E. the water that comes up on its outer parts and on the
rope wound round its neck and on the rope that is needed [in
dipping it] —lo, this is under the law, If water be put on.

[Maimonides, *Uncleanness of Foodstuffs* 12:5: "And
water on that part of the rope that is more than is needful in
handling it is not deemed to be detached with approval."]
  F. And how much is needed [in handling it] ?
  G. R. Simeon b. Eleazar says, "A handbreadth."
  H. [If] one put it under the water-spout, [the water on its
outer parts and on the rope, now not needed in drawing wa-
ter] is not under the law, If water be put.

M. 4:1

The principle of M. 3:8 is given two further illustrations. What
must get wet in order to accomplish one's purpose is deemed wet
down by approval. But water not needed in one's primary goal is
not subject to approval. The pericope consists of A-C and D-H, the
latter in two parts, D-E + F-G, and H. The point of A-C is clear.
Since, D-E, in dipping the jug into the water, it is not possible to
draw water without wetting the outer parts and the rope, water on
the rope and the outer parts is deemed affected by one's wishes.
Simeon b. Eleazar glosses. At H one does not make use of the rope
and does not care to have the water on the outer parts, since he
can draw the water without recourse to either. Accordingly, water
on the rope and on the outer parts does not impart susceptibility
to uncleanness.

מִי שֶׁיָּרְדוּ עָלָיו גְּשָׁמִים, אֲפִלּוּ אַב הַטֻּמְאָה – אֵינָן בְּכִי יֻתַּן.
וְאִם נָעַר – בְּכִי יֻתַּן. עָמַד תַּחַת הַצִּנּוֹר לְהָקֵר, אוֹ לְדוֹחַ:
בַּטָּמֵא – טְמֵאִין. וּבַטָּהוֹר – בְּכִי יֻתַּן.

  A. He on whom rains fell,
  B. even [if he is] a Father [principal source] of unclean-
ness—
  C. it [the water] is not under the law, If water be put
[since even in the case of B, the rainfall was not wanted].
  D. But if he shook off [the rain], it [the water that is
shaken off] is under the law, If water be put.
  E. [If] he stood under the water-spout to cool off,
  F. or to rinse off,

G. in the case of an unclean person [the water] is unclean.

H. And in the case of a clean person, [the water] is under the law, If water be put.

M. 4:2

The pericope again is in two parts, A-D and E-H, each in two units. The point of A + C is that the rain does not come under the person's approval. Therefore the rain is not capable of imparting susceptibility to uncleanness. If by some action, however, the person responds to the rain, for example, if he shook off his garments, then it falls under his approval. B is certainly a gloss, and not an important one. The principal source of uncleanness, e.g., the *Zab* of Leviticus, Chapter Fifteen, derives no benefit from the rain and therefore need not be explicitly excluded.

At E, however, the person obviously does want to make use of the water. Therefore it is rendered both susceptible to uncleanness and capable of imparting susceptibility to other things. G makes the former point, H, the latter. Perhaps it is G that has generated B, since the distinction between unclean and clean is important at G-H and then invites the contrast between A + B and E + G, that is, falling rain *versus* rain-water pouring through the waterspout and deliberately utilized.

Maimonides' restatement of the rule (*Uncleanness of Foodstuffs* 12:6) is as follows:

If rain falls upon someone, even if he is a Father of uncleanness, the water on him remains clean, even though it passes all the way down him, *provided that he shakes it off himself with all his might;* but if it is still dripping off from him as it leaves him, it is rendered unclean. Such time as it is clean, it does not render foodstuffs susceptible, since it has not come down upon him with his approval; *but if he shakes it off,* the water that he shakes off is deemed to be where it is with his approval and can render foodstuff susceptible.

At the italicized words we see a rather fine reading of the rule. At the first point, Maimonides wants the man by a deed to indicate his disapproval of the presence of the rain. At the second, he brings us to M. 4:2D. Now the issue is how the water can be subject to approval if it is shaken off, and Maimonides solves that problem by having the man deliberately place the water in its new location.

הַכּוֹפֶה קְעָרָה עַל הַכֹּתֶל בִּשְׁבִיל שֶׁתִּדּוֹחַ, הֲרֵי זֶה בְּכִי יֻתַּן.
אִם בִּשְׁבִיל שֶׁלֹּא יִלְקֶה הַכֹּתֶל – אֵינָן בְּכִי יֻתַּן.

A. He who puts a dish on end against the wall so that it will rinse off, lo, this [water that flows across the plate] is under the law, If water be put.

B. If [he put it there] so that it [rain] should not harm the wall, it [the water] is not under the law, If water be put.

M. 4:3

The established distinction is repeated once more, with reference to an inanimate object. Now we make use of the water for rinsing off the plate. Accordingly, the water is detached with approval. But if the plate is so located as to protect the wall, then the water clearly is not wanted and therefore does not have the capacity to impart susceptibility to uncleanness.

חָבִית שֶׁיָּרַד הַדֶּלֶף לְתוֹכָהּ – בֵּית שַׁמַּאי אוֹמְרִים: יְשַׁבֵּר.
בֵּית הִלֵּל אוֹמְרִים: יְעָרֶה. וּמוֹדִים שֶׁהוּא מוֹשִׁיט אֶת יָדוֹ
וְנוֹטֵל פֵּרוֹת מִתּוֹכָהּ, וְהֵם טְהוֹרִים.

עֲרֵבָה שֶׁיָּרַד הַדֶּלֶף לְתוֹכָהּ, הַנִּתָּזִין וְהַצָּפִין – אֵינָן בְּכִי יֻתַּן.
נְטָלָהּ לְשָׁפְכָהּ – בֵּית שַׁמַּאי אוֹמְרִים: בְּכִי יֻתַּן. בֵּית הִלֵּל
אוֹמְרִים: אֵינָן בְּכִי יֻתַּן. הִנִּיחָהּ שֶׁיֵּרַד הַדֶּלֶף לְתוֹכָהּ, הַנִּתָּזִין
וְהַצָּפִין – בֵּית שַׁמַּאי אוֹמְרִים: בְּכִי יֻתַּן. בֵּית הִלֵּל אוֹמְרִים:
אֵינָן בְּכִי יֻתַּן. נְטָלָהּ לְשָׁפְכָהּ – אֵלּוּ וָאֵלּוּ מוֹדִים שֶׁהֵן בְּכִי יֻתַּן.
הַמַּטְבִּיל אֶת הַכֵּלִים, וְהַמְכַבֵּס אֶת כְּסוּתוֹ בַּמְּעָרָה: הַמַּיִם
הָעוֹלִים בְּיָדָיו – בְּכִי יֻתַּן; בְּרַגְלָיו – אֵינָן בְּכִי יֻתַּן. רַבִּי
אֶלְעָזָר אוֹמֵר: אִם אִי אֶפְשָׁר לוֹ שֶׁיֵּרַד, אֶלָּא אִם כֵּן נִטַּנְּפוּ
רַגְלָיו, אַף הָעוֹלִין בְּרַגְלָיו – בְּכִי יֻתַּן.

I. A. A jug into which water leaking from the roof came
down—
   B. The House of Shammai say, "It is broken."
   C. The House of Hillel say, "It is emptied out."
   D. And they agree that he puts in his hand and takes
pieces of fruit from its inside, and they [the drops of water,
the pieces of fruit] are insusceptible to uncleanness.

M. 4:4

II. F. A trough into which the rain dripping from the roof
flowed [without approval] —
   G. [water in the trough and (GRA)] the drops [of water]
that splashed out and those that overflowed are not under
the law, If water be put.
   H. [If] one took it to pour it out—
   I. The House of Shammai say, "It is under the law, If
water be put."
   [Segal, p. 485, n. 10: Since he poured the water away
only when the tub was moved to another place, it may be said
that he did not object to the water when the tub was in its
original place.]
   J. The House of Hillel say, "It is not under the law, If
water be put."
   [Segal, p. 485, n. 11: His pouring away showed that he
did not want the water even in the tub's original place.]
III. K. [If] one [intentionally] left it out so that the rain
dripping from the roof would flow into it—
   L. the drops [of water] that splashed out and those that
overflowed—
   M. The House of Shammai say, "They are under the law,
If water be put" [all the more so what is in the trough] .
   N. The House of Hillel say, "They [the drops that splashed
or overflowed] are not under the law, If water be put."
   O. [If] one took it in order to pour it out, these and those
agree that [both kinds of water] are under the law, If water
be put.
   [Maimonides, *Uncleanness of Foodstuffs* 12:8: "For
since the owner did not empty it where it stood, the water is
deemed to be detached with his approval."]

P. He who dunks the utensils,
and he who washes his clothing in a cave [pond] —
Q. the water that comes up on his hands is under the law,
If water be put.
R. [And the water that comes up] on his feet is not under
the law, If water be put.
S. R. Eleazar says, "If it is impossible for him to go down
[into the water] unless his feet become muddy, even [the
drops of water] that come up on his feet are under the law,
If water be put [since he wants to clean his feet] ."

M. 4:5

The composite is in the following parts: A-D, a complete and
well balanced Houses' dispute, in which the apodosis exhibits exact
balance in the number of syllables, F-G, which set the stage for the
second Houses' dispute, at H-J; K-L, the protasis for the third dispute, which depends upon F (+ G = L)—a trough that happens to
receive rain *versus* one deliberately left out to collect rain, and the
standard apodosis, M-N; and a final agreement, O, parallel to D.
R-S form a separate pericope entirely, dealt with as an autonomous
unit in many MSS.

The issue of A-D is this: We have left a jug containing fruit in
such a position that water leaking from the roof fills it. We want
to empty the fruit out of the jug. But we want to do so in such a
way that the water in the jug does not receive the capacity to impart susceptibility to uncleanness to the fruit contained in the jug.
There are these considerations. (1) Clearly, in its present location,
the water is insusceptible. Why? Because it did not fall into the jug
with approval. (2) If then we break the jug, we accomplish the
purpose of treating the water as unwanted and this is what the
Shammaites say we should do (B). (3) But if we merely empty
out the fruit, we stir the water with approval; the fruit in the jug
forthwith is wet down by the water, with approval, and becomes
susceptible.

The Hillelites (C) say that if we pour out the fruit, that suffices.
Why? Because the man wants the fruit, not the water. So the water
does not have the capacity to impart susceptibility to uncleanness.
In its original location it is not subject to approval.

The Shammaites and Hillelites agree that, so long as the fruit in the jug is unaffected by the water, the fruit is insusceptible to uncleanness. It is not made susceptible even by the water which is removed with the fruit. Maimonides *(Uncleanness of Foodstuffs,* 12:7) at the italicized words adds a valuable clarification:

If a jar is full of fruit and water leaking from the roof drips into it, the owner may pour off the water from the fruit, and it does not render the fruit susceptible, *even though it was with his approval that the water remained in the jar until he should pour it off the fruit.*

Accordingly, Maimonides not only follows the Hillelite position but (quite reasonably) imposes that position upon the Shammaite agreement at D.

The second Houses' dispute, F-J, goes over the ground of the first. There is no significant difference between water that has leaked into the jug and water that has fallen into the trough, A/F. But the issue, G, is different. Now we ask about water that overflows. Does this water flow with approval? Certainly not, both parties agree. None of this water is wanted. What if the man then takes up the trough with the intention of pouring the water out? We already know the Hillelite position. It is the same as at C. There is no reason to be concerned about moving the trough in order to empty it. The man pours out the water. By his deed he therefore indicates that he does not want it. The Shammaites are equally consistent. The man has raised the trough to pour out the water. In moving the water, he (retrospectively) imparts the stamp of approval on the original location of the water. The reference at G is only to set the stage for K-L, since the water in the trough of F itself is insusceptible.

At K the problem is that the man deliberately does collect the water. Accordingly, he certainly has imparted his approval to it. The problem of L is that part of the water splashes out or overflows. Clearly, the man wanted the water and, therefore, what overflowed or splashed out has not conformed to his original wishes. That is, if he shook the tree to bring down the water, all parties agree that the water that falls is subject to the man's approval. But the water that does not fall is a problem. Here too the Shammaites say that what has been in the trough and overflowed has been subject to the man's intention. Therefore, like the water in the trough, the drops that splash out or overflow are under the law, If water be put. But the House of Hillel maintain that the water not in the location where the man has desired it is not subject to his wishes, and therefore does not impart susceptibility to uncleanness.

O completes the elegant construction by bringing the Hillelites over to the Shammaite position. If the man lifted up a trough of water that he *himself* has collected, then this is water that at one point in its history has surely conformed to the man's wishes and therefore has the capacity to impart susceptibility to uncleanness. The Hillelites of N clearly will agree that the water in the trough is subject to the law, If water be put, just as the Shammaites at L-M will maintain the same. The dispute of M-N concerns only the liquid referred to at L.

P-R go over the ground of M. 4:1. That is, water necessary to accomplish the man's purpose is subject to the law, If water be put. That which is not important in the accomplishment of his purpose is not subject to the law. Eleazar's gloss, S, adds that if the man's feet grow muddy in the process of getting the water, then he will want to clean his feet, and even the water on his feet therefore is subject to the law, If water be put. There is nothing surprising in this unit.

קֻפָּה שֶׁהִיא מְלֵאָה תֻּרְמוֹסִין וּנְתָנוּהָ לְתוֹךְ מִקְוֶה – מוֹשִׁיט יָדוֹ
וְנוֹטֵל תֻּרְמוֹסִין מִתּוֹכָהּ, וְהֵם טְהוֹרִים. הֶעֱלָם מִן הַמַּיִם:
הַנּוֹגְעִים בַּקֻּפָּה – טְמֵאִים, וּשְׁאָר כָּל הַתֻּרְמוֹסִים – טְהוֹרִים.
צְנוֹן שֶׁבַּמְּעָרָה–נִדָּה מַדִּיחַתּוּ, וְהוּא טָהוֹר. הֶעֱלַתּוּ כָּל שֶׁהוּא
מִן הַמַּיִם – טָמֵא.

A. A basket that is full of lupines and [that happens to be] placed into an immersion-pool —

B. one puts out his hand and takes lupines from its midst, and they are insusceptible to uncleanness.

C. [If] one took them out of the water [while still in the basket] —

D. the ones that touch the [water on the sides of the] basket are susceptible to uncleanness.

E. And all the rest of the lupines are insusceptible to uncleanness.

F. A radish that is in the cave-[water] —

G. a menstruant rinses it off, and it is insusceptible to uncleanness.

H. [If] she brought it out of the water in any measure at all, [having been made susceptible to uncleanness in the water], it is unclean.

M. 4:6

We go over the point on which the Houses agree at M. 4:4D. The lupines in the basket are wet on account of the water in the pool, but that does not render them susceptible to uncleanness. Accordingly, since the water is not detached with approval, when one takes the lupines out of the basket, they remain insusceptible. The water on the basket, however, is detached with approval, since presumably the basket has been immersed to render it clean from uncleanness. (The lupines—being food—in any event cannot be cleaned in the pool.) Accordingly, at C, the ones in the basket that touch the sides of the basket are in contact with water capable of imparting susceptibility to uncleanness, having been used with approval. The others, however, although wet, remain clean. Why? Because they have not touched water that has been detached with approval. The sentence-structure is slightly strange, since A sets the stage for a thought, but the thought begins afresh at B. This is then extreme apocopation at A-B, less clear-cut apocopation at C-D.

The same form is followed at F-H. The radish in the water is insusceptible to uncleanness. The menstruant rinses it off. While the radish is in the water, it remains insusceptible. But the woman has rinsed her hands and the radish. Accordingly, the water on the radish is detached with approval. It renders the radish susceptible to uncleanness, and as soon as the radish is taken out of the water, the woman's touch imparts uncleanness.

פֵּרוֹת שֶׁנָּפְלוּ לְתוֹךְ אַמַּת הַמַּיִם, פָּשַׁט מִי שֶׁהָיוּ יָדָיו טְמֵאוֹת

וּנְטָלָן – יָדָיו טְהוֹרוֹת, וְהַפֵּרוֹת טְהוֹרִים. וְאִם חִשֵּׁב שֶׁיְּדוֹחוּ
יָדָיו – יָדָיו טְהוֹרוֹת, וְהַפֵּרוֹת בְּכִי יֻתַּן.

A. Pieces of fruit that fell into a water-channel—

B. he whose hands were unclean reached out and took them—

C. his hands are clean, and the pieces of fruit are insusceptible to uncleanness.

D. But if he gave thought that his hands should be rinsed off [in the water], his hands are clean, and the [water on the] pieces of fruit is under the law, If water be put.

M. 4:7

The pericope is in the severe apocopation characteristic of the present set, A, B, and C being out of clear syntactical relationship to one another. We should have to add, at A, *as to pieces . . .* , then at B, *if he whose hands . . .* , and C would follow as a complete sentence. But A is not continued at B-C. Rather, we have apocopation.

We have a further illustration of the principle of the foregoing. The owner wants to retrieve the fruit. Even though his hands are unclean, he reaches out and takes the fruit. What is the result? The hands are made clean by the water-flow. But the fruit remains insusceptible to uncleanness. Why? Because it was not the man's intent to rinse off his hands in the water channel and so to clean them. If, D adds, that was his intent, then his hands of course are clean, but the fruit now has been rendered susceptible to uncleanness. Maimonides adds a reference to the fact that it is the owner who reaches out (*Uncleanness of Foodstuffs* 12:10):

If fruit falls into water and [*the owner*] stretches in his hand and takes it out, the fruit is not rendered susceptible; but if his purpose was that his hands should thereby be rinsed, the fruit is rendered susceptible by the water on his hands, for the water on his hands and on the fruit is deemed to be detached with his approval.

Maimonides omits reference to the unclean hands of B, and the
cleaning of the hands in C, but goes directly from A to D, presumably because he does not want to commit himself here on whether
immersion requires intention. B-C are clear that it does not.

קְדֵרָה שֶׁהִיא מְלֵאָה מַיִם וּנְתוּנָה לְתוֹךְ הַמִּקְוֶה, וּפָשַׁט אַב
הַטֻּמְאָה אֶת יָדוֹ לְתוֹכָהּ – טְמֵאָה; מַגַּע טְמֵאוֹת – טְהוֹרָה.
וּשְׁאָר כָּל הַמַּשְׁקִין – טְמֵאִין, שֶׁאֵין הַמַּיִם מְטַהֲרִים אֶת שְׁאָר
הַמַּשְׁקִין.

A. A [clay] dish that is full of water and placed in an
immersion-pool,
   B. and into [the airspace of] which a Father of unclean-
ness put his hand,
   C. is unclean [but the water remains clean].
   D. [If he was unclean only by reason of] contact with un-
clean things, it is clean.
   E. And as to all other liquids—they are unclean.
   F. For water does not effect cleanness for other liquids.

M. 4:8

The present pericope is not phrased in the expected apocopation,
for C refers to the dish and so completes the thought of A. We have
an exercise in several distinct rules. First, a clay pot is made unclean
only by a Father of uncleanness. Second, it is not cleaned by immersion in the pool but only by breaking. But the sides of the pot
are porous, as at M. 3:2. Therefore, third, the water in the pot is
deemed in contact with the immersion-pool. The dish is touched
by a Father of uncleanness and is therefore made unclean. But, D,
someone in the first remove of uncleanness is not able to contaminate the pot. The liquid in the pot is not referred to at A-D, but E
demands that we understand the liquid in A-C and D to be clean.
Why? Because the water referred to at A certainly is cleaned and
kept clean in the pool, along the lines of M. 4:6-7. E then simply
registers the fact that liquids apart from those enumerated at M. 6:4
are not cleaned in an immersion-pool. E-F should also tell us that
if other liquids are in the pot, the pot also is unclean, because liquids

in the first remove of uncleanness do impart uncleanness to clay or earthenware utensils. Accordingly, E-F form either a slightly awry gloss, taking for granted that A-C have said *the water is clean, even though it* [the pot] *is unclean,* or they belong to a pericope other than the present one, which is highly unlikely. Maimonides (*Uncleanness* 2:25) states:

If the pot is full of water, the pot remains clean, since one who suffers first-grade uncleanness never renders an earthenware vessel unclean [D], while the water inside it is not unclean, since it is mingled with the water of the immersion-pool [F]. If a Father of uncleanness stretches out his hand and touches it [B], the pot becomes unclean, since the immersion-pool does not render an earthenware vessel clean.

הַמְמַלֵּא בַּקִּילוֹן, עַד שְׁלשָׁה יָמִים – טְמֵאִין. רַבִּי עֲקִיבָא אוֹמֵר: אִם נִגְּבוּ – מִיָּד טְהוֹרִים; וְאִם לֹא נִגְּבוּ, אֲפִלּוּ עַד שְׁלשִׁים יוֹם – טְמֵאִים.

A. He who draws water with a swape-pipe [or bucket] [and pieces of fruit later fell into the moisture or water remaining in the pipe or bucket],

B. up to three days [the water] imparts susceptibility to uncleanness. [Afterward it is deemed to be unwanted (Maimonides).]

C. R. 'Aqiba says, "If it has dried off, it is forthwith incapable of imparting susceptibility to uncleanness, and if it has not dried off, up to thirty days it [continues to] impart susceptibility to uncleanness."

M. 4:9

The dispute poses A-B against C. We deal now with a wooden pipe or bucket. Do we deem the bucket to be dried off as soon as it is empty? No, B says, the water in the bucket, detached with approval (by definition) remains able to impart susceptibility for three days. 'Aqiba qualifies the matter. If the water drawn with approval was dried out of the bucket, whatever moisture then is

found in the bucket is not wanted; the man has shown, by drying
out the bucket or pipe, that he does not want moisture there. If it
is not dried out, then whatever liquid is there is deemed to be detached from the pool with approval and therefore able to impart
uncleanness for a very long time. Only after thirty days do we assume
that the wood is completely dry of the original water detached
with approval.

עֵצִים שֶׁנָּפְלוּ עֲלֵיהֶם מַשְׁקִין וְיָרְדוּ עֲלֵיהֶם גְּשָׁמִים, אִם רַבּוּ –
טְהוֹרִים. הוֹצִיאָם שֶׁיֵּרְדוּ עֲלֵיהֶם גְּשָׁמִים, אַף עַל פִּי שֶׁרַבּוּ –
טְמֵאִים. בָּלְעוּ מַשְׁקִים טְמֵאִים, אַף עַל פִּי שֶׁהוֹצִיאָם שֶׁיֵּרְדוּ
עֲלֵיהֶן גְּשָׁמִים – טְהוֹרִין. וְלֹא יַסִּיקֵם אֶלָּא בְיָדַיִם טְהוֹרוֹת
בִּלְבַד. רַבִּי שִׁמְעוֹן אוֹמֵר: אִם הָיוּ לַחִין וְהִסִּיקָן, וְרַבּוּ
הַמַּשְׁקִין הַיּוֹצְאִין מֵהֶן עַל הַמַּשְׁקִין שֶׁבָּלָעוּ – טְהוֹרִים.

A. Pieces of wood on which liquids fell and on which rains
fell-

B. if [the rains] were more [than the liquids], [the pieces
of wood] are insusceptible to uncleanness.

C. [If] he took them outside so that the rains might fall
on them, even though they [the rains] were more [than the
liquids], they [the pieces of wood] are [susceptible to uncleanness and] unclean.

D. [If] they absorbed unclean liquids, even though he took
them outside so that the rains would fall on them, they are
clean [for the clean rain has not had contact with the unclean
absorbed liquid].

E. But he should kindle them only with clean hands alone
[to avoid contaminating the rain-water of D].

F. R. Simeon says, "If they were wet [freshly cut] and he
kindled them, and the liquids [sap] that exude from them were
more than the liquids that they had absorbed, they are clean"

[Segal, p. 488, n. 10: "The unclean liquid is neutralized
by the sap."].

M. 4:10

We begin with Maimonides, *Uncleanness of Foodstuffs* 13:2, who states the rule as follows:

If liquid falls with approval on pieces of wood, and then rain falls on them without approval, and the rain is the greater in quantity, all is deemed to have fallen without approval. If they have been taken out for the rain to fall on them, even if the rain is greater in quantity, all is deemed to have fallen with approval. If they have been taken out for the rain to fall on them, even if the rain is greater in quantity, all is deemed to have fallen with approval.

At *ibid.*, 9:6, he goes over the matter of kindling the wood:

If unclean liquid has soaked into pieces of wood and they are set alight to heat an oven, the oven remains clean, since the liquid is made of no account by the wood. Even if a man takes out the wood so that rain should fall on it, and it falls to his liking, and he sets the wood alight, the oven remains clean; and the water on the wood does not contract uncleanness from the liquid that has soaked into it.

But he may not kindle the wood except with clean hands, a precautionary measure lest an unclean person kindle it and the liquid thereon render the oven unclean.

With this overview in mind, we turn to the pericope.

The pericope is in the following parts: A-B balanced by C; and D, qualified by E. F is an important gloss of D-E. The point of A-B is familiar from M. 2:3. If we have a mixture of unclean and clean liquids, we determine matters in accord with the relative quantity of each. If the clean liquids are the greater part, the whole is deemed clean. Accordingly, since the rain, which is insusceptible and does not impart susceptibility to uncleanness unless it falls with approval, forms the greater part, B, the liquids on the pieces of wood are deemed clean. But if, C, the man deliberately arranged for the rain to fall on the pieces of wood, then the rain falls on the wood with approval, is susceptible to uncleanness, and is made unclean by the unclean liquids already on the wood.

D raises a separate question. What if pieces of wood have absorbed unclean liquids? The answer is that what is absorbed does not have contact with what is on the surface—that is the meaning of absorption. Therefore if rain falls on wood that has absorbed unclean liquids, the rain does not impart susceptibility to uncleanness if it has not fallen with approval. D does not treat that matter; it wishes to say something additional. Even if the rain falls with approval, the wood remains clean. Why? Because nothing has made the rain unclean.

That secondary point then invites E—or E imposes the detail, *even if*, on D: Even though he took them outside, so the rain falls with approval, E adds, since the rain *has* fallen with approval, it is susceptible to uncleanness. Accordingly, the man should kindle the wood only with clean hands, lest he make the rain-water unclean.

Simeon deals then with a still further point. If the wood is freshly cut when kindled, then the unclean absorbed liquids are deemed neutralized by the sap. If the exuded liquid caused by the heat is more than the still-absorbed liquid, then the clean, exuded liquid forms the greater part, and the whole is clean, just as at A-B. Simeon, Maimonides says, differs from D (+ E). We hold, as at A-D, that if unclean liquids are absorbed by the wood, they are deemed clean and do not impart uncleanness to the oven, *only* in the case in which the wood is wet. Then, when it is heated, it produces sap in greater quantity than the unclean liquids that it absorbed. But if not, the wood imparts uncleanness to the oven when it is heated because of the unclean liquid that has been absorbed.

v. Mishnah Makhshirin Chapter Five

מִי שֶׁטָּבַל בַּנָּהָר, וְהָיָה לְפָנָיו נָהָר אַחֵר וְעָבַר בּוֹ – טְהֲרוּ
שְׁנִיִּים אֶת הָרִאשׁוֹנִים. דָּחָהוּ חֲבֵרוֹ לְשָׁכְרוֹ, וְכֵן לִבְהֶמְתּוֹ –
טְהֲרוּ שְׁנִיִּים אֶת הָרִאשׁוֹנִים. וְאִם כִּמְשַׂחֵק עִמּוֹ, הֲרֵי זֶה בְּכִי
יֻפַן.

A. He who immersed in a river, and there was before him another river [and] that he crossed—

B. [the water of] the second [river] renders insusceptible [the water of] the first.

C. [If] his fellow in drunkenness (LSKRW) [alt.: LŠWBRW: to hurt him] pushed him in [to the second river],

D. and so [if his drunken fellow pushed in] his beast,

E. [the water of] the second [river] renders insusceptible [the water of] the first.

F. And if [he did so] as he was wrestling with him, lo, this [second immersion's water is not applied in constraint and therefore] is under the law, If water be put.

M. 5:1

The unit is in two parts, A-B and C-F, both in the expected apocopation. The point of A-B, as at M. 4:2, is that the water of the first river was detached with approval, therefore imparts susceptibility to uncleanness. But the man gave no thought to the second river, which was incidental to his purpose. That water does not render the man susceptible to uncleanness and moreover washes off the first. Maimonides adds (in italics) valuable clarifying language (*Uncleanness of Foodstuffs* 13:6):

If a man immerses himself in one river and another river lies before him and he passes through that, the second water *makes the first water of no account, and so the water that remains on him is not deemed to be detached with approval.*

Exactly the same point is made at C-E. The first immersion was intentional, the second was not. The second water, as at M. 4:10, annuls the first. But if it could have been expected that the man would be thrown into the water, the second immersion does not remove the effects of the first; again, Maimonides (*Uncleanness of Foodstuffs* 13:6B):

So too if a man has immersed himself and then his fellow pushes him *to do him hurt or to hurt* his beast and he falls

into the water, *the first water is made of no account;* but if
he has pushed him in play, the first water is not made of no
account *and the water that remains on him is deemed to be
detached with approval.*

It is clear that C-F depend for context and meaning on the opening
unit, A-B.

הַשָּׁט עַל פְּנֵי הַמַּיִם, הַנִּתָּזִין – אֵינָן בְּכִי יֻתַּן. וְאִם נִתְכַּוֵּן לְהַתִּיז
עַל חֲבֵרוֹ, הֲרֵי זֶה בְּכִי יֻתַּן. הָעוֹשֶׂה צִפּוֹר בַּמַּיִם, הַנִּתָּזִין וְאֶת
שֶׁבָּהּ – אֵינָן בְּכִי יֻתַּן.

A. He who swam in the water—
B. the water that splashed is not under the law, If water be
put.
   [Maimonides, *Uncleanness of Foodstuffs* 13:7: "But
water that comes away with him is deemed to be detached with
approval."]
   C. And if [the splashing was because] he intended to splash
his fellow,
   D. lo, it is under the law, If water be put.
   E. He who makes a "bird" [a bubble, a squirt, a waterspout.
Jastrow, II, p. 1296: "a bird" . . . producing bubbles by
blowing through a tube . . .] in the water—
   F. the water which [accidentally] splashes out and that
[water] which is in it are not under the law, If water be put.

M. 5:2

The first unit, A-B + C-D, makes no new point. C-D run parallel
to M. 5:1F. The "bird" seems to be an inflated object, like a rubber
duck, used to support the swimmer. Water that splashes out of the
duck and water that happens to be located in it are not wanted,
since the water will impair the duck's flotation.

פֵּרוֹת שֶׁיָּרַד הַדֶּלֶף לְתוֹכָן וּבְלָלָן שֶׁיְּגּוּבוּ – רַבִּי שִׁמְעוֹן
אוֹמֵר: בְּכִי יֻתַּן. וַחֲכָמִים אוֹמְרִים: אֵינָן בְּכִי יֻתַּן.

A. Pieces of fruit into which rain dripping from the roof fell [without approval] and that one mixed together [with dry fruit] for drying [Segal, p. 489, n. 10: The owner mixed up the wet fruit with the dry fruit, so as to accelerate the drying of the moisture by spreading it over a wider space] —

B. R. Simeon says, "It is under the law, If water be put."

C. And sages say, "It is not under the law, If water be put."

M. 5:3

The dispute runs parallel to that of the Houses, M. 4:4-5. The man mixes the fruit up, so that it will dry more rapidly. In so doing, he wets some of it. His ultimate purpose is that the fruit dry, so what happens in the meantime is of no effect, so far as the sages are concerned. But Simeon, like the House of Shammai, stresses that once the man has stirred up the water and wet down the dry fruit, his ultimate intention is of no consequence. What is intentionally done imparts approval upon the water, even though, later on, the water is not wanted. So far as the sages are concerned, the water never was wanted and is going to be removed. What is done to remove it is adjudged by its ultimate purpose; parallel to M. 4:1, the main purpose is paramount.

הַמּוֹדֵד אֶת הַבּוֹר בֵּין לְעָמְקוֹ בֵּין לְרָחְבּוֹ, הֲרֵי זֶה בְּכִי יֻתַּן;
דִּבְרֵי רַבִּי טַרְפוֹז. רַבִּי עֲקִיבָא אוֹמֵר: לְעָמְקוֹ – בְּכִי יֻתַּז,
וּלְרָחְבּוֹ – אֵינוֹ בְּכִי יֻתַּז.

A. He who measures the cistern —

B. "whether for depth or for breadth —

C. "lo, this [water which is on the measuring rod] is under the law, If water be put," the words of R. Tarfon.

D. R. 'Aqiba says, "[If he measured it] for depth, [the water on the measuring rod] is under the law, If water be put. And [if he measured it] for breadth, [the water on the measuring rod] is not under the law, If water be put."

M. 5:4

The dispute is acutely well-balanced. 'Aqiba declares to be susceptible water that is on the rod, because it is needed to ascertain the exact depth of the water in the cistern. In measuring the breadth, water on the rod is immaterial. 'Aqiba's principle applies at M. 4:1.

פָּשַׁט יָדוֹ, אוֹ רַגְלוֹ, אוֹ קָנֶה לַבּוֹר, לֵידַע אִם יֵשׁ בּוֹ מַיִם–אֵינָן
בְּכִי יֻתַּן; לֵידַע כַּמָּה מַיִם יֵשׁ בּוֹ, הֲרֵי זֶה בְּכִי יֻתַּן. זָרַק אֶת
הָאֶבֶן לַבּוֹר, לֵידַע אִם יֵשׁ בּוֹ מַיִם: הַנִּתָּזִין–אֵינָן בְּכִי יֻתַּן,
וְאֶת שֶׁבָּאֶבֶן – טְהוֹרִים.

A. [If] one stuck his hand or his foot or a reed into the cistern to know whether there is water in it—

B. [water that comes up on the hand, foot, or reed] is not under the law, If water be put.

C. [If he did so] in order to find out how much water is in it, lo, this [water on hand, foot, or reed] is under the law, If water be put.

D. [If] one threw a stone into the cistern to find out whether there is water in it—

E. the water that splashed out is not under the law, If water be put. [GRA: It *is* under the law . . . , because the man wants to hear the splash or see the drops.]

F. And that which is on the stone is insusceptible to uncleanness.

M. 5:5

A-D, in apocopation, conform to 'Aqiba's distinction at M. 5:4. D-F hold that the water in both situations, E and F, is insusceptible. Neither is detached with approval, perhaps because, if we hear the splash, we accomplish our purpose; GRA's reading is preferable.

הַחוֹבֵט עַל הַשֶּׁלַח: חוּץ לַמַּיִם – בְּכִי יֻתַּן; לְתוֹךְ הַמַּיִם –
אֵינָן בְּכִי יֻתַּן. רַבִּי יוֹסֵי אוֹמֵר: אַף לְתוֹךְ הַמַּיִם – בְּכִי יֻתַּן,
מִפְּנֵי שֶׁהוּא מִתְכַּוֵּן שֶׁיֵּצְאוּ עִם הַצּוֹאָה.

A. He who beat upon [a wet] pelt—

B. [if he beat on it] outside the water—

C. [what is splashed from it] is subject to the law, If water be put.

D. [If he beat] in the water [itself], [the water that is beaten out] is not under the law, If water be put.

E. R. Yosé says, "Even [if he beat the pelt] in the water, [what is splashed out] is under the law, If water be put,

F. "because he intends that it flow out together with the excrement." [Segal, p. 491, n. 3: "In order to get on it fresh clean water and complete its cleansing."]

M. 5:6

The usual apocopation, A-C, is used to express the view that since the man wants to beat the water out, the water that splashes out is subject to approval. D holds that if the hide is in the water, the man obviously cannot expect to remove it, since other water will flow in. Yosé does not differ in principle.

הַמַּיִם הָעוֹלִין בַּסְּפִינָה, וּבָעֵקֶל, וּבַמְּשׁוֹטוֹת – אֵינָן בְּכִי יֻתַּן.
בַּמְּצוֹדוֹת, וּבָרְשָׁתוֹת, וּבַמִּכְמָרוֹת – אֵינָן בְּכִי יֻתַּן. וְאִם
נָעַר – בְּכִי יֻתַּן. הַמּוֹלִיךְ אֶת הַסְּפִינָה לַיָּם הַגָּדוֹל, לְצָרְפָהּ,
הַמּוֹצִיא מַסְמֵר לַגְּשָׁמִים, לְצָרְפוֹ, הַמַּנִּיחַ אֶת הָאוּד בַּגְּשָׁמִים,
לְכַבּוֹתוֹ – הֲרֵי זֶה בְּכִי יֻתַּן.

A. The water that comes up on (1) [the hull of] the ship and (2) on the bilge [Rosh: anchor] and (3) on the oars is not under the law, If water be put.

B. [The water that comes up] (1) on the snares, (2) and on the gins, and (3) on the nets is not under the law, If water be put.

C. And if he shook [them to remove the water], it [the water that is detached] is under the law, If water be put.

D. (1) He who takes out a ship onto the Great Sea in order to tighten [the seams] —

E. (2) he who takes out a [hot] nail into the rain to temper it—

F. (3) he who leaves the burning brand in the rain in order
to extinguish it—
G. lo, this is under the law, If water be put.

M. 5:7

The pericope is in two units, A-C and D-G, a set of well-balanced
declarative sentences at A-C, and an apocopated one at D-G. The
pericope unfolds in sets of threes, A and B, then, what is unusual,
a triplet of protases, D, E, and F, all served by the single apocopated
apodosis, G. That fact and the subject of the entire group strongly
suggest the whole is a unitary construction. The point hardly requires specification: Water at A is not wanted, so too at B. We
should have expected a contrast here, but the contrast is between
A-B and D-G. C is familiar from M. 4:2. If one shook them off to
remove the water as at M. 4:2, 4:5, etc., then we have done something to the water; it is located where we want it.

קַסְיָא שֶׁלַּשֻׁלְחָנוֹת, וְהַשִּׁיפָא שֶׁלַּלְּבֵנִים – אֵינָן בְּכִי יֻתַּן. וְאִם
נָעַר – בְּכִי יֻתַּן.

A. A covering for tables [spread out to protect food],
B and matting for bricks—
C. [rain that falls on these] is not under the law, If water
be put.
D. And if he shook [these objects off], [the water that is
detached] is under the law, If water be put.

M. 5:8

The form, apocopation (A-B, C), expresses a familiar point
(M. 4:3). The water is not wanted. There is intention, D, to shake
off the moisture, so it is now susceptible.

כָּל הַנִּצּוֹק – טָהוֹר, חוּץ מִדְּבַשׁ הַזִּיפִין, וְהַצַּפַּחַת. בֵּית שַׁמַּאי
אוֹמְרִים: אַף הַמִּקְפָּה שֶׁלַּגְּרִיסִין, וְשֶׁלַּפּוֹל, מִפְּנֵי שֶׁהִיא
סוֹלֶדֶת לְאַחֲרֶיהָ.

A. Any unbroken stream [of water] is clean [insusceptible to uncleanness],

B. except for the thick honey and porridge.

C. The House of Shammai say, "Also: one of porridge made from grits or beans,

D. "because [like the items of B] it shrinks backwards [at the end of its flow]."

M. 5:9

We shift the topic and also the formulary pattern. We turn from whether or not liquid is wanted, and apocopated sentences, to the traits of a stream of water, and declarative sentences. At issue, A, is a stream of liquid poured from one utensil to another. If the bottom part of the stream of liquid is unclean (or if it has the capacity to impart susceptibility to uncleanness because it is detached with approval [Albeck]), the upper part of the stream is not deemed to be unclean (or to impart susceptibility to uncleanness). Why not? Because, as we know from M. Toh. 8:8-9 (*Purities*, Part XI, pp. 198-202), a stream of liquid does not constitute a connector from bottom to top, but only from top to bottom.

The matter of whether the uncleanness climbs back up the stream fits the conditions of the case. In fact, the problem, pure and simple, is that of the jet as connective. Why are thick honey and porridge excluded? Maimonides gives the answer (*Uncleanness of Foodstuffs* 7:4):

The stream from a hive of Zifin-honey or Sappahat [B] honey serves as a connective [= A, unclean] even if it is poured cold into something cold [M. 5:10B], because it is slimy and shrinks back like glutinous stuff. Accordingly, it is not of every foodstuff that its stream serves as a connective, even if it is very thick, such as grits, porridge [versus C], or melted fat and the like, since they are not slimy.

Maimonides thus applies D to B.

הַמְעָרֶה מֵחַם לְחַם, וּמִצּוֹנֵן לְצוֹנֵן, וּמֵחַם לְצוֹנֵן – טָהוֹר.
מִצּוֹנֵן לְחַם – טָמֵא. רַבִּי שִׁמְעוֹן אוֹמֵר: אַף הַמְעָרֶה מֵחַם
לְחַם, וְכֹחוֹ שֶׁלַּתַּחְתּוֹן יָפֶה מִשֶּׁלָּעֶלְיוֹן – טָמֵא.

A. He who empties (from) hot [clean water] into hot
[unclean water],
B. and (from) [clean] cold into [unclean] cold
C. and (from) hot into cold—
D. it [the remaining upper, clean liquid] is clean.
E. [He who empties] (from) cold into hot [water] —
F. it is unclean.
[Segal, p. 492, n. 3: "The hot water in the unclean vessel
causes steam to rise that mixes with the water in the clean
vessel and renders it unclean."]
G. R. Simeon says, "Also: He who empties (from) hot into
hot [versus A] ,
H. "and the force [of the heat] of the lower [water] was
stronger than that of the upper —
I. "it is unclean."

M. 5:10

We have a problem of connectives, pure and simple. Surely *clean*
is preferable to "insusceptible to uncleanness." This is proved by
the present rule and M.5:11, which exemplifies M. 5:10's principle.
The formulaic pattern of apocopation is applied, A completed by
D, which refers to what is poured, not to the pourer. Maimonides
states the rule as follows (*Uncleanness of Foodstuffs* 7:1-2):

A jet of liquid does not serve as a connective either for uncleanness or for cleanness. Thus if a man pours clean liquid
into an unclean vessel, even onto a dead creeping thing, the column of the jet remains clean; and if he collects some of the
poured-out liquid while it is in the air, what he collects is
clean, and, needless to say, the liquid from which it is poured
remains clean.

This applies if he pours cold liquid into cold, or hot into
hot, or hot into cold. But if he pours clean cold liquid into

unclean hot liquid, the jet serves as a connective, and all the cold liquid from which he pours becomes unclean, and the vessel from which he pours becomes unclean, because of the unclean liquid inside it.

And why have the sages said that if he pours cold liquid into hot that it serves as a connective? Because the steam of the hot liquid rises like columns of smoke and mingles with the jet and with the water in the upper vessel and renders the vessel unclean, because the steam rising from hot liquid counts as liquid.

Simeon simply carries that same point forward, G-H. If the lower liquid is hotter than the upper, then we do have transmission of uncleanness through the steam. I suppose he might like to say, "Also: He who empties (from) hot into hotter," which is no different from "cold(er) into hot(ter)."

הָאִשָּׁה שֶׁהָיוּ יָדֶיהָ טְהוֹרוֹת, וּמְגִיסָה בִּקְדֵרָה טְמֵאָה: אִם הִזִּיעוּ יָדֶיהָ – טְמֵאוֹת. הָיוּ יָדֶיהָ טְמֵאוֹת, וּמְגִיסָה בִּקְדֵרָה טְהוֹרָה: אִם הִזִּיעוּ יָדֶיהָ – הַקְּדֵרָה טְמֵאָה. רַבִּי יוֹסֵי אוֹמֵר: אִם נִטְּפוּ. הַשׁוֹקֵל עֲנָבִים בְּכַף מֹאזְנַיִם – הַיַּיִן שֶׁבַּכַּף טָהוֹר, עַד שֶׁיְּעָרֶה לְתוֹךְ הַכְּלִי. הֲרֵי זֶה דוֹמֶה לְסַלֵּי זֵיתִים וַעֲנָבִים כְּשֶׁהֵן מְנַטְּפִין.

A. The woman whose hands were clean,

B. and who stirred the unclean cooking pot [with a spoon] —

C. if her hands sweated,

D. they are unclean.

[Segal, p. 492, n. 6: "The perspiration caused by the steam of the unclean pot renders her hands unclean."]

E. [If] her hands were unclean,

F. and she was stirring the clean cooking pot,

G. if her hands sweated,

H. [what is in] the pot is unclean [versus M. 5:10A: Hot to hot].

I. R. Yosé says, "If they dripped [then what is in the pot becomes unclean]."

J. He who weighs grapes in a cup of a balance—

K. the wine that is in the cup [after the weighing] is insusceptible to uncleanness,

L. until one will pour it out into [another] utensil.

M. Lo, this is like baskets of olives and grapes when they
drip [sap].

M. 5:11

The foregoing rule, that the mixture of cold and hot produces
uncleanness *via* the steam coming up from below, is illustrated here.
The steam from the pot imparts uncleanness to the woman's hands,
as shown by the hands' sweating. Since, E-H, the hands sweated
because of the heat of the pot, we regard the sweat on her hands
as mingled with the hot liquid in the pot, parallel to M. 2:1D. Since
E-H present the reverse, I suppose Simeon would be pleased with
this case.

Yosé rejects this view, because he does not deem the sweat on
the hands to be joined to the contents of the pot unless liquid actually drips from the unclean hands into the clean liquids in the
pot. He surely will disagree with Simeon. Yosé agrees with the
anonymous authority of M. 5:10A, who says that if there is pouring from hot to hot, there is no connection. In Yosé's view, steam
is not liquid and does not form a connector. He demands actually
congealed steam, that is, liquid.

Maimonides, *Uncleanness of Foodstuffs* 7:3, quite logically explains M. 5:11 in terms of M. 5:10:

Therefore, if a woman whose hands are clean stirs an unclean
cooking pot, and her hands sweat from the vapor of the cooking pot, her hands become unclean as though she had touched
the liquid in the cooking pot. So too if her hands are unclean
and she stirs the cooking pot and her hands sweat, all that is
in the cooking pot becomes unclean as though she had touched
the liquid itself.

At J-M, we do not want the wine in the weighing cup. Therefore it
is insusceptible. But if one pours it out, then it is detached with

approval, L. M explains K. When olives or grapes drip moisture in a basket, that moisture is not regarded as with approval, as at M. Toh. 9:1, *Purities* XI, pp. 205-208.

vi. Mishnah Makhshirin Chapter Six

הַמַּעֲלֶה פֵּרוֹתָיו לַגַּג מִפְּנֵי הַכְּנִימָה, וְיָרַד עֲלֵיהֶם טַל – אֵינָם
בְּכִי יֻתַּן. אִם נִתְכַּוֵּן לְכָךְ, הֲרֵי זֶה בְּכִי יֻתַּן. הֶעֱלָן חֵרֵשׁ שׁוֹטֶה
וְקָטָן, אַף עַל פִּי שֶׁחָשַׁב שֶׁיֵּרֵד עֲלֵיהֶן הַטַּל – אֵינָן בְּכִי יֻתַּן;
שֶׁיֵּשׁ לָהֶן מַעֲשֶׂה, וְאֵין לָהֶן מַחֲשָׁבָה.

A. He who brings up his produce to the roof because of the maggots [Danby: "To keep it free from maggots"],

B. and dew fell on it—

C. it is not under the law, If water be put.

D. If he intended such, lo, this is under the law, If water be put.

E. [If] a deaf-mute, an imbecile, or a minor brought it up, even though he gave thought that dew should fall on it—

F. it is not under the law, If water be put.

G. Because they have the power of deed, but not the power of intention.

M. 6:1

A-D go over the ground of M. 3:5's treatment of dew, and D = M. 3:5. E-G = M. 3:8. The man, A-C, never intended dew to fall on the produce.

הַמַּעֲלֶה אֶת הָאֲגֻדּוֹת, וְאֶת הַקְּצִיעוֹת, וְאֶת הַשּׁוּם לַגַּג, בִּשְׁבִיל
שֶׁיַּמְתִּינוּ – אֵינָן בְּכִי יֻתַּן. כָּל הָאֲגֻדּוֹת שֶׁלְּבֵית הַשְּׁוָקִים –
טְמֵאִיז. רַבִּי יְהוּדָה מְטַהֵר בַּלַּחִים. אָמַר רַבִּי מֵאִיר: וְכִי
מִפְּנֵי מַה טִמְּאוּ? אֶלָּא מִפְּנֵי מַשְׁקֵה הַפֶּה! כָּל הַקִּמְחִין,
וְהַסְּלָתוֹת שֶׁלְּבֵית הַשְּׁוָקִים – טְמֵאִים. הַחִילְקָה, הַטְּרָגִיס,
וְהַטִּסְנִי – טְמֵאִים בְּכָל מָקוֹם.

A. He who brings up bundles [of vegetables] and blocks [of figs] and garlic to the roof

B. so as to keep them fresh—

C. they are not under the law, If water be put.

D. All bundles [of vegetables] in the market place are susceptible to uncleanness.

E. R. Judah declares insusceptible to uncleanness in the case of those that are fresh.

F. Said R. Meir,"And on what account have they been declared unclean? But because of the liquid of the mouth."

G. All kinds of meal and flour in the market place are susceptible to uncleanness.

H. Pounded wheat and groats and grits are susceptible to uncleanness in all circumstances [being dampened before milling] .

M. 6:2

The pericope is in two units, A-C, and D-H. A-C repeat the foregoing, simply giving us a new illustration of the familiar principle that when dew falls without a person's wanting it, then it does not impart susceptibility to uncleanness. Maimonides (*Uncleanness of Foodstuffs* 14:3) adds interesting clarifying language:

If a man takes up to the roof bundles of vegetables or blocks of figs or garlic in order to keep them fresh, and the dew falls upon them, they are not thereby rendered susceptible; *and we may not say that inasmuch as everyone knows that the dew falls, this is with his approval, for he has taken them up only that they might remain fresh.*

D, G, and H are three simple declarative sentences, in which all the apodoses are the same. No one has bothered to construct a single list, so I take it the sentences originally are separate from one another. The point in all three instances is that these are things people routinely wet down and therefore are deemed susceptible to uncleanness. Judah and Meir, E-F, differ as to the reason behind D, and therefore disagree on the law as well. In Judah's view, people do not wet down fresh vegetables. Meir regards them as susceptible to uncleanness because people may have tasted them, or spit on them, or put them into their mouth when binding them. In Meir's view, however, we have to say that the vegetables not only are susceptible to uncleanness but are in fact unclean, inasmuch as a person who is unclean may have put the bundle in his mouth. The reason behind G is that it it customary to soak the items in water before milling. They are therefore susceptible to uncleanness and, again, presumed to be made unclean by people who pass by and touch them. In the view of H, pounded wheat and groats and grits are unclean even not in the market.

Maimonides (*Uncleanness of Foodstuffs* 16:1) states the rule of D-H as follows:

Any bundles of vegetables in the market place and any meal or flour in the market places are presumed to have been made susceptible to uncleanness: the bundles of vegetables because the custom is to sluice them constantly with water; and meal and flour, because these are first moistened and then ground. So too wheat part-ground in the millstones, one grain into two, or one into two or three, in order to make of them a sort of pottage, such as grits or the like, is everywhere presumed to have been made susceptible to uncleanness whether in market places or in private houses, *since it is moistened to free it from the husk.*

כָּל הַבֵּיצִים בְּחֶזְקַת טַהֲרָה, חוּץ מִשֶּׁלְמוֹכְרֵי מַשְׁקֶה. וְאִם הָיוּ
מוֹכְרִין עִמָּהֶן פֵּרוֹת יְבֵשִׁים – טְהוֹרוֹת. כָּל הַדָּגִים בְּחֶזְקַת
טֻמְאָה. רַבִּי יְהוּדָה אוֹמֵר: חֲתִיכַת אִילְתִית וְדַג הַמִּצְרִי הַבָּא
בַקֻּפָּה, וְקוּלְיַס הָאִסְפָּנִין – הֲרֵי אֵלּוּ בְּחֶזְקַת טַהֲרָה. כָּל
הַצִּיר בְּחֶזְקַת טֻמְאָה. וְעַל כֻּלָּם עַם הָאָרֶץ נֶאֱמָן לוֹמַר:
טְהוֹרִים הֵן, חוּץ מִשֶּׁלַּדָּגָה, מִפְּנֵי שֶׁהֵן מַפְקִידִין אוֹתָהּ אֵצֶל
עַם הָאָרֶץ. רַבִּי אֱלִיעֶזֶר בֶּן יַעֲקֹב אוֹמֵר: צִיר טָהוֹר שֶׁנָּפַל
לְתוֹכוֹ מַיִם כָּל שֶׁהֵן – טָמֵא.

A. All eggs are assumed to be insusceptible to uncleanness,

B. except for those of dealers in liquids [who handle the eggs with dripping hands].

C. And if they were selling along with them [the eggs] dry produce [and therefore keep their hands dry], they are insusceptible to uncleanness.

D. All kinds of fish are assumed to be susceptible to uncleanness [made susceptible by water shaken off from nets].

E. R. Judah says, "A piece of the Iltith-fish, Egyptian fish that comes in a basket, and Spanish mackerel, lo, these are in the assumption of being clean [since they are kept dry, being spoiled by water]."

F. All kinds of brine are assumed to be susceptible to uncleanness [since it is made by liquid].

G. And in the case of all of them [eggs, fruit, brine], an 'am ha'ares is believed to testify, "They are insusceptible to uncleanness,"

H. except for that of [small] fish,

I. because they [G] are stored with an 'am ha'ares..

J. R. Eliezer b. Jacob says, "Insusceptible brine [made by crunching salt and fruit juice] into which fell any amount at all of water is deemed susceptible to uncleanness."

M. 6:3

What makes this construction interesting is the addition of G-I, which gloss the whole of the antecedent construction. The rules are stated in simple declarative sentences, A-B, C, D, glossed by E, and F, four in all. Then I explains G or H, and J glosses F. I do not know why the insertion of G-I comes before J.

The point of A-B is that eggs are kept dry. But dealers in liquids touch the eggs with already-dripping hands. C limits B and returns us to A. D-E require no comment. F + J are obvious as well. If the fish is assumed to be susceptible to uncleanness, D, so too is the fish-brine assumed to be susceptible. Eliezer then speaks of brine that is unsusceptible; then this is presumably brine that has no water mixed in with it, and the rest follows.

There are two readings for H, *except for that*—the brine—*of fish,* and *except for fish* (see TYT). The 'am ha'ares is believed, G, if he says that these products have not been rendered susceptible to uncleanness. If I refers to G, then the reason if that people keep such objects with the 'am ha'ares (Bert.). If so, then I simply re-

peats the point of G. Perhaps I explains H (TYY, n. 25, MA). If an
'am ha'areṣ is believed, it is because the aforenamed substances
have *not* been stored with him, so he has no interest in declaring
them clean. But in the case of fish or brine of fish, the fish itself is
stored with him, and so he is interested in declaring it clean or insusceptible to uncleanness.

שִׁבְעָה מַשְׁקִין הֵן: הַטַּל, וְהַמַּיִם, הַיַּיִן, וְהַשֶּׁמֶן, וְהַדָּם, וְהֶחָלָב,
וּדְבַשׁ דְּבוֹרִים. דְּבַשׁ צְרָעִים – טָהוֹר, וּמֻתָּר בַּאֲכִילָה.

תּוֹלָדוֹת לַמַּיִם: הַיּוֹצְאִין מִן הָעַיִן, מִן הָאֹזֶן, מִן הַחֹטֶם, מִן
הַפֶּה, מֵי רַגְלַיִם, בֵּין גְּדוֹלִים בֵּין קְטַנִּים, לְדַעְתּוֹ וְשֶׁלֹּא
לְדַעְתּוֹ. תּוֹלָדוֹת לַדָּם: דַּם שְׁחִיטָה בַּבְּהֵמָה וּבַחַיָּה וּבָעוֹפוֹת
הַטְּהוֹרִים, וְדַם הַקָּזָה לִשְׁתִיָּה. מֵי חָלָב – כֶּחָלָב, וְהַמֹּחַל –
כַּשֶּׁמֶן, שֶׁאֵין הַמֹּחַל יוֹצֵא מִידֵי שֶׁמֶן; דִּבְרֵי רַבִּי שִׁמְעוֹן. רַבִּי
מֵאִיר אוֹמֵר: אַף עַל פִּי שֶׁאֵין עִמּוֹ שֶׁמֶן. דַּם הַשֶּׁרֶץ – כִּבְשָׂרוֹ,
מְטַמֵּא, וְאֵינוּ מַכְשִׁיר; וְאֵין לָנוּ כַּיּוֹצֵא בוֹ.

A. There are seven liquids [to which the law, If water be
put, applies] :
B. (1) dew, and (2) water, and (3) wine, and (4) oil, and
(5) [human] blood, and (6) milk, and (7) bee-honey.
C. The honey of hornets is insusceptible to uncleanness
but is permitted for eating.

M. 6:4

D. [These are the kinds of liquids that are] subspecies of
water [and impart susceptibility to uncleanness as does water] :
E. [liquids that] exude from (1) the eye, (2) the ear, (3)
the nose, (4) from the mouth, (5) urine,
whether of adults or children [Sens, Bert.: "whether
from the anus or the penis"] ,
whether [excreted] knowingly or unknowingly.
F. [These are liquids that are] subspecies of blood:
G. (1) blood from the slaughtering of cattle and beast and
fowl that are clean,

and (2) blood let out from the veins for drink [which is desired].

H. Whey is like milk.

I. And sap is like oil,

J. "for sap is not wholly freed from particles of oil," the words of R. Simeon.

K. R. Meir says, "Even though there is no oil with it, [it is like oil]."

L. The blood of the creeping thing is like its flesh. It imparts uncleanness but does not impart susceptibility to uncleanness.

M. And we have nothing that is like it [that blood is deemed equivalent to flesh].

M. 6:5

The composite is in the following parts: A-B, with the interpolation at C; D-E, which gloss B2; F-G, which gloss B5; H, which lacks the expected superscription and serves B6; I, in equivalent form and serving B4, with the appended explanations of J-K; and, finally, L-M, which are autonomous of the foregoing but relate to B5. The composite thus is somewhat complex; the glosses are not systematic, since some of the items of B are left without comment, and glosses of the items that are dealt with are not set forth in their original order. The matter of blood is taken up again, as we shall see in a moment.

The listed liquids are those that impart susceptibility to uncleanness. Simeon's view, J, is that the sap of olives contains particles of oil, on which account it is deemed equivalent to oil, as at M. Toh. 9:3 (*Purities* Part XI, pp. 209-211). Meir says it is deemed equivalent to oil even though it lacks all evidence of the presence of oil. The blood of the creeping thing, L-M, is deemed flesh, which is to say, it contributes to the requisite bulk at which the creeping thing imparts uncleanness. But then it is not equivalent to blood in imparting susceptibility to uncleanness, a consistent view of the matter.

Maimonides (*Uncleanness of Foodstuffs* 1:2) adds to the list the following observation:

And they render foodstuffs susceptible to uncleanness only if they fall upon the foodstuffs with the approval of the owner, and if they have not turned foul; for liquid that has turned foul does not render foodstuffs susceptible to uncleanness.

As to G2, Maimonides (*Uncleanness of Foodstuffs* 10:3) states the entire corpus of pertinent materials, part of which is below, as follows:

The blood which is numbered among the seven liquids is the blood which flows from cattle permitted for food, wild animals and birds when they are slaughtered; but the blood which spouts out in a jet does not make them susceptible, since they are still alive, and it counts as blood from a wound or blood let out from the veins. If during the slaughtering blood splashes foodstuffs and the blood is wiped off between the cutting of one tube and the other, it is in doubt; therefore such foodstuff is held in suspense, being neither eaten nor burnt.

Under "blood" is included blood let out from a man's veins to be given as a drink; but if it is let for healing, it is not susceptible to uncleanness, nor does it render foodstuffs susceptible.

So too the blood of slaughtering that flows from cattle forbidden for food, wild animals, and birds, and the blood that issues with secretions or excrement and the blood from a boil or a blister and what is squeezed out of flesh—all these neither contract uncleanness nor render foodstuffs susceptible, but count as no more than the other fruit juices.

And the blood of a dead creeping thing is deemed to be like its flesh: It conveys uncleanness and does not render foodstuffs susceptible. And we have nothing else that is like it.

אֵלוּ מְטַמְּאִין וּמַכְשִׁירִין: זוֹבוֹ שֶׁלַּזָּב, וְרֵקוֹ, וְשִׁכְבַת זַרְעוֹ,
וּמֵימֵי רַגְלָיו, וּרְבִיעִית מִן הַמֵּת, וְדַם הַנִּדָּה. רַבִּי אֱלִיעֶזֶר
אוֹמֵר: שִׁכְבַת זֶרַע אֵינָהּ מַכְשֶׁרֶת. רַבִּי אֶלְעָזָר בֶּן עֲזַרְיָה
אוֹמֵר: דַּם הַנִּדָּה אֵינוֹ מַכְשִׁיר. רַבִּי שִׁמְעוֹן אוֹמֵר: דַּם הַמֵּת
אֵינוֹ מַכְשִׁיר. וְאִם נָפַל עַל הַדְּלַעַת – גּוֹרְדָהּ, וְהִיא טְהוֹרָה.

אֵלוּ לֹא מְטַמְּאִין וְלֹא מַכְשִׁירִין: הַזֵּעָה, וְהַלֵּחָה סְרוּחָה,
וְהָרָאִי, וְהַדָּם הַיּוֹצֵא עִמָּהֶם, וּמַשְׁקֶה בֶּן שְׁמוֹנָה. רַבִּי יוֹסֵי

אוֹמֵר: חוּץ מִדָּמוֹ. וְהַשׁוֹתֶה מֵי טְבֶרְיָה, אַף עַל פִּי שֶׁיּוֹצְאִין
נְקִיִּים, דַּם שְׁחִיטָה בַּבְּהֵמָה בַּחַיָּה וּבָעוֹפוֹת הַטְּמֵאִים, וְדַם
הַקָּזָה לִרְפוּאָה. רַבִּי אֱלִיעֶזֶר מְטַמֵּא בָּאֵלּוּ. רַבִּי שִׁמְעוֹן בֶּן
אֶלְעָזָר אוֹמֵר: חֲלֵב הַזָּכָר – טָהוֹר.

A. These impart uncleanness and impart susceptibility to uncleanness.

B. (1) the flux of the *Zab*, (2) and his spit, and (3) his semen, and (4) his urine;

C. (5) and a quarter-*log* [of blood] from the corpse;

D. (6) and the blood of the menstruating woman.

E. R. Eliezer says, "Semen does not impart susceptibility to uncleanness."

F. R. Eleazar b. 'Azariah says, "The blood of the menstruating woman does not impart susceptibility to uncleanness."

G. R. Simeon says, "The blood of the corpse does not impart susceptibility to uncleanness.

H. "And if it fell on the gourd, one scrapes it off [since it cannot be eaten], and it is deemed insusceptible to uncleanness."

M. 6:6

I. These do not become unclean and do not impart susceptibility to uncleanness:

J. (1) sweat [= M. 2:1], and (2) stinking pus, and (3) excrement, and (4) blood which exudes with them, and (5) liquid [that is excreted with a still-born child] at the eighth month.

K. R. Yosé says, "Except for its blood."

L. (6) And [the discharge from the bowels of] him who drinks Tiberias-waters [which is a purgative], even though it comes out clean,

M. (7) blood from the slaughtering of cattle and beast and fowl which are unclean,

N. and (8) blood from blood-letting for healing.

O. R. Eliezer declares unclean in the case of these [=M, N].

P. R.Simeon b. Eleazar says, "The milk of the male is insusceptible to uncleanness."

M. 6:7

A is balanced by I, which should mean that the lists will be correlated. I count six items at B-D. But B3 is removed by Eliezer, E, and D6 by Eleazar b. 'Azariah, F. Simeon further wishes to remove C6. I do not see how B can lose B3 in any case. When we come to the specification of I at J, we have five items. L6 clearly is separate from J, since its form is quite at variance. M speaks to M. 6:5G1, and N to M. 6:5G2. Accordingly, the primary lists that should be balanced against one another are as follows:

M. 6:6	*M. 6:7*	*M. 6:5*
These impart both uncleanness and susceptibility to uncleanness [( ) = subject to dispute] :	These do not become unclean and do not impart susceptibility to uncleanness:	Subspecies of water [and impart susceptibility to uncleanness and become unclean as does water] :
1. Flux of *Zab*	1. sweat	1. [Liquid that exudes from] the eye
2. his spit	2. stinking pus	2. the ear
(3. his semen)	3. excrement	3. the nose
4. his urine	4. blood that exudes with them	4. the mouth
(5. quarter-*log* of blood from a corpse)	5. liquid excreted with stillborn child at the eighth month	5. urine
(6. blood of menstruating woman)	6. [discharge from bowels of] him who drinks Tiberias-waters, even though it comes out clean	[Subspecies of blood]

M. 6:6	*M. 6:7*	*M. 6:5*
	7. blood of slaughtering of cattle and beast and fowl which are unclean	6. blood from slaughtering of cattle and beast and fowl that are clean
	8. blood from bloodletting for healing	7. blood let out from veins for drink

In fact, M. 6:6 bears no relationship to its formal counterpart at M. 6:7. But M. 6:7 and M. 6:5 invite comparison at the final two items on each list, M. 6:7, Nos. 7-8 and M. 6:5, Nos. 6-7, and, therefore, at the opening items: Liquids of (1) eye, (2) ear, (3) nose, (4) mouth, and (5) urine are susceptible to uncleanness and impart susceptibility, but (1) sweat, (2) pus, (3) excrement, and (4) blood with them do not. Bodily excretions are not subject to uncleanness, but body-water is subject to uncleanness. M. 6:4, 5, and 6 go over the same matter, but M. 6:4-5 and M. 6:6 do not relate to one another. The formal history of the set thus is exceedingly difficult to imagine. At one point, the superscription of M. 6:7 or of M. 6:5 has been revised—I do not know which —and therefore the superscriptions come at the end of the process of making up the lists. Of these, the following clearly form cogent units: M. 6:6, Nos. 1-4, M. 6:7, Nos. 1-4, and M. 6:5, Nos. 1-4. Originally, therefore, perhaps the several lists began with matched sets of four items each.

Let us turn to the substance of the rules, considerably less difficult than the form. The original list of M. 6:6 certainly is at B. The quarter-*log* of blood from the corpse is disputed by Simeon; G. Eleazar b. 'Azariah would remove D6 from the list; and Eliezer wishes to exclude semen, which, given the antecedent materials, can only be semen of the *Zab*. Maimonides states the rule (*Uncleanness of Foodstuffs* 10:5) as follows:

Liquids which issue from those unclean persons whose liquids are Fathers of uncleanness convey uncleanness, and what they render unclean need not first be rendered susceptible, for the

uncleanness and the rendering susceptible befall at the same
time. And these are they: the issue of a man with flux, his
semen, his urine, a quarter-*log* of the blood of a corpse, the
blood of a menstruant, the blood issuing from the wound of
a man with flux or of his kind, a woman's milk, the tears of
the eyes, together with the other things included under 'water'
which issue from them — all these convey uncleanness in the
manner of unclean liquids which convey uncleanness without
needing intention; for unclean liquids convey uncleanness
whether they fall with or without approval [M. 1:1D] .

As to the items of M. 6:7, Maimonides says (*Uncleanness of
Foodstuffs* 10:7):

Sweat, foul secretion, excrement, liquid pertaining to an
eight months' abortion, the excrement of one who drinks the
water of Tiberias and the like, even though it comes forth
clear — none of these is deemed to be a liquid, and they neither
convey uncleanness nor render foodstuffs susceptible.

חֲלֵב הָאִשָּׁה מְטַמֵּא לְרָצוֹן וְשֶׁלֹּא לְרָצוֹן, וַחֲלֵב הַבְּהֵמָה אֵינוֹ
מְטַמֵּא אֶלָּא לְרָצוֹן. אָמַר רַבִּי עֲקִיבָא: קַל וָחֹמֶר הַדְּבָרִים:
מָה אִם חֲלֵב הָאִשָּׁה שֶׁאֵינוֹ מְיֻחָד אֶלָּא לַקְּטַנִּים, מְטַמֵּא
לְרָצוֹן וְשֶׁלֹּא לְרָצוֹן, חֲלֵב הַבְּהֵמָה שֶׁהוּא מְיֻחָד לַקְּטַנִּים
וְלַגְּדוֹלִים, אֵינוֹ דִין שֶׁיְּטַמֵּא לְרָצוֹן וְשֶׁלֹּא לְרָצוֹן? אָמְרוּ לוֹ:
לֹא, אִם טִמֵּא חֲלֵב הָאִשָּׁה שֶׁלֹּא לְרָצוֹן, שֶׁדַּם מַגֵּפָתָהּ טָמֵא,
יְטַמֵּא חֲלֵב הַבְּהֵמָה שֶׁלֹּא לְרָצוֹן, שֶׁדַּם מַגֵּפָתָהּ טָהוֹר? אָמַר
לָהֶם: מַחְמִיר אֲנִי בְּחָלָב מִבְּדָם, שֶׁהַחוֹלֵב לִרְפוּאָה, טָמֵא,
וְהַמַּקִּיז לִרְפוּאָה, טָהוֹר. אָמְרוּ לוֹ: סַלֵּי זֵיתִים וַעֲנָבִים יוֹכִיחוּ,
שֶׁהַמַּשְׁקִים הַיּוֹצְאִין מֵהֶן לְרָצוֹן, טְמֵאִים, וְשֶׁלֹּא לְרָצוֹן,
טְהוֹרִים. אָמַר לָהֶן: לֹא, אִם אֲמַרְתֶּם בְּסַלֵּי זֵיתִים וַעֲנָבִים,
שֶׁתְּחִלָּתָן אֹכֶל וְסוֹפָן מַשְׁקֶה, תֹּאמְרוּ בֶחָלָב שֶׁתְּחִלָּתוֹ וְסוֹפוֹ
מַשְׁקֶה? עַד כָּאן הָיְתָה תְשׁוּבָה. אָמַר רַבִּי שִׁמְעוֹן: מִכָּאן
וְאֵילָךְ הָיִינוּ מְשִׁיבִיז לְפָנָיו: מֵי גְשָׁמִים יוֹכִיחוּ, שֶׁתְּחִלָּתָן

וְסוֹפָן מַשְׁקֶה, וְאֵינָן מְטַמְּאִין אֶלָּא לְרָצוֹן. אָמַר לָנוּ: לֹא,
אִם אֲמַרְתֶּם בְּמֵי גְשָׁמִים שֶׁאֵין רָבִּוּ לְאָדָם אֶלָּא לָאֲרָצוֹת
וְלָאִילָנוֹת, וְרֹב הֶחָלָב לְאָדָם.

A. Woman's milk imparts susceptibility to uncleanness whether it is subject to approval or not subject to approval.

B. But the milk of the beast imparts susceptibility to uncleanness only [when it is detached] with approval. [Cf. M. 6:7P.]

C. Said R. 'Aqiba, "The matter produces an argument from the less to the greater [which proves that B is false].

D. "Now if the woman's milk, which is intended for infants alone, imparts uncleanness whether [detached] with approval or not with approval, the milk of cattle, which is intended for both infants and adults—is it not logical that it imparts susceptibility to uncleanness whether [detached] with approval or not with approval?"

E. They [= A-B] said to him, "No. If milk of the woman imparts uncleanness when [it is detached] without approval, [the reason is] that the blood of her wound is [automatically] unclean [like the blood of a corpse].

"But will the milk of cattle when [it is detached] without approval impart uncleanness, since the blood of its wound is clean?"

F. He said to them, "I rule more stringently in the case of milk than of blood,

G. "for "he who milks [a cow] for healing [the cow by relieving it of its milk] — it is susceptible to uncleanness.

H. "But he who draws blood for healing [= M. 6:7N, versus M. 6:7/0] — it is deemed insusceptible to uncleanness."

I. They said to him, "Baskets of olives and grapes will prove the case.

[Segal, p. 497, n. 4: Animal's milk may be compared to the juice flowing from such baskets, since both serve as human food.]

J. "For liquids that exude from them with approval are susceptible to uncleanness, [and those that exude] not with approval are insusceptible to uncleanness."

K. He said to them, "No. If you have so stated in the case of baskets of olives and grapes,which in the beginning are solid food and at the end become liquid, will you say so in the case of milk, which both in the beginning and at the end is a liquid?"

L. To this point was [his] reply.

M. Said R. Simeon, "From this point on we should reply before him:

N. "Rain will prove the matter, for in the beginning and at the end it is a liquid, and it imparts susceptibility to uncleanness only when it falls with approval."

O. He said to us, "No. If you have said so in the case of rain, in which instance most of it is only for lands and trees and not for man,

[Segal, n. 497, n. 9: The use of rain for man is limited, therefore rain cannot render human food susceptible to uncleanness unless a man desires it flow upon his food]

"[will you say so in the case of] milk, in which instance most of it is for the use of man?"

M. 6:8

Continuing M. 6:7P, the statement of the dispute, A-B, is slightly defective. 'Aqiba should have an equivalent, for which, following B, R. 'Aqiba says, 'P ŠL' LRŚWN should suffice. The dispute then is augmented with a debate, in two obvious parts, C-K and M-O. Since M-O do not raise a fresh issue but carry forward the analogy of C-K, I am inclined to see the gloss of L as important. There is no obvious reason to separate what is in fact a logical continuation unless the primary materials indeed are as described, formulated in two distinct units. But that is not a probative consideration.

'Aqiba's argument, D, begins in the subject-matter of the dispute, milk of the beast, demonstrating that it should be subjected to at least as stringent a rule as woman's milk. But E, the opposition shows that, in another aspect, the woman is subject to more stringent uncleanness-rules, and that is therefore the case here too. 'Aqiba then has to distinguish from the present one that aspect of the woman's uncleanness-rules which is more severe, which is to say, to distinguish milk from blood. Milk in any event is subject to a more severe rule than blood, an argument that incidentally attests M. 6:7N to the period after A.D. 70 at the latest.

The reply is based on the comparison between baskets of olives and grapes, justified for the reason given by Segal. This is an analogy not quite to the point and shifts the flow of argument. 'Aqiba, K, deals adequately with the case. But I-K seem to be a somewhat secondary level of discourse. Simeon's addition, M-O, proposes an argument along the lines of I-J. He too leaves behind milk and blood, animals and women, to which the matter of liquid and solid is impertinent. So Simeon depends on the immediately antecedent element in the construction. At O 'Aqiba succeeds in showing the relevance of the analogy to rain and at the same time turns the analogy to his own advantage. In all, therefore, 'Aqiba is given the opening argument, C-D, answered by E, and supported by F-H; the opposition has I-J, successfully refuted at K; and M-N, successfully overturned at O. At no point is the opposition allowed to reply to 'Aqiba's arguments, and all three analogies—milk and blood, olives and grapes, and rain-water—serve his view. The 'Aqibans' hand is clearly discerned in this formally balanced, but clearly one-sided construction.

vii. Conclusion

Now that we have undertaken a protracted exercise in the form-analytical interpretation of Mishnah, we should specify those aspects of the required exegetical program to which this approach in no way contributes. These are important and are not few.

First, the explanation of the meaning of individual words, in context or otherwise, rarely is affected by the use of those words in sentences, let alone by the formal and syntactic meaning imputed to them in context. Philology (let alone archaeology) in this work remains untouched.

Second, we have made very little of matters of variant readings, only rarely alluding to them (except in Chapter 4). For deciding the law, these variants will be of critical importance. For an exercise of the present sort, they make little material difference, and, as we shall see later on, when it comes to the study of history, history of ideas, and history of religions, they make no difference at all. Text-criticism is curiously unaffected, and the unimportance for diverse legitimate purposes of exegesis and history is underlined.

Third, where we find problems of readings that do affect the meaning of a pericope, e.g., at M. 3:7W-X, form-analysis makes no contribution at all. This is disappointing. We should have hoped that recognition of patterns internal to the expression of Mishnah's ideas would facilitate the proposal of improved readings, on the one side, and the solution of long-standing problems of textual variants of an important character, on the other. Perhaps that is so on a large scale. For example, we are able to determine points of development of language beyond the expected pattern. But when matters come down to the parsing of a self-evidently defective sentence, so far as I can see, form-analysis makes no difference at all. Perhaps as the inventor of the method, I take too conservative a position, and, in time to come, others may devise more precise criteria so as to permit solution of problems of parsing sentences. But, in my view, I have carried as far as they should go the matter of analysis of forms and formulary patterns, the unpacking of con-structions of complete units of thought within a given pattern, the inquiry into the repetition of that pattern in carefully counted-out numbers of exempla, the shifting of that pattern to some other with a change in the subject, and similar matters explored in the preceding pages.

Form-analytical exegesis therefore is one approach among many, solving certain long-standing problems, not approaching others. It does only what it claims to do. It therefore is to be judged solely in accord with one criterion. Its purpose is to recover the original, historical sense or meaning of a pericope through the analysis of the syntactic traits, formal and formulary usages, and related evi-dences of how the framer of a pericope chooses to express his ideas: that way, not in some other way, to say that thing, not some other thing. This supposition, on the foundations of which the earliest strata of the Talmudic exegesis of Mishnah also are constructed, further lays the way open to other sorts of analysis of Mishnah, other exercises of exegesis of large-scale phenomena of Mishnah. But before turning to the reconstructive enterprise, let us turn aside and undertake the difficult task we have postponed until now: the problem of Makhshirin Chapter One. That chapter permits two exercises in method, both (1) a systematic reading of the received exegetical literature and (2) an account of the problem of Tosefta. Makhshirin Chapter One indeed presents us with an ample opportunity to do both.

What we shall now do is to turn aside to that thicket of thorns and brambles represented by the established exegesis of the tractate and its problems. That inherited approach is in two parts.

First, as we shall see, Tosefta (see glossary, under Mishnah) contains its own reading of Mishnah, complete with its own original formulations of the laws covered by Mishnah. For the entire history of the interpretation of Mishnah, exegetes who had access to Tosefta (or to the Talmuds, and all of them had that, but there is no Talmud to our tractate) took for granted that Tosefta (and the Talmuds) would define Mishnah's meaning. Tosefta was not perceived as what it is, the first systematic *commentary* to Mishnah, certainly the greatest commentary ever composed for Mishnah. Tosefta was perceived as a corpus of authoritative and definitive statements of what Mishnah meant. Tosefta was deemed correlative to Mishnah, not dependent on it. Since Tosefta was not a commentary, other commentators did not imagine they might take fresh initiatives in approaching Mishnah. For the earlier exegetes, Tosefta in fact defined the initiatives to be taken in explaining Mishnah, said what there is to be said, solved all problems. So there is no way of reaching back to the first, historical meaning of Mishnah, except to see how Tosefta understands matters. This is for two reasons: the legitimate reason, as I said, which is that Tosefta constitutes Mishnah's greatest commentary; and the illegitimate reason, which is that one will never understand the whole of the established exegetical literature of Mishnah without knowing Tosefta. Governing, as it did, what everyone after Tosefta would assume Mishnah meant, Tosefta must be seen as a problem in Mishnah's exegesis.

Second, once we have reviewed Tosefta on one chapter of the tractate at hand, we shall turn to a statement of the problems to be solved by any exegete who approaches that same wretchedly difficult chapter, as well as a solution of those problems. Then we shall proceed to review how the principal prior exegetes of the same chapter answered precisely the same questions we have considered. Obviously, no "final" answers are possible. There are only more plausible or adequate ones. In no way are we able to claim that form-analytical reading of the document answers all questions. It surely does not answer questions better than people who to begin with asked different questions and who took note of different characteristics of the text from those important to us. But in no way shall we concede that what we have inherited exhausts what there is to be said. So we enter that part of the forest in which brambles and thickets bar the way, progress is slow and painful, and just where we are heading and why is not always clear.

PART II   Brambles and Thorns
           The Problem of Tosefta
           The Received Exegesis

CHAPTER 3

A Sample of the Analysis of Tosefta's Relationship to Mishnah

i. Introduction

Now that we have completed our first encounter with the tractate under study, examining each of its units, the logical next step should be to take up the problem of how these individual units are put together into chapters. But before we move onward, we turn aside to take up two questions not considered in the exegesis of the tractates's pericopae. These are, first, the matter of Tosefta, and second, the issue of the received exegetical literature of Mishnah. The reason is that all commentaries to Mishnah prior to this one treat as authoritative the meanings imputed to Mishnah by Tosefta, a compilation I shall describe in a moment. Consequently, if Tosefta treats a Mishnah-pericope and states an interpretation of that pericope, and if, further, a later commentator to Mishnah had access to Tosefta, then invariably what Tosefta says will define the meaning of Mishnah for that commentator, and for the many who later copied what he said. Furthermore, obviously, Mishnah already has a sizable corpus of commentaries. Any claim to approach the document from an essentially untried direction must be accompanied by an account of what remains, from the tried and true perspectives, to be learned and how this is to be learned. Thus we have to turn aside for the moment to consider two significant questions. We treat together the problem of Tosefta and the utilization of the received exegesis of Mishnah because, as is clear, the two are simply inseparable. The latter is shaped by the former.

95

Tosefta, emerging in the two hundred years after the formation of Mishnah, serves as an extended commentary on, and supplement to, Mishnah. It is one of the three types of exegetical literature generated by Mishnah. (The other two are the two Talmuds, on the one side, and the Scriptural-exegetical compilations, Sifra and Sifré, aimed at bringing Mishnah into relationship to the written Torah of Moses, on the other.) The Toseftan compilation closely models its language and organization on the language and order of Mishnah, while the other two sorts of exegeses of Mishnah go their own way. Tosefta joins together materials that, in themselves, stand in one of two distinct relationships to Mishnah (in various gradations). Some of Tosefta's pericopae cite Mishnah verbatim, or nearly verbatim, and systematically gloss Mishnah; or they restate Mishnah's problems and propositions in other terms and in accord with other principles than those of Mishnah. Other pericopae of Tosefta will present ideas generally relevant to Mishnah's topics but substantively independent therefrom. The former sort of Toseftan materials may be said to complement Mishnah, the latter, to supplement it.

Now when we come to that later stage of Mishnah-exegesis, after the age of the Talmuds, Sifra and Sifré, and Tosefta, we enter the world of what generally are called "the traditional commentaries." In an unsystematic way, the reader already has encountered here a great many of the approaches and ideas of these commentaries. In the chapter following this one, we shall systematically consider how many commentators deal with a single, extremely complicated problem of interpretation. Calling these commentaries "traditional" seems to me inappropriate. To some, "tradition" implies a claim to authority that is absolutely incongruous with the work of reasoned and principled exegesis ("our holy rabbis would not lie," "the ancients must have had a reason to say what they did, even if we do not know what it was," "they said it, so we have to accept it"). To others, what is "traditional" may be dismissed because "the ancients" came to their conclusions on grounds unacceptable to "modern," or to "scientific," minds. The reader already knows that out of the established commentaries—not only the incomparable Maimonides—we gain much insight into the reasoning encapsulated in the texts before us. Possessed of minds of surpassing intelligence and unequaled mastery of the texts themselves, the rabbinical exegetes of ancient, medieval, and modern times provide penetrating guidance into the heart of matters. To ignore them is simply unthinkable. At the same time, to turn their opinions into a kind of revelation and endow them with supernatural authority, or to suppose that what they had to say exhausts for all time what there is to be said is equally unthinkable. If we choose to study Mishnah, it is because we suppose there is something interesting to be learned there. Both our predecessors and we ourselves have a role to play in finding out what that is and in reporting it.

Now the first lesson to be learned about the received exegetical literature is its highly *traditional* character. By *traditional* I mean, its tendency to receive and accept what is in earlier authorities—to copy what is said earlier. That is not to say that no fresh minds and unanticipated initiatives existed in the intellectural history of Mishnah-exegesis. On the contrary, we already have noticed many interesting ideas, and, it goes without saying, Maimonides' choice of writing a Mishnah-commentary was itself daring, inventive, and revolutionary. Nonetheless, where there is a comment on a Mishnah-pericope in Tosefta or in the Babylonian Talmud, or, for some of the post-Talmudic exegetes, in the Palestinian Talmud or even (for a very few) in Sifra and Sifré (and related compilations), that comment finally and exhaustively decides matters. From that point onward, the exegetical decision has been completed. What there is to say has been said. It remains only to copy, amplify, repeat.

So before one may approach the received exegetical literature to find out what the ages have had to say, we have first to examine what they regarded as the definitive sources of the exegesis of the document before them. Since the established exegetical literature deems Tosefta, the Talmuds, and related writings of the centuries following Mishnah's formation to be not *also* exegetical in character, but canonical and normative, what in fact is subject to their exegetical effort is something other than Mishnah ("as such"). That is why, for our part, *approaching Tosefta as itself a work of interpretation*, and not as *part* of what is to be interpreted, we effect a revolution that places us outside of the framework of the established exegesis. If this book succeeds, we shall find ourselves not only outside of what is in place, but also at the beginning of a quite new and different enterprise of Mishnah-study. Form-analysis is the least of what is new.

We come now to the opening chapter of the tractate under study, an unusually difficult essay. I have to specify the problems of a literary and conceptual character that await attention and to propose solutions to each one of them (or to specify those I cannot solve). In the next chapter we shall then go over a single difficult matter and review the approaches to the problem taken by a number of earlier exegetes. This will require rereading what is said in this chapter.

The procedure established in Part One thus varies in a single important respect. In addition to the sequence of Mishnah-pericopae, we now shall also consider what Tosefta has to say. For this purpose I have divided Tosefta into units corresponding to the Mishnah-pericope to which each is relevant. So we shall analyze a Mishnah-pericope, then turn to Tosefta's corresponding unit, and proceed, thereafter, to the next unit of Mishnah.

ii. Mishnah-Tosefta Makhshirin Chapter One

כָּל מַשְׁקֶה שֶׁתְּחִלָּתוֹ לְרָצוֹן, אַף עַל פִּי שֶׁאֵין סוֹפוֹ לְרָצוֹן, אוֹ
שֶׁסּוֹפוֹ לְרָצוֹן, אַף עַל פִּי שֶׁאֵין תְּחִלָּתוֹ לְרָצוֹן – הֲרֵי זֶה בְּכִי
יֻתַּן. מַשְׁקִין טְמֵאִים מְטַמְּאִין לְרָצוֹן וְשֶׁלֹּא לְרָצוֹן.

A. Any liquid that in the beginning is acceptable, even though at the end it is not acceptable,

B. or that at the end is acceptable, even though at the beginning it is not acceptable—

[Segal, p. 469, n.2 (= Rosh, Sens, Bert., Rashi, B. Hul. 16a): . . . the meaning is that the owner was pleased with the beginning of the flow of the liquid for some other purpose, but was displeased when in the end the liquid settled on the produce, or the reverse]

C. lo, this is under the law, If water be put.

[Maimonides, *Uncleanness of Foodstuffs* 12:2: " . . . But if it in no wise falls with his approval, it does not render the foodstuff susceptible. Even if a man makes his produce wet out of danger or necessity, while in fact he does not wish

it to be made wet, such produce is not rendered susceptible"
(= M.1:6).]

D. Unclean liquids [e.g., the flux of a *Zab* (GRA) simul-
taneously] impart [susceptibility to uncleanness and] uncleanness [whether they are] acceptable or not acceptable.

[MS, Bert.: What is unclean imparts uncleanness whether
wanted or not, likewise here.]

M. 1:1

A-C set the stage for the Houses' disputes, M. 1:2-4. D formally
is autonomous, for it shifts from the singular of A-C to the plural
and makes use of the participle, MṬM'YN, in place of BKY YTN,
which has exactly the same meaning. But the secondary link between
A-C and D is firm, since LRṢWN/ŠL' LRṢWN, is shared by both,
and, moreover, while A and B distinguish the two (THLTW/SWPW),
D pointedly does not (L . . . WŠL' . . .). Accordingly, the
contrast has invited joining, by a balanced predicate, laws that
originally were phrased as separate and distinct statements.

The point of A-C is clear. If liquid at some point is wanted, its
capacity to render something susceptible to uncleanness is activated.
Once the liquid can make dry food susceptible, it does so, whether
or not, at some other point in the process, the liquid is wanted,
e.g., when it wets down the food. Accordingly, if one drew water
intentionally, put it on the food intentionally, or allowed rain to
fall on food and considered making use of the food in its wet-down
condition, but later on too much water came down or for some
other reason the man changed his mind about wanting the food to
be wet, or wanting to make use of the water he drew, that does
not matter. Alternatively, if when the rain fell on the food the
man did not want it, but he then changed his mind and decided
that he did, we do not take account of the former fact, the lack of
prior intention. Under both circumstances, we deem the water and
its application to the food to be desired—at some point in its
origination or in its application to the food—and therefore it has
the capacity to impart susceptibility to uncleanness. We have already
seen many pericopae that illustrate this conception.

D's independent rule is clear as stated. Unclean liquids both render something susceptible to uncleanness and also (simultaneously)

impart uncleanness. This is the case even if the unclean liquids fall
on the food contrary to the owner's wishes. The double meaning
of MṬM'YN should not be missed.

הַמַּרְעִיד אֶת הָאִילָן לְהַשִּׁיר מִמֶּנּוּ אֳכָלִין, אוֹ אֶת הַטֻּמְאָה –
אֵינָן בְּכִי יֻתַּן. לְהַשִּׁיר מִמֶּנּוּ מַשְׁקִין – בֵּית שַׁמַּאי אוֹמְרִים:
הַיּוֹצְאִין, וְאֶת שֶׁבּוֹ – בְּכִי יֻתַּן. בֵּית הַלֵּל אוֹמְרִים: הַיּוֹצְאִין –
בְּכִי יֻתַּן, וְאֶת שֶׁבּוֹ – אֵינָן בְּכִי יֻתַּן, מִפְּנֵי שֶׁהוּא מִתְכַּוֵּן שֶׁיֵּצְאוּ
מִכֻּלּוֹ.

הַמַּרְעִיד אֶת הָאִילָן וְנָפַל עַל חֲבֵרוֹ, אוֹ סוֹכָה וְנָפְלָה עַל
חֲבֶרְתָּהּ, וְתַחְתֵּיהֶן זְרָעִים אוֹ יְרָקוֹת הַמְחֻבָּרִין לַקַּרְקַע –
בֵּית שַׁמַּאי אוֹמְרִים: בְּכִי יֻתַּן. בֵּית הַלֵּל אוֹמְרִים: אֵינָן בְּכִי
יֻתַּן. אָמַר רַבִּי יְהוֹשֻׁעַ מִשּׁוּם אַבָּא יוֹסֵי חֲלִיקוֹפְרִי אִישׁ
טִבְעוֹן: תְּמַהּ עַצְמָךְ אִם יֵשׁ מַשְׁקֶה טָמֵא בַּתּוֹרָה עַד שֶׁיִּתְכַּוֵּן
וְיִתֵּן, שֶׁנֶּאֱמַר׳: ׳וְכִי יֻתַּן מַיִם עַל זֶרַע׳.

הַנּוֹעֵר אֲגֻדָּה שֶׁלַּיָּרָק, וְיָרְדוּ מִצַּד הָעֶלְיוֹן לַתַּחְתּוֹ – בֵּית
שַׁמַּאי אוֹמְרִים: בְּכִי יֻתַּן. בֵּית הַלֵּל אוֹמְרִים: אֵינָם בְּכִי יֻתַּן.
אָמְרוּ בֵית הַלֵּל לְבֵית שַׁמַּאי: וַהֲלֹא הַנּוֹעֵר אֶת הַקֶּלַח,
חוֹשְׁשִׁין אָנוּ שֶׁמָּא יָצְאוּ מִן הֶעָלֶה לֶעָלֶה? אָמְרוּ לָהֶן בֵּית
שַׁמַּאי: שֶׁהַקֶּלַח אֶחָד, וַאֲגֻדָּה קְלָחִים הַרְבֵּה. אָמְרוּ לָהֶם
בֵּית הַלֵּל: הֲרֵי הַמַּעֲלֶה שַׂק מָלֵא פֵרוֹת וּנְתָנוֹ עַל גַּב הַנָּהָר,
חוֹשְׁשִׁין אָנוּ שֶׁמָּא יָרְדוּ מִצַּד הָעֶלְיוֹן לַתַּחְתּוֹן? אֲבָל אִם
הֶעֱלָה שְׁנַיִם וּנְתָנָן זֶה עַל גַּב זֶה – הַתַּחְתּוֹן בְּכִי יֻתַּן. וְרַבִּי יוֹסֵי
אוֹמֵר: הַתַּחְתּוֹן טָהוֹר.

A. He who shakes the tree to bring down from it fruit,

B. or [shakes the tree to bring down from it] that which
is unclean [e.g., a piece of corpse-matter left by a bird in the
tree] —

C. it [water that falls with the fruit or the unclean thing]
is not under the law, If water be put.

I. D. [If one shakes the tree] to bring down from it liquids —

E. The House of Shammai say, "Those [drops] that fall and [those] that [remain] on it are under the law, If water be put."

F. The House of Hillel say, "Those that fall are under the law, If water be put. And those that [remain] on it are not under the law, If water be put,

G. "because [the man] intends that they [the drops of liquid] should fall from it in its entirety."

[Maimonides, *Uncleanness of Foodstuffs* 13:15 at the end: "What is left thereon, although it has fallen from one place to another, is not deemed to be detached with approval because his purpose has been that it should come away from all of the tree. So too if it splashes something attached to the ground, it is not deemed to be detached with approval."]

M. 1:2

II. H. He who shakes the tree, and it [GRA: liquid] fell on its fellow —

I. or [if he shakes] a bush and it fell on another bush,

J. and under them are (1) seeds or (2) vegetables which are attached to the ground —

K. The House of Shammai say, "They are under the law, If water be put."

L. The House of Hillel say, "They are not under the law, If water be put."

M. Said R. Joshua in the name of Abba Yosé Holi Qofri of Tibe'on, "Be surprised if there is a liquid in the Torah which is unclean before a person actually intends [to make use of it] and puts it on, as it said, *And if water be put on seed* (Lev. 11:18)."

M. 1:3

III. N. He who shakes a bunch of herbs [so deliberately detaching the water (MA)], and [drops of water] fell from the topside to the bottom —

O. The House of Shammai say, "[They are] under the law, If water be put"

[Segal, p. 470, n. 10: Because the water fell on the lower side by the owner's deliberate act.]

P. The House of Hillel say, "They are not under the law, If water be put."

[Segal, p. 470, n. 11 (=MA): His intention was to shake off the water altogether, and not to wet the lower side]."

Q. Said the House of Hillel to the House of Shammai, "And is it not so [that in the case of] one who shakes off the stalk [of a plant] —do we take thought of whether they dropped from leaf to leaf?"

[Segal, n. 12: . . . But if no susceptibility is caused in the case of a stalk, why should it be caused in the case of a bundle.]

R. Said to them the House of Shammai, "For the stalk is one, but the bunch [of vegetables] is [made up of] many stalks."

S. Said to them the House of Hillel, "Lo, he who brings up [from the river] a sack full of produce and puts it on the bank of the river [so that the water will flow back into the river] —do we take thought of whether it [the water] descends from the topside to the bottom?"

T. But: If he brought up two and put them one on top of the other, the bottom one [indeed] is under the law, If water be put.

[Segal, p. 471, n. 5: Because by placing one sack upon the other he must have intended that the water should flow from the upper sack upon the lower sack (= Maharam).]

U. And R. Yosé says, "The bottom one is insusceptible to uncleanness."

M. 1:4

The Houses now will ask the correlative, but secondary question after M.1:1: What if part (in origin and application) of the water is wanted (all the time, beginning and end), and part is never wanted (all the time, beginning and end)? That is to say, once we declare that we do not make distinctions within the time, that is, the intervals, at which the water is applied to the food, we ask whether we distinguish water wanted all the time from water not wanted all the time. Clearly, the position consistent with M. 1:1A-C will hold that, just as we do not distinguish water wanted at one point from that (same) water not wanted at some other, but regard the whole process of the infusion of water as single and indivisible, so, if we want part of a quantity of water, then the whole of that quantity is deemed to activate the process of susceptibility to uncleanness. This in fact is the Shammaite position. The Hillelites will distinguish that which is wanted from that which is not wanted, though, as we shall see, the matter is phrased with somewhat greater subtlety.

This handsome construction is introduced by a single rule, A + C, glossed by B. This sets the stage for the tripartite dispute, D-F, glossed at G, H + K-L, with an interpolation at I, a major gloss at J, and an appended autonomous saying, M. Then comes the third dispute, N-P, with an appended debate, Q-S, giving the Hillelites an opening and closing argument. The Shammaites are permitted only to set up the decisive statement at S. As we shall see, the debate presupposes a text or versions of the matter other than the one before us, and Tosefta "corrects" accordingly. T should not be regarded as a continuation of the Hillelite saying at S, both for formal reasons, which are obvious, and for substantive ones. The Hillelites need make no concession whatsoever; U clearly intends to reject the foregoing stich, with which, therefore, it should be read as a single unit, a dispute unto itself. The language of the Houses' apodoses invariably is acutely balanced, the operative predicate, KY YTN +/- *not*. Yosé's, by contrast, sets KY YTN against ṬHWR, an odd mixture.

To begin with, we observe a curious disjuncture between M. 1:1 and M. 1:2-4. M. 1:1A-C are clear that, if we want liquid at the outset but not at the end, or vice versa, the liquid falls under the law, If water be put. Yet what do we have in the cases of M. 1:2-4 if not exactly that? The man shakes the tree to bring down fruit, but liquid falls along with the fruit. Here the liquid is not wanted at all. All parties therefore agree that the liquid, which never falls with approval, is not subject to the law, If water be put. But at M. 1:2D we do want some of the liquids. Are all covered by it? No, that is not the case, the Hillelites say. Why not? Because the water in the tree *never* was wanted where it is. At M. 1:3H, we shake the tree and the water does not fall directly onto the ground. Is it then wanted? No, the Hillelites say, it is not wanted. Why not? Because the water did not fall *where* it is wanted. At M. 1:4N, once more, we go over the same ground, with the same result. In all cases, therefore, the Shammaites consistently stand within the plain and obvious meaning of M. 1:1. It is only the Hillelites who propose to refine that meaning and limit its application. That is one way of viewing matters. But the other is to regard M. 1:1 as a rule quite outside the framework of Hillelite thought.

If we see the set, M. 1:1-4, as essentially harmonious, with the Houses in agreement on M. 1:1, then the Houses are understood to debate a gray area of the law. That is, A-C set up one pole, with the other, opposite view left unstated. The point is that if we shake the tree to bring down the fruit, we certainly do not want any of the water that falls along with it. Our clear intent is for fruit, not moisture. The question at D is whether we can differentiate water we want from that which we do not want. The House of Shammai say we cannot. Accordingly, the drops that fell and those that remain on the tree but fall later on (Rosh, Sens, Albeck, among all commentaries) all have been subjected to the man's approval. All falling drops now are deemed water that can render susceptible whatever pertinent foodstuffs of the man are touched by it. The contrary view of the Hillelites is explained at G. The man wants all the water – but he wants it to fall *out* of the tree. That which remains in the tree therefore has not conformed to his wishes.

Clearly, the issue of M. 1:2 concerns rendering the water capable of imparting susceptibility to something else. This brings us to M. 1:3, a pericope exhibiting more problems than appear on the surface. (In the next chapter we shall survey the diverse approaches taken by the great commentaries to these same problems. Clearly, there can be no final solutions.) The analysis of the distinct components of the complex will show the layers of meaning to be uncovered in the whole.

We proceed to the problem of substantive interpretation, phrase by phrase. H, to begin with, should be read in the context of A, D and N:

A. He who shakes (HMR'YD) the tree to bring down from it fruit—

D. (He who shakes the tree) to bring down from it liquids—
H. He who shakes the tree and it fell on its fellow—
N. He who shakes (NW'R) a bunch of herbs and they fell from the topside [of the herbs] to the bottom—

The formulation imposes its own discipline: *he who shakes,* implied at D. The repetition of the participle proves beyond doubt that we have a unitary construction and therefore shows that we should have a progression of problems, (for example) simple to complex. Certainly A and N address the problem of falling moisture. This is explicit at N, which is incomprehensible in any other terms, and equally certain at A, since E and F refer *to those which exude* and *those which remain,* once more, liquids. M. 1:2 cannot be a debate about the status of fruit, on the tree and off. And the excellent gloss at G leaves no doubt of that matter. (We observe, then, that M is parallel in function to G and therefore the redactor who placed it wants us to see Joshua's saying as an explanation for the foregoing.)

Can H then support the meaning, "He who shakes the tree and it—*liquid*—fell on its fellow?" The problem here is the use of the singular verb for *fell,* and again at I. But the Hillelite saying, L, takes for granted we have had a plural antecedent. The referent of K-L can only be liquids. But more decisive still, if we posit that H speaks of liquids, we have a handsome sequence from A to D, H, and N:

A. He who shakes the tree to bring down pieces of fruit—
1. *What about liquid that comes down along with the fruit, but that the man has not intended to bring down at all?*
D. He who shakes the tree to bring down from it liquids—
2. *What about the liquids that do not fall as a direct result of the shaking?*
H. He who shakes the tree and it fell on its fellow—
3. *What about liquids that do fall, but that do not fall directly onto the ground, but first fall onto an intervening object* [= those that remain of D-G!] ?
N. He who shakes a bunch of herbs and they fell from top to bottom (on the bunch itself)—
4. *What about liquids that do not fall even indirectly onto the*

ground, but fall onto another part of their own original loca-
tion — a refinement of the foregoing?

In other words, the problem of the three disputes is, in sequence, (1) not falling, (2) not falling directly but falling onto another object, and (3) not falling onto another object but falling onto another place in the original object. That seems a fairly tight sequence of problems. The Houses' opinions are constant throughout. Self-evidently, the whole is a major expansion of a single dispute, best represented by D-G, which is given two further and more subtle, but essentially repetitious, exemplifications. The construction appears therefore to be a secondary expansion of a primary and simple dispute.

Let us now turn to M. By the formal analogy to G, as I said, M should be asked to explain the Hillelite position. The Hillelite view, G says, is that the drops that do not fall from the tree are not under the law, If water be put. Why not? Because the man intended everything to fall. That which has not fallen is not subject to his intention. Joshua proposes to explain the Hillelite saying at L: Why is water that falls onto an intervening tree or bush and thence to the ground not subject to the law, If water be put? Asked in this way, the question Joshua answers is straightforward: The water on the intervening area is not subject to the law, If water be put, *because the man never intended the water to fall where it actually did fall.* He did not put it where it fell by a deliberate act. Accordingly, M really does say in reference to L exactly what G says in reference to F, just as the redactor's formal care in placing M clearly intends.

To summarize: We take full account of the intention of the man, at D/H, who has shaken the tree. He intended all the water to fall. That which does not fall has not accorded with his intent. He intended the water to fall to the ground. That which has not fallen directly to the ground likewise has not conformed to his intent. He did not intend to shake the water from tree to tree but from tree to ground. The man's own action, moreover, has not accomplished the intention. He intended to shake water onto the ground and he shook the tree, but he did not actually put the water onto the ground at all.

This brings us to J. Clearly, J breaks the well-established and sensible form of D, H, and N. In no case do we need to be told what is under the tree. If the water is not deemed to have fallen "with approval," what difference does it make where it falls or upon what it falls? The specification of seeds or vegetables attached to the ground is decidedly secondary. J1 in particular adds nothing, except from the viewpoint of M's citation of Scripture. That is to say, if we did not have the reference to seed at M, why should we want it at J1?

J2, however, is another matter. J2 presents not merely a repetition of J1 — something else lying under the tree, now unplucked, in the ground. (The reference to *attached to the ground* applies to seeds as much as to the vegetables. But this is secondary.) J necessarily distinguishes between the status of the water (does it render something susceptible to uncleanness?) and the produce upon which the water falls (has it been made susceptible to uncleanness?). It clearly sees a distinction between (1) the water's capacity to render something susceptible to uncleanness, and (2) the status of the object on which the water has fallen. Specifying that the unplucked vegetables are part of the superscription is the way clearly to establish this distinction. For why should J2 tell us that the vegetables are still in the ground? Because it wishes to stress: the vegetables are *not* themselves made susceptible to the uncleanness. The issue at hand concerns *only* the status of the water itself, that is, the water's capacity to impart susceptibility to uncleanness. If the water that has fallen on the seeds in the ground or on the vegetables in the ground *touches something else*, which can be susceptible to uncleanness by reason of having been detached from the ground, that latter object is indeed affected by the water and so made susceptible to uncleanness. Obviously, the consideration important to J is secondary to the larger construction. Just as the form of J requires us to treat J as an interpolation, so its issue, properly interpreted, likewise is interpolated, not conceptually integral to the larger problem of the construction of which it is part.

The third unit, N-S, poses few new problems. N-S go over the ground of I. We see another instance in which an inanimate object intervenes between the shaking of the tree or bunch and the ultimate destination of the falling water. The Shammaites say that the man has detached the water, even though it has not exuded, parallel to M. 1:2E. The Hillelites take a position consistent with the foregoing. Their argument in principle serves M. 1:3 as much as M. 1:4. But the details of the argument are distinctive to the third dispute, which therefore is integrally served by the debate.

The force of the Hillelite argument is simply to underline the absurdity of the Shammaite position. That is, we do not take account of the falling of water from one stalk to another. But where have the Shammaite conceded that point? Not in the pericope before us. We should have a statement, for instance, after L, "And they agree [= the Shammaites concede] in the case of shaking a stalk, and water fell from one leaf to another, (that) it is not under the law, If water be put." Then the bunch of herbs forms an intermediate and unclear case, and the rest follows. As it is, however, the Shammaites explicitly accept the Hillelites' assumption of a Shammaite concession: We do *not* take account of water's dripping from one leaf to another on the stalk of a plant. The Shammaites therefore must distinguish the stalk of a plant from a bunch of herbs. The present statement of the debate is slightly askew.

The closing argument of the Hillelites, S, is equally difficult to interpret. The Hillelites now assume that, in a sack full of produce that is wet through and through, if water drips from the top of the sack to the bottom, it is *not* deemed to drip with approval. We do not take thought of whether drops of water fall from top to bottom. The water that drips is not subject to the law, If water be put. But this is as close as we can come to N without actually restating the case. The Hillelites have no answer but repeat their original position, so far as I can see.

Obviously, T could bear the formula, *And they agree that . . .* In this case the Hillelites go over to the Shammaite position. But that is not how matters are formulated. As it is, we treat two separate sacks as different from one sack's top and bottom. The Hillelite position is correct, but only for one sack. If we have two, then there is dripping with effect. Yosé denies that position, taking the principle of the Hillelites to its ultimate conclusion. T. correctly sees Yosé as revising the Hillelite position. Take note in the Tosefta-passage that follows, and in many others, that Tosefta often cites

Mishnah verbatim, or nearly so. When that is done, I present the Tosefta's translation of a lemma of the Mishnah in italics, so that the process of citation and gloss will be visually striking. This first occurs in the presentation of the following pericope of Tosefta.

¹המרעיד את האילן להשיר ממנו משקין ונפלו על תלושין שבו ועל מחוברין שתחתיו בית שמאי אומר׳ בכי יותן ובית הלל אומ׳ על התלושין בכי יותן ועל המחוברין אינן בכי יותן:

A. *He who shakes the tree in order to bring down liquids from it —*

B. and they fell on those [pieces of fruit] that were detached, that were on it [the tree], and on those [vegetables] that were attached [to the ground], that were under it [that tree] —

C. The House of Shammai say, "It is under the law, If water be put."

D. And the House of Hillel say, "As to those [drops of moisture falling on those] that were detached, [they are] under the law, If water be put.

E. "And as to those [drops falling on those] that were attached [to the ground], they are not under the law, If water be put."

[Maimonides, *Uncleanness of Foodstuffs* 13:15: . . . water splashed from it is not deemed to be detached with approval. . . . What is left thereon, although it has fallen from one place to another, is not deemed to be detached with approval, because his purpose has been that it should come away from all of the tree. So, too, if it splashes something attached to the ground, it is not deemed to be detached with approval.]

T. 1:1

At A T. cites M. 1:2D and then introduces an interesting distinction, already familiar to us from M. 1:3J, into the analysis of M. 1:2. M. 1:2D-G speaks of drops that fell from the tree and drops that remain on the tree. We know that the Hillelites of M. 1:2 regard the drops of water that remain on the tree as insusceptible, and the Shammaites deem all of the water to be subject to the man's intent. Now, T. asks, what about fruit that was in the tree but *not* attached to it? Water has fallen on that fruit. The Shammaite position requires no exposition. The Hillelites say that the water is not subject to the law, If water be put. The man intended the water to fall on the ground, not on fruit still in the tree, as Maimonides explains.

The issue of the vegetables attached to the ground, by contrast, is interesting from the Shammaite viewpoint. Water has fallen on these vegetables. The Hillelites, we know, deem that water not to fall under the rule, If water be put. Why not? Because the water was not intended for the vegetables. The same rule applies here; E contains no surprises. How do the Shammaites view the water on vegetables attached to the ground? They hold that such water is no different from the rest. Even though this water has fallen on what is not capable of being susceptible to uncleanness and what therefore is not subject to the water to begin with, when the vegetables are picked, they are made susceptible to the water. Or when other produce touches the water on the insusceptible vegetables in the ground, it is indeed affected by the water. This expansion of M. 1:2 governs the interpretation of M. 1:3J.

²אמר ר' יוסי בר' יהודה לא נחלקו בית שמאי ובית הלל על המרעיד את האילן להשיר הימנו משקין ונפלו על התלושין שבו ועל מחוברין שתחתיו שאינן בכי יותן ועל שפקין משנגבו שאינן בכי יותן על מה נחלקו על המרעיד את האילן להשיר מהן אוכלין ונפלו מבד לבד ומסוכה לחברתה באותו אילן שבית שמאי אומרים בכי יותן ובית הלל אומרים אינן בכי יותן:

    A. Said R. Yosé b. R. Judah, "The House of Shammai and the House of Hillel did not dispute concerning the case of one who shakes the tree in order to bring down from it liquids,

    B. "and they fell on the detached [pieces of fruit] that were on it, and on those that were attached to the ground that were beneath it,

    C. "that they are (GRA deletes: *not*) subject to the law, If water be put.

    D. "[Nor did they dispute the case in which] one detached them after they were dried off, that they are *not* subject to the law, If water be put.

    E. "Concerning what did they differ?

F. "Concerning the case of him *who shakes the tree* [Sens lacks:] *to bring down from it pieces of fruit,* and they [drops of moisture] fell from one press to another, or from one branch to another, in that very same tree—

G. "for the House of Shammai say, 'It is subject to the law, If water be put.'

H. "And the House of Hillel say, 'It is not subject to the law, If water be put.' "

T. 1:2

Yosé b. R. Judah rejects the picture of T. 1:1. (GRA's revision at C is necessary, or C contradicts D.) Now, Yosé says, the Houses agree on the Shammaite position at T. 1:1. But in line with our interpretation of T. 1:1, if we pick the vegetables attached to the ground after they are dry, the vegetables are not deemed susceptible to uncleanness. Why not? Because when they were in the ground, they were insusceptible. The process of contamination could not affect them at all. Then they dried off. They now are not susceptible, for when we actually pick them, they are dry. Accordingly, the law at D conforms to the Hillelite view. The reason is that the water has never subjected the vegetables attached to the ground to susceptibility. Yosé b. R. Judah thus insists that the two specified disputes of T. 1:1 in fact find the Houses in agreement with one another, in the first, with the Shammaites, in the second, with the Hillelites.

What then *is* the point of disagreement? It is at M. 1:2A-C! The man shakes the tree to bring down pieces of fruit, verbatim as at M. 1:2A. Drops of moisture fall along with the fruit. M. 1:2A-C has the Houses agree (implicitly) that water which falls with the fruit, all the more so that which remains in the tree, is not under the law, If water be put. But, Yosé says, that is not the case. The drops remain in the very same tree—which is exactly the issue of M. 1:2D-F, "Those that fall . . . those that remain. . . "! The House of Shammai regard the drops that fall within the tree's foliage as subject to the law, If water be put. The Hillelites, consistent with M. 1:2F-G, say the man wants the fruit to fall out of the tree. Since that has not happened, his intention has not been wholly carried out. Accordingly, M. 1:2A-C reject Yosé b. R. Judah's opinion of the dispute, as given at T. 1:2, and T. 1:1 reads the Houses' dispute pretty much as do M. 1:3D-G, but in a somewhat more complicated framework.

Clearly, Yosé b. R. Judah's intent here is to have the Houses disagree on the most fundamental problem, rather than the secondary and subtle ones that M. and T. 1:1 have them debate. The man shook the tree to get fruit. How do we regard the moisture that is not even shaken down with the fruit but that remains on the same tree and does not fall at all? Surely the man was after fruit, never giving thought to moisture shaken within the tree itself. No, that is not so. Even in this latter case, the Shammaites deem the water to be under the law, If water be put. That is a most extreme statement of their position. The Hillelite position is of less interest, of course. Accordingly, while M. works out the limits of the Hillelite viewpoint, carried to their extremes by Yosé and Simeon (below), T. gives us Yosé b. R. Judah's equivalent exercise in the logical extension of the Shammaite view. This is a very refreshing exercise in the Ushan philosophical imagination.

³אמרו בית הלל לבית שמאי הכל מודין
במעלה שק אחד מעודר ונתנו על גב הנהר שאף על פי שהמים יורדין מצד העליון
לתחתון שאינן בכי יותן אמרו להן בית שמאי אי אתם מודין במעלה שני שקין
מעודרון ונתן זה על גבי זה שהמים יורדין מן העליון לתחתון שהתחתון בכי יותן:

A. Said the House of Hillel to the House of Shammai, "All agree [Sens: *Do you not agree*] concerning *one who brings up a single upright sack* (M'WDD—tied up), *and who placed it on the side of the river,*

B. "that, even though the *water descends from the upper side to the lower side,* (that) it is *not* subject to the law, If water be put."

C. The House of Shammai said to them, "Do you not agree concerning *one who brings up two sacks* that are upright *and placed them on the bank, one on top of the other,* and the water descends from the upper to the lower, (that) *the lower is under the law, If water be put?*"

T. 1:3

T. Augments M. 1:4S. The House of Hillel there assume that, in the case of a single sack, we do not take thought of the moisture's descending from top to bottom. T. 1:3A simply asserts that the Hillelites claim all agree to that proposition, just as M. assumes. The reply of the Shammaites is that all agree about two sacks, just as M. 1:4T alleges. There we have two sacks. M. 1:4T says, not in the name of the Hillelites but as an anonymous rule, that if there are two, the bottom one indeed is subject to susceptibility to receive uncleanness. T. therefore takes the curious construction of M. 1:4T and explains that, on this point, all are in agreement.

Standing by itself, T. is incomprehensible, of course, and the purpose of the Shammaite saying at C is difficult to fathom. The purpose of the person who made up T. 1:3, by contrast, is perfectly clear. He wants us to understand M. 1:4T in the proper context, which is to say, as a point on which all parties are in agreement. Yosé must now deny T. 1:3's version of the matter. But the disagreement surely is not primary to Yosé's saying at M. 1:4U. For, as I said, what M. gives us is a dispute between Yosé at M. 1:4U and the viewpoint of M. 1:4T. There is no need for the Houses to be given sayings on the same matter, unless it is our intent to show that, in fact, the purpose of M. 1:4T is to conclude the Houses' dispute. In other words, T. revises M. to improve its sense, and therefore must give Yosé a new version of his saying, which, so far as I can see, is original in M. and changed in T. 1:4A-C, to which we proceed.

⁴ר' יוסי אומר אחד שק אחד ואחד שני שקין בית שמאי אומ' בכי יותן ובית הלל אומר' אינן בכי יותן ר' יהודה אומר ר' אליעזר אומר זה וזה בכי יותן ר' יהשע אומר זה וזה אינן בכי יותן ור' עקיבא אומר התחתון בכי יותן והעליון אינו בכי יותן:

A. R. Yosé says, "All the same is the law covering one sack and two sacks:

B. "The House of Shammai say, 'It is under the law, If water be put.'

C. "And the House of Hillel say, 'It is not under the law, If water be put.' "

D. R. Judah says, "R. Eliezer says, 'This and that are under the law, If water be put.'

E. "R. Joshua says, 'This and that are not under the law, If water be put.'

F. "R. 'Aqiba says, 'The lower one is under the law, If water be put, and the upper is not under the law, If water be put.' "

T. 1:4

Yosé's saying requires no further comment. All we have at A-C is another way of stating what Yosé says at M. 1:4U, but, for reasons just now given, T. 1:4 presents Yosé's view at M. 1:4U as the position of the House of Hillel.

Judah then presents an unexpected version of the matter. First, he knows nothing about the Houses. His attributions are to Yavneans. Second, he gives us three positions, instead of the two of T. 1:3 and Yosé alike. That is, so far as T. 1:3 is concerned, in the case of a single sack, all parties agree that what is on the bottom of the sack is unaffected by water dripping down from the top. In the case of two sacks, all parties agree that what is on the bottom is affected. So far as Yosé is concerned, in the case of two sacks, the Hillelites maintain the bottom is likewise unaffected by water dripping down from the top.

Now, Judah claims, in the case of two sacks, Eliezer deems both to be affected. Joshua says that in the case of two sacks, both are unaffected, just as Yosé says at M. 1:4U and as the House of Hillel, in Yosé's view, also maintain. 'Aqiba then stands behind the distinction taken for granted by both T. 1:3 and Yosé at T. 1:4 between the top and the bottom sack. I can understand Joshua's and 'Aqiba's view of the top sack, for both agree it is unaffected by dripping water.

But how, in Eliezer's view, is the top sack affected by dripping water? Perhaps Eliezer will have in mind water dripping from the top of the top sack to the bottom of the top sack. Or, to put it differently, Eliezer radically differs from M. 1:4's Hillelites at S. The Hillelites take for granted that we do not take thought of whether, in the case of a single sack, water drips from top to bottom. Eliezer holds that we indeed *do* take exactly that flow of water into account. In Judah's version, Eliezer will stand with the Shammaites of M. 1:4N-P—for if we speak of a sack, then why not a bunch of herbs? Joshua then is in agreement with the Hillelites of M 1:4N-P, and for the same reason. And Judah's 'Aqiba accords with the Hillelites of the debate of M. 1:4S.

הַמְמַחֵק אֶת הַכְּרֵישָׁה, וְהַסּוֹחֵט שְׂעָרוֹ בִּכְסוּתוֹ – רַבִּי יוֹסֵי
אוֹמֵר: הַיּוֹצְאִין – בְּכִי יָתַּן, וְאֶת שֶׁבּוֹ – אֵינָן בְּכִי יָתַּן, מִפְּנֵי
שֶׁהוּא מִתְכַּוֵּן שֶׁיֵּצְאוּ מִכָּלּוֹ.

A. He who rubs [the wetness off] the leek—

B. and he who wrings out his hair with his garment—

C. R. Yosé says, "Those that exude are under the law, If water be put.

[Segal, p. 471, n. 8: It renders produce susceptible to uncleanness, because it came out by his deliberate act.]

D. "And those that remain in it are not under the law, If water be put,

E. "because he intends that they exude from its entirety."

M. 1:5

Yosé continues his earlier lemma. We lack the expected dispute. But that is no problem, because all Yosé gives us is the apodosis of the House of Hillel at M. 1:2F-G, word for word. We should have been glad to have Simeon or Meir or sages say, "Those that exude *and* those that remain are under the law. . . . " That is what obviously is demanded for the contrary opinion. The sole point of interest is the superscription. Distinctions may be drawn between M. 1:5A and B and M. 1:2D's tree. But there can be no material difference between shaking a tree, rubbing the leek, and wringing out the hair.

⁶המטחיק את הגג ואת הכרישה אף על פי שהטים יורדין מצד העליון לתחתון
אינן בכי יותן נתלשו הרי זה בכי יותן ר׳ יוסי אומר זב וטמא שהיו מהלכין בדרך
וירדו גשמים על שערו ועל כסותו אף על פי שהטים נתלשין מצד העליון לתחתון
אלו טהורין שאין נחשבים אלא לאחר שיצאו מכולו יוצא מכולו הרי אלו מוכשרין
וטהורין שאין נחשבין אלא לאחר יציאתן:

A. *He who rubs off [the wetness]* of the press (GT for GG) *and of the leek,*

B. even though the water descends from the upper side to the lower side—it is not under the law, If water be put.

C. If they [the drops of moisture] were detached [from the leek or press] , lo, this is under the law, If water be put.

D. R. Yosé says, "A *Zab* or a *Zabah* who was walking along, and rain fell on his hair and on his garment,

E. "even though the water is detached from the upper side to the lower, lo, they are clean.

F. "For they are taken into account only after they have exuded from all of him.

G. "[Supply: *Once they have exuded from all of him*] , lo, these are susceptible to uncleanness, but they are clean.

H. "For they are taken into account only after they have exuded."

T. 1:5

T.'s issue differs from that of M. 1:5. It asks about the equivalent to the single stalk of M. 1:4, thus linking M. 1:5 to M. 1:4. The Hillelites assume all parties agree that we do not take account of dripping from the upper to the lower part of the stalk. Yosé, M. 1:5, is clear on the same point. Then T. has the water detached from the leek in its entirety, C, just as at M. 1:5C. B. Ker. 15b reads E as follows: "Though the water was squeezed by him from the upper toward the lower part [of his clothes] ," it is clean. Why? Because it is of no consequence until it is wholly removed from the clothes. Once it is removed, however, then it imparts susceptibility to uncleanness. G therefore should begin, "Once they have exuded," and the rest follows as given. The relevance to M. 1:5 is primarily through Yosé, who is assigned T. and M. T. 1:5A presents exactly the same view as Yosé's at M. but in different words and in Yosé's name. We seem therefore to have two versions of materials deriving originally from Yosé's circle.

הַנּוֹפֵחַ בָּעֲדָשִׁים, לְבָדְקָן אִם יָפוֹת הֵן – רַבִּי שִׁמְעוֹן אוֹמֵר:
אֵינָן בְּכִי יֻתַּן, וַחֲכָמִים אוֹמְרִים: בְּכִי יֻתַּן. וְהָאוֹכֵל שֻׁמְשְׁמִין
בְּאֶצְבָּעוֹ, מַשְׁקִין שֶׁעַל יָדוֹ – רַבִּי שִׁמְעוֹן אוֹמֵר: אֵינָן בְּכִי
יֻתַּן. וַחֲכָמִים אוֹמְרִים: בְּכִי יֻתַּן. הַטּוֹמֵן פֵּרוֹתָיו בַּמַּיִם מִפְּנֵי
הַגַּנָּבִים – אֵינָן בְּכִי יֻתַּן. מַעֲשֶׂה בְּאַנְשֵׁי יְרוּשָׁלַם שֶׁטָּמְנוּ דְבֵלָתָן

בַּמַּיִם מִפְּנֵי הַסִּיקָרִיז – וְטִהֲרוּ לָהֶן חֲכָמִים. הַנּוֹתֵן פֵּרוֹתָיו
בְּשִׁבֹּלֶת הַנָּהָר לַהֲבִיאָן עִמּוֹ – אֵינָן בְּכִי יֻתַּן.

A. He who blows on lentils to test whether they are good—

B. R. Simeon says, "They [drops of moisture in the breath]
are not under the law, If water be put. [since they were not
subject to his intention (Sens)]."

C. And sages say, "They are under the law, If water be put
[for breath-moisture is a liquid (M. 6:5) (MA)]."

D. He who eats sesame with his [wet] finger [wetting his
finger so as to pick up the sesame-grains] —

E. liquids that are on [the palm of] his hand—

F. R. Simeon says, "They are not under the law, If water be
put [since the man intended to wet the finger, not the palm]."

G. And sages say, "They are under the law, If water be put."

H. He who hides away his fruit in water because of the
thieves—

I. they are not under the law, If water be put.

J. M'SH B: People in Jerusalem hid away their fig-cakes in
water because of thugs.

K. And sages declared [them] clean for them.

L. He who puts [floats] his fruit [along] in the stream of
the river to bring them along with himself—they are not under
the law, If water be put.

M. 1:6

A-G continue the issues of the foregoing. H-L make an important
new point. The issue of A is simply whether or not the moisture of
one's breath is wanted. Since the moisture is part of the process of
blowing on the lentils, sages hold, it is wanted, and the lentils are
made susceptible by the moist breath. Simeon does not see the
moisture as desired; it simply cannot be avoided. No significant
difference appears at E-G, which say the same thing in the same
words. The important point of H-I is that when the fruit is wet
down under constraint, that is not placing water with approval—by
definition. The subtle issue is whether the person is understood as

doing so because necessity requires it, therefore whether "approval" can be imposed by necessity. It cannot. J-K then give us a precedent for the foregoing. L adds that the fruit floated on the stream is not deemed deliberately wet down, an extremely lenient statement of the matter. Even natural necessity is a kind of constraint. Certainly Simeon and the sages of K and the authorities behind L all carry forward the tendency of the Hillelite position in the earlier pericopae.

Maimonides (*Uncleanness of Foodstuffs* 12:2) neatly ties the chapter's closing and opening pericopae:

> If any liquid fell upon foodstuff with the owner's approval at the beginning, even though in the end it is·not with his approval; or if in the end it is with his approval but at the beginning it was not with his approval, such foodstuffs are rendered susceptible to uncleanness; but if it in no wise falls with his approval, it does not render the foodstuff susceptible. Even if a man makes his produce wet out of danger or necessity, while in fact he does not wish it to be made wet, such produce is not rendered susceptible. Thus if a man hides his fruit in water because of thieves or puts his produce on the stream of a river to bear it along with him, it is not rendered susceptible.

iii. Conclusion

If we may now review Tosefta's contribution to the exegesis of Mishnah, we recognize that we are in the hands of truly formidable and profound masters of Mishnah's text. Tosefta's authorities do not hesitate to read "their own" problems and conceptions into the interpretation of Mishnah, evidence of their remarkable freedom from subservience to "tradition." This is strikingly clear at T. 1:1, which takes up the relationship of the conceptions of M. 1:2 to those of M. 1:3 and makes its own quite original comment on those relationships. At T. 1:2 Tosefta contributes to the interpretation of Mishnah the opinion of an authority not cited in Mishnah at all. On the surface, this unit stands independent of, and correlative with, Mishnah, that is, at the very time of Mishnah's own formation. The attribution to Yosé, Judah's son, places the saying in the generation of the making of Mishnah itself, so the conclusion that Tosefta's materials in this instance are of the same period as Mishnah's is hardly farfetched. T. 1:3, for its part, provides us with an augmentation of M.'s version of the debate appended to the Houses' dispute. This improves the clarity of M.'s materials, an example of how Tosefta may restate what Mishnah has said, to improve on Mishnah's formulation of its own ideas (or, in many instances, to impose on Mishnah Tosefta's ideas of what Mishnah should have said). T. 1:4 is of the same type as T. 1:3. T. 1:5 again cites and glosses M. It does that same sort of redactional criticism as we noted above, showing the connections between two unconnected Mishnah-pericopae, this time, M. 1:5 and M. 1:4. Those who have worked their way patiently through Tosefta's treatment of Mishnah will concur that Mishnah's first also are its greatest exegetes, because their work is far more daring, intellectually independent, and imaginative than anything to come thereafter.

CHAPTER 4

A Sample of the Received Exegesis: A Second Look at Makhshirin 1:2-4 and Its Problems

i. Introduction

It is time to systematically consider the way in which the received exegesis treats a problem of the interpretation of Mishnah. Without doing so, the reader will not have a clear picture of the ways in which the methods illustrated in this book produce new and significant results, and the ways in which they do not. Before proceeding, therefore, the reader may want to review what I have already said about M. 1:2-4 (above, pp. 100-109), since what follows is a survey of what others have said about the same set of problems. What we shall now do is state the principal problems in interpreting M. Makhshirin 1:2-4 and then survey the opinions and solutions of the important commentators to Mishnah. This time around I shall specify in my translation the variant readings for the pericope, since what the several commentators say is governed in part by the reading they have before them or by what on the basis of their own reasoning they impute to the passage. In the abbreviations the symbols of the various manuscripts are given.

ii. Mishnah Makhshirin 1:2-4 and Its Problems

הַמַּרְעִיד אֶת הָאִילָן לְהַשִּׁיר מִמֶּנּוּ אֹכָלִין, אוֹ אֶת הַטֻּמְאָה –
אֵינָן בְּכִי יֻתַּן. לְהַשִּׁיר מִמֶּנּוּ מַשְׁקִין – בֵּית שַׁמַּאי אוֹמְרִים:

הַיּוֹצְאִין, וְאֶת שֶׁבּוֹ – בְּכִי יָתַן. בֵּית הִלֵּל אוֹמְרִים: הַיּוֹצְאִין –
בְּכִי יָתַן, וְאֶת שֶׁבּוֹ – אֵינָן בְּכִי יָתַן, מִפְּנֵי שֶׁהוּא מִתְכַּוֵּן שֶׁיֵּצְאוּ
מִכֻּלּוֹ.

הַמַּרְעִיד אֶת הָאִילָן וְנָפַל עַל חֲבֵרוֹ, אוֹ סוֹכָה וְנָפְלָה עַל
חֲבֶרְתָּהּ, וְתַחְתֵּיהֶן זְרָעִים אוֹ יְרָקוֹת הַמְחֻבָּרִין לַקַּרְקַע –
בֵּית שַׁמַּאי אוֹמְרִים: בְּכִי יָתַן. בֵּית הִלֵּל אוֹמְרִים: אֵינָן בְּכִי
יָתַן. אָמַר רַבִּי יְהוֹשֻׁעַ מִשּׁוּם אַבָּא יוֹסֵי חֲלִיקוֹפְרִי אִישׁ
טִבְעוֹן: תְּמַהּ עַצְמְךָ אִם יֵשׁ מַשְׁקֶה טָמֵא בַּתּוֹרָה עַד שֶׁיִּתְכַּוֵּן
וְיִתֵּן, שֶׁנֶּאֱמַרº: 'וְכִי יֻתַּן מַיִם עַל זֶרַע'.

הַנּוֹעֵר אֲגֻדָּה שֶׁלַּיָּרָק, וְיָרְדוּ מִצַּד הָעֶלְיוֹן לַתַּחְתּוֹן – בֵּית
שַׁמַּאי אוֹמְרִים: בְּכִי יָתַן. בֵּית הִלֵּל אוֹמְרִים: אֵינָם בְּכִי יָתַן.
אָמְרוּ בֵּית הִלֵּל לְבֵית שַׁמַּאי: וַהֲלֹא הַנּוֹעֵר אֶת הַקְּלַח,
חוֹשְׁשִׁין אָנוּ שֶׁמָּא יָצְאוּ מִן הֶעָלֶה לֶעָלֶה? אָמְרוּ לָהֶן בֵּית
שַׁמַּאי: שֶׁהַקְּלַח אֶחָד, וַאֲגֻדָּה קְלָחִים הַרְבֵּה. אָמְרוּ לָהֶם
בֵּית הִלֵּל: הֲרֵי הַמַּעֲלֶה שַׂק מָלֵא פֵּרוֹת וּנְתָנוֹ עַל גַּב הַנָּהָר,
חוֹשְׁשִׁין אָנוּ שֶׁמָּא יָרְדוּ מִצַּד הָעֶלְיוֹן לַתַּחְתּוֹן? אֲבָל אִם
הֶעֱלָה שְׁנַיִם וּנְתָנָן זֶה עַל גַּב זֶה – הַתַּחְתּוֹן בְּכִי יָתַן. וְרַבִּי יוֹסֵי
אוֹמֵר: הַתַּחְתּוֹן טָהוֹר.

A. He who shakes the tree to bring down from it fruit,

B. or [shakes the tree to bring down from it] that which is unclean [e.g., a piece of corpse-matter left by a bird in the tree] —

C. it [water that falls with the fruit or the unclean thing] is not under the law, If [water] be put.

I. D. [If one shakes the tree] to bring down from it liquids—

E. The House of Shammai say, "Those [drops] that fall and [those] that [remain] on it are under the law, If water be put."

F. The House of Hillel say, "Those that fall are under the law, If water be put. And those that [remain] on it are not under the law, If water be put,

G. "because [the man] intends that they [the drops of liquid] should fall from it in its entirety (MKWLW; V:MKLLW)."

M. 1:2

II. H. He who shakes the tree, and it [GRA: liquid] fell on its fellow (NPL, NPLH [= the tree or the bush] : C, M, T, N, K, Katsh, Plate 148, PB, V, Pa; NPLW [= the water] :P)—

I. or [if he shakes] a bush and it fell on another bush,

J. and under them are (1) seeds or (2) vegetables that are attached to the ground—

K. The House of Shammai say, "They are under the law, If [water] be put."

L. The House of Hillel say, "They are not under the law, If water be put."

M. Said R. Joshua (P, Maimonides, Mishnah-commentary: Yosah) in the name of Abba Yosé Qofri of Tibeon, "Be surprised if there is a liquid in the Torah that is unclean before a person actually intends [to make use of it] and puts it on, as it is said, *And if water be put on seed* (Lev. 11:18)."

III. N. He who shakes a bunch of herbs [so deliberately detaching the water (MA)] and they [drops of water] fell from the topside to the bottom—

O. The House of Shammai say, "They are under the law, If water be put on."

P. The House of Hillel say, "They are not under the law, If water be put on."

Q. Said the House of Hillel to the House of Shammai, "And is it not so (HL'; C, P, Pa, K: WHRY) [that in the case of] one who shakes off the stalk [of a plant] ,—do we take thought of whether they dropped from leaf to leaf (Katsh, Plate 148, M, Pa, C, K, V: MN H'LH L'LH)?"

R. Said to them the House of Shammai, "For the stalk is one, but the bunch [of vegetables] is [made up of] many stalks."

S. Said to them the House of Hillel, "Lo, he who brings up [from the river] a sack full of produce and puts it on the bank of the river [so that the water will flow back into the river] —do we take thought of whether it [the water] descends from the topside to the bottom?"

T. But: If he brought up two and put them on top of the other, the bottom one [indeed] is under the law, If water be put.

U. And R. Yosé says, "The bottom one is insusceptible to uncleanness."

M. 1:4

At the outset I specify the problems that any exegete must confront in interpreting this unusually difficult pericope.

1. What is the antecedent of *(it) fell* at H? Is it (a) the fruit, (b) the liquid, or (c) the tree itself? (The same problem arises at I.)

2. How can things attached to the ground be referred to as susceptible to uncleanness, J, when, in fact, that which is not yet plucked is not susceptible at all?

And this leads to 3. *What* of K-L is under the law, If water be put? The Hillelite saying, L, is stated in the plural, so this should mean, they—*the liquids*—are (K) or are not (L) under the law, If water be put.

4. Does Joshua at M support (a) the Hillelites, or (b) both Houses' opinions, or (c) neither—that is, is his opinion more extreme than the principle they share?

The solutions to these problems will not be settled by the "right" manuscript-reading, first, because the commentators routinely take for granted readings that support (and presumably generate) their diverse interpretations; and, second, because the MSS are too few, too late, and too episodic to supply definitive information. Accordingly, we shall have to rely on the context as to both its forms and its sequence of thought.

Formal analysis reveals two clear facts. First, M is an autonomous saying, despite its attributive formula, *said,* which ordinarily means that the redactor has placed the saying in such a way as to serve as a commentary to antecedent materials. But the attributive is redactional. Why? Because, in fact Joshua's saying is comprehensible out of the context of H-L. Its interpretation is possible without regard to the preceding dispute. Again, why? Because if it were set after G, rather than after L, it would make as much, or as little, sense. If Joshua's quotation is a gloss, it obviously explains the

Hillelite position, in the formal analogy of G. But the protasis of H-J leaves no doubt that the Shammaites concur in the basic principle: The issue of approval is common to both Houses. The Shammaites simply place a narrow construction on the meaning of approval. Joshua's real dispute is with someone who holds that liquid is susceptible to uncleanness even when it is *not* applied with approval. (I think it highly unlikely that Joshua rejects M. 1:1D.)

Second, H-J form a highly complex superscription to the dispute. The model for the whole is either A-B, in which case I serves as a gloss formally parallel to B, or D and N, in which case both B and I are excessive. But neither B nor I poses any problem of interpretation, being mere, formal repetitions of A and H, respectively.

J, third, does present a problem, both because J1 serves as a second gloss to H's statement of the problem, and because J2 duplicates the gloss, parallel again to B/I. So much for the problems of substance and form awaiting attention.

Before proceeding, let me now review and summarize the proposed exegesis that I have already given: The complex as a whole is secondary to M. 1:1. The primary principle, shared by all parties, is that water that falls with approval imparts susceptibility to that on which it falls. M. 1:1 has told us that we cannot distinguish "temporally" between the moment at which the man wants the water and the moment at which he does not want it. The rule disputed by the Houses is whether we may make any other distinctions in the effects of the man's intent and in its effects on the water. The Shammaites hold, quite consistently, that we cannot. The Hillelites maintain, in successive cases, that we can make such distinctions: (1) if the man wants only part of the water, only that part he wants is under the law, If water be put; (2) if the man wants the water to fall in a particular place, only the water that falls in the desired location is under the law, If water be put; (3) and this (=2) is the case both if the water falls on a place outside the object that is shaken and if it falls from one to another part of the object itself.

The whole is an essay on Hillelite conceptions. After D-F, there is no reason to explore implications of the Shammaite position. J raises the secondary distinction, perhaps in response to M, of whether the activation of the power of the water to impart susceptibility is treated separate from the effect of the water in imparting susceptibility to a formerly insusceptible object. J claims that the Houses agree that there is such a two-part process.

Let us now follow the great commentators as they analyze the pericope both in the light of Tosefta and ignoring Tosefta, with singular and with plural verbs for H, and above all, in the assumption that each and every element in construction has always been present and imposes its meaning upon all other elements.

1. At his Mishnah-commentary, Maimonides says that just as water that is on the ground is not rendered capable of making something susceptible to uncleanness, so water that is detached from the ground not with approval does not render something susceptible, even if this water is intentionally mixed with fruit. If a man shook the tree and *it* — the tree-branch — fell on its fellow, or if he shook a branch of the tree and it fell on its fellow, and water fell from that second tree or second branch on seeds or vegetables on the ground, the water on those seeds and vegetables on the ground does not render susceptible to uncleanness fruit that then falls on it, because the water was detached with the approval of the owner. The Shammaites hold that the water was detached with approval because the man did, after all, shake the first tree so that liquid would exude from it. Yosé (Joshua in most versions) then *supports* the view of the House of Hillel. At *Uncleanness of Food-stuffs* 13:16, Maimonides states:

> If a man shakes a tree and the drops of rain on it fall on
> another tree, or if he shakes a branch and the drops of rain
> on it fall on another branch, and below them are seeds of
> unplucked vegetables, and the water falls on the unplucked
> produce below, the water on the seeds or the vegetables is
> not deemed to be detached with approval.

Accordingly, the issue of M. 1:3 is fresh, since it concerns *water* that lands on the vegetables, still in the ground, and the effect of the water, once located on the vegetables in the ground or seeds on the ground, on other produce that may afterward touch it. Maimonides thus interprets matters in terms of two stages, (1) the water that falls and itself has to be rendered capable of *imparting* susceptibility to uncleanness, which is separate and distinct from (2) the status of objects on which the water falls, to which susceptibility is imparted, in which case the wetting down of the objects likewise must be with the approval of the owner. The advantage of this position is that we are not required to explain how vegetables that are attached to the ground can become unclean. The rule is, that still in the ground is susceptible to uncleanness. The issue, Maimonides states, is not the uncleanness of the vegetables in the ground but the "uncleanness" of *water* (that is, capacity to impart susceptibility to uncleanness) that falls on them. Only that first stage in the two-stage process is now under discussion, he holds.

2. Rabad (super-commentary to Maimonides' *Uncleanness of Foodstuffs* 13:16) sees the issue of the vegetables on the ground quite differently, for he will not distinguish the two stages in the process. He says that the vegetables on the ground do not receive susceptibility to uncleanness while they are in the ground. But if they are rendered susceptible with the owner's approval *while* they are in the ground, and then, later on, they are plucked up, and there *still* is moist liquid on them, which the owner wants, they are rendered susceptible to uncleanness. The Shammaites hold that since the man intended to shake and bring down the tree or bush, there is no longer any need for the liquid to remain on them. Or the intention to bring down the liquid and the tree is a single, indivisible intention. It is as if the man shook the tree to make the liquids render susceptible the seeds that are under them. The Hillelites hold that, even so, when the man shakes the tree to bring down its fruit, he does not intend to bring down the tree or branch itself. The matter of seeds or unplucked vegetables under them introduces a second point for each party. Even though the vegetables are attached to the ground when they are rendered susceptible to uncleanness, once they are plucked up with liquid on them, they forthwith fall under the law, If water be put. If they are plucked up with the falling of the bush and the liquid on them, the Shammaites see the preparation and the uprooting as taking place at the same moment (equivalent to M. 1:1C).

3. GRA has the man shaking the tree to bring down liquids. His reading for the verb is plural, thus *they*, namely, the liquids, fall on another tree, and so with a bush that the man shook to remove

liquids. The liquids fall on another bush. Under them are seeds or unplucked vegetables. The liquids fall on the vegetables or seeds. The House of Shammai rule that, even though the liquids fall on unplucked vegetables, the *liquid* on the vegetables falls under the law, If water be put. The Hillelites hold that the liquid does not impart susceptibility to uncleanness unless it falls on that which is detached from the ground. Accordingly, GRA reads M. in the light of T. 1:1, that is, he focuses the entire dispute on J2 (as if J1 were not present). Joshua, GRA says, then refers to the entire pericope, not merely to the Hillelite position. Can a liquid impart susceptibility to uncleanness unless one intentionally puts it on, by his own deed? No, it cannot, so that if the liquid falls by accident, the consequent susceptibility to uncleanness is not based upon the Torah's rule, but on rabbinical decree. GRA stresses that the operative word in Joshua's sayings is *in the Torah.*

4. Sens reads J2 as the center of the matter. When the fruit on the ground dries off before being plucked, the Hillelites say it remains insusceptible. But if wet when picked, all parties agree, the vegetables are susceptible. Joshua then takes a still more extreme view: Even if plucked, the vegetables on the ground are insusceptible unless the owner now deliberately will wet them down (!).

5. TYY sees the issue as a refinement of M. 1:2. The House of Hillel do not regard water that is not shaken from the tree but remains in it and falls later as having fallen with the approval of the man who originally shook the tree. The water that has remained in the tree therefore does not fall into the category of that which renders something susceptible to uncleanness. Now at M. 1:3 the issue is expressed by the singular verb, the man shook *the tree.* The tree fell (or the bush, and the bush fell). The tree has touched the neighboring tree (or the bush touched a second bush). The fruit on the tree or bush touched by the falling tree or bush is made wet by water that originates in the tree that the man shook. Now we return to the Hillelites' position. Water remaining on the tree shaken by the man does not fall under the rule, If water be put on, as at M. 1:2. This is the case if the water remains on the original tree and afterwards falls directly onto fruit. But if, when the man shook the tree, the water fell not onto the ground but onto other fruit, then, again, we have to specify the Hillelite position,

which is exactly as it was before. There are two factors: (1) The fruit was wet down without approval, but the fruit also was shaken from the tree with approval; (2) the vegetables on the ground are unplucked. In the view of the Shammaites, that which is attached to the ground *is* capable of being made susceptible to uncleanness. The Hillelites deny that what is attached to the ground can be made susceptible to uncleanness. Accordingly, TYY reads T. into M., which is not unreasonable, since T.'s purpose, we have seen is to make some sense of M. Joshua's point is that even if the vegetables on the ground were not attached, they would not be made susceptible when the water fell on them, because it was not by intent and deed—thus an extreme statement of the original rule, A-C, as the Hillelites read it.

6. MA comes at the problem in the light of the opening dispute. There we are told that if one shakes a tree to bring down water, the water is deemed detached with approval. Here too we deal with the same matter. The foregoing rule, M. 1:2, applies when the man did not intend for the water to fall on something attached to the ground. The man, indeed, did not want the water to fall to the ground. Before the water reaches the ground it is deemed detached with approval, while it is still in the air. When it reaches the ground, it is as if it is attached to the ground and is not deemed detached with approval. We have seeds or vegetables attached to the ground. The House of Hillel hold that, when the man shook the tree, it was for the sake of these very vegetables. Then it is water that is used to wet down that which is attached to the ground, and whatever serves that which is attached to the ground is *not* under the law, If water be put. The House of Shammai hold that, since the man did not originally intend to water what was attached to the ground, he has not registered the intention to do that, and, accordingly, the water is and remains deemed subject to the law, If water be put. This surely is far more subtle than is required.

7. Albeck (p. 416) has the man shake the tree to bring down liquids. He does not commit himself as to what it is that falls on the other tree. But he clearly understands that the issue is the liquids: "Even if he had brought down liquids on vegetables which are attached to the ground, the liquids or unplucked vegetables fall under the law, If water be put, and render susceptible to uncleanness

food which falls on them"—namely, which fall on liquids on vegetables attached to the ground. That is the Shammaite view. The
Hillelites hold that since the liquids fall on vegetables attached to
the ground, the liquids are not subject to the law, If water be put.
But if afterward the liquids had not fallen on vegetables attached
to the ground but had remained on the other tree or on the other
bush, the House of Hillel would have agreed that the liquids do fall
under the rule, If water be put, "since they fell from tree to tree
even though they did not fall on the ground." Joshua's position is
that the man must himself intentionally put the water on the seed,
and if the water fell on its own, it does not impart susceptibility to
uncleanness. Albeck's reading of Joshua's position places him outside
of, and in disagreement with, the positions of both Houses. At his
additional note, pp. 592-3, Albeck adds that Joshua holds that the
Houses differ only where the liquids fell on attached, unplucked
vegetables and seeds. But if the liquids fell on plucked vegetables,
all agree that they render the seeds themselves susceptible to uncleanness. Joshua expresses his surprise at this state of affairs, for
liquid that itself is susceptible to uncleanness does not impart susceptibility to uncleanness unless the man himself puts it on the seeds.

iii. Conclusion

The inescapable conclusion is that one's theory of the literary traits
of a pericope will govern one's definition and consequent interpretation of its constituent parts and therefore the determination of
the meaning of the whole. There is no exegesis not grounded in
literary analysis. That is the fact—whether or not literary analysis is
articulately carried out. The only difference between the approaches
taken elsewhere and the approach taken here, in which I spell out
my theory of the division, constituents, and exegetical limits of a
pericope and how they relate to one another, is simple. I state why
I conceive a given line of a pericope to relate to some other line
thereof and how the whole works syntactically and formally.

Now an approach to this set of materials that takes for granted
that they form a unity imposes one set of problems and disposes
of some other. It is clear that if you read M. 1:2-4 as essentially

independent of M. 1:1, or if you conceive Joshua's saying to follow from and explain the position of the House of Hillel, then one set of results is dictated. Another also is made impossible. Furthermore, if you bring to the pericope a long-standing argument, as do Maimonides and Rabad, about the two-stage character of the process of imparting susceptibility (Maimonides' theory of the *power* of the water to impart susceptibility, which is distinct from the *actual* step of imparting of susceptibility to uncleanness), then you are going to shape your interpretation around that long-standing and encompassing dispute of principle. What you will find important to observe within the pericope will not be the issues and problems of the pericope. What will attract attention is how the pericope addresses itself (or may be made to express itself) to an extraneous issue. Indeed, the single most important thing to notice in the materials just considered is how a long-standing dispute in theory between Maimonides and Rabad will be brought to bear on the interpretation of a pericope rich in its own, but by them neglected, problems.

What makes GRA of special interest is his insistence on reading Mishnah in the light of Tosefta, a characteristic of his approach to Mishnah-exegesis in general. The power of his commentary (even without reference to his surpassing genius) is in his consistent attention to Mishnah's companion and closest associate. MA is the other truly noteworthy exegete of Mishnah (he writes on the divisions of Purities and Agriculture), because of his grasp of the larger context and attention to the place of a given dispute in its encompassing literary-redactional framework. Clearly, my own approach to the interpretation of M. 1:2-4 comes closest to his because of a shared commitment to the consideration of context and attention to matters of redactional framework—therefore purpose as well. Albeck's commentary lacks a certain measure of articulation. Because of its abbreviated character, as footnotes, it is not always easy to follow how he reads a problem or why he says what he does. Even in his extended notes his exegetical work tends to be spotty and unsustained. No clear approach or method is available that would help us to predict what he will find worth noting, or how he will define problems requiring attention. But even though it sometimes appears that he makes things up as he goes along, his commentary in fact is episodically acute and thoughtful. Its strengths are his own; its weaknesses characterize the genre—the formal character as atomistic and harmonistic comments, and the setting of Mishnah-commentary in the larger framework of the law.

The strength of the received exegesis is by no means fully exposed in this brief survey. The wide-ranging erudition, the acute grasp of detail, the capacity to think out successive stages of a process of reasoning—and the perfect mastery of the classic sources—these are only the more obvious virtues. But the weakness of the established tradition also is fairly evident. There is a general indifference to literary questions. Lower criticism is carried out only occasionally, higher criticism never. The whole is diffuse and lacks focus. I have spared the reader an extensive account of the irrelevant issues that have been thought pressing in the confrontation with this passage (and all the others treated in this book). The repetitiousness of the exegetes, their assumption that theirs is the entire task and that no one has done any part of it (or, that readers have no access to anyone's book but theirs), the utter silence on all questions of method (except for Maimonides, who makes up for the rest)— these and other intellectual failings characterize the received exegesis. To be sure, no commentator will concede that there is nothing left to do. That is by definition. So in the end what each one who wants to study Mishnah must achieve is his or her own commentary. In the act of study, that is what we all do all of the time.

Before going onward, we should ask ourselves why we care about the received exegesis at all. The people whose opinions we have studied lived over a period of more than a thousand years. Unless we take the position of traditionalists ("orthodox"), who hold that because something was said a long time ago and bears the approval of "the tradition," its claim on our minds is self-evident, we have to ask why we are able to take seriously the opinions we have now surveyed. For what we have done—I wish to make it explicit—is to enter into conversation, on a single plane and program of discourse, with people who lived at varying times and in diverse places over a very long period of time. That fact should be found truly astonishing. One would not imagine talking with these same sorts of authorities about the original meaning of Scripture, about what happened in the history of the Jewish people, let alone about questions of science, technology, aesthetics, literature, or politics. From our perspective, in most of the great intellectual adventures of our day, these men are ignorant and primitive. Yet in the framework of interpretation of Mishnah, they are sophisticated, fresh, imaginative, interesting. Why should that be so?

The reason will be found when we realize that, for its part, Mishnah casts them and us upon a single plane of discourse. Its problems, in the process of analyzing arcane and picayune matters, are phrased in an eternally contemporary frame of reference. They are problems of logic, within certain established rules and givens. "If A, then B"—that kind of logic is not bound within a particular culture or time-frame. It is Mishnah's own language of discourse that permits, indeed demands, the participation of people in diverse times and places, from the end of the second century to the end of the twentieth. Mishnah lays forth that plane of discourse, on which all participants to the conversation are equal and able to speak of some one thing contained within some one established construction of logic. Whether GRA lived before or after Maimonides in this context hardly matters. What is probative and persuasive is the argument and the mode and elegance of proof, not the mere proposition and the formal authority of the one who holds it. What we have before us is to be compared to a problem of logic or mathematics, utterly separate from differentiating traits of culture, society, and history. There is a given set of logical possibilities. One may opt for this one or that one. There is no possibility of stepping outside the frame of logic and yet remaining inside the realm of reasoned discourse.

So we care about the opinions of the received exegesis not because we hear the words of holy men, men wiser than ourselves (though they are). We care about them because they represent logical potentialities. They use imagination and stimulate ours. So the received exegesis is important because it lays before us the potentialities of the pericope. It tells us what a brilliant imagination is able to perceive within the logical givens of a problem accessible to everyone everywhere, a problem on which we have thought too.

Now when you consider, once again, what we are discussing— a drop of water on a stalk of leek—you realize the true achievement of the framers and philosophers of Mishnah. For Socrates to speak about eternal issues of truth, justice, and virtue in such a way that we may listen to what he says and join in the argument is one thing. For Meir, Judah, and Yosé to talk about absurd matters of an obsessive-compulsive world of imagined "uncleanness" and fantasized "cleanness"—we might as well speak of *bleep* and *blope,* for all the concrete meaning these categories have for us—in such a way that we even care to listen is quite another thing. As we shall now see, what they really accomplish is a stunning essay on the logical limitations and potentialities of human intentionality—the power of the will of the human being to shape and affect the natural world.

Underlying Mishnah's sustained discussion is whether what I *want* to do is to be taken into account, or whether only what I actually *do* is what matters. Every time you say, "I didn't *mean* it," and are told, "But you *did* it," you enter into that range of issues phrased before us in this peculiar tractate. So, as I said, we can both join the discourse of the established exegesis and listen to what Tosefta has to tell us, because the framers of Mishnah so formed their document that such discourse,—a conversation in eternity about eternal issues, in a forever-present-tense utopia— they so formed Mishnah that such discourse would be plausible, would be wanted, would be logical, would be compelling, would make a difference.

In so stating the underlying issues of our tractate, I have moved beyond the exegesis of its individual units that we have just now completed. Let us ask ourselves how we put these units together into more substantial and encompassing statements of meaning. Only then will be fully exposed and explained that power of Mishnah to join us in a common conversation on a common and perennial human concern.

PART III The Groves. The Forest

CHAPTER 5

Groves of Trees:
Seeing Chapters Whole

i. Introduction

Mastering a Mishnah-tractate requires more than learning in sequence each of the smallest units of thought (pericopae). That work constitutes only the first stage of what should be a three-part process. The second stage is to reexamine the tractate, giving special attention to how the individual units relate to one another and so form intermediate units ("chapters"). The third and final stage is to attempt to lay hold of the tractate as a whole and explain how "chapters" are put together with one another. In this chapter we shall accomplish that second stage, and in the next, the third.

The purpose of seeking out the larger framework of the individual units is twofold. First, we need to ask how the redactors of the tractate have grouped their materials, so that we may reconsider each item in the light of others, fore and aft in particular, that discuss the same or closely related problems. Second, if we wish to know a tractate, we have to review it and so attempt to master it as a whole, not merely bit by bit. There is no better way for reviewing and seeing things whole and in perspective than to ask a fresh set of questions of materials already mastered from one viewpoint.

Now when we speak of "chapters" or intermediate divisions, we refer to conglomerates of small units of material. I place quotation-marks around "chapter" because the divisions of tractates into chapters and pericopae have been established by the copyists and printers. Theirs are the judgments on what constitute those larger groups of units of thought (pericopae) and of how these are discerned and delineated. Whether or not these judgments correspond to the original opinions of the people who framed the document is an open question. For the present designations of chapters may or may not reflect the intentions of the original framers of the document. Occasionally, we already have seen, the forms and themes of a given sequence of pericopae break off within a single "chapter." Sometimes they continue across the limits of one "chapter" and into another "chapter." So when we wish to define the natural conglomerates of materials, collections made up of individual pericopae (let us say: "paragraphs"), we must not confuse what the copyists or printers have done with what the original framers of the tractate thought *they* were doing.

The natural divisions of the tractate in fact are defined by the confluence of theme and form. That is to say, pericopae form a conglomerate when they share (1) a common form or formulary pattern, on the one side, and (2) a single problem, theme, or principle, on the other. This is not a definition that I made up; it emerges from the examination of the traits of the document itself. There we see that, as soon as we ask about relationships between one pericope and some other, we observe the simple fact that when a pericope is like some other, nearby one in form, it also is like that same neighbor in opinion, theme, problem, or principle. When a pronounced formal or formulary trait ceases to occur, the subject (opinion, theme, problem, principle) also changes. A mere glance at M. 2:3-11 shows precisely what I mean. Now I also should not present this definition on the basis of one "probative" example, or even of the evidence of one tractate. I have examined the whole of the division of Purities and specified what I believe to be the internal evidence behind the breaking up of that division's tractates into distinct "chapters" or, as I prefer to say, intermediate units of tradition. So what is stated here emerges from an entirely inductive examination of a vast corpus of materials—twelve tractates, one hundred twenty-six chapters, nearly a third of the whole Mishnah.

In my *Purities. XXI. The Redaction and Formulation of the Order of Purities in Mishnah and Tosefta,* pp. 113-164, I have spelled out the several criteria revealed solely through *internal* traits, by which we may designate and define these intermediate divisions of Mishnah. There are four possible criteria.

1. We may find an intermediate division defined by a single coherent theme, on the one side, and by the presence of a single set of formulary traits *internal* to the expression of that single coherent theme, on the other. That is to say, a single idea will be stated three or five times (or in multiples of three or five times) in a single formulary pattern, internal to the syntax of sentences.

2. Second, we may find an intermediate division defined by a single theme and by the presence of repeated formal traits. But the traits will be *external* to the expression of that single coherent theme. For example, we shall have a key-word running through, or the repetition of a participial construction. But what follows that single shared trait in each of the sub-units of the intermediate division will be syntax particular to each sub-unit and not shared among them. This criterion tends to be the more commonplace of the two.

3. Third, there will be intermediate divisions defined by a shared theme, but lacking all formulary coherence whatever. These are very few in number.

4. Finally, there will be intermediate divisions defined by unitary formulary traits but lacking coherent themes. These are still less common.

Examples of each of these formal-redactional types are given in my book on the subject. There I have catalogued all of what I conceive to be the intermediate divisions of the entire division of Purities, including the present tractate. I have further specified the grounds for claiming that each of them does indeed constitute an intermediate division, or a "chapter."

It would not be a useful exercise to repeat that program here. Our principal task is to learn a single tractate in the way in which I believe it should be learned. For that purpose what is called for is a review of the tractate as a whole, from the larger perspective, this time, of how the numerous individual pericopae are to be grouped together. Following the existing order of the printed chapters will be considerably easier for students than making up our own divisions, along the lines of the criteria just now explained. The printers' judgments are by no means useless, and it is sufficient if we accept them for the present purpose. The main point is to see how individual pericopae are linked into conglomerates, and for that purpose, the established division of the tractate, while not perfect, is adequate. The alternative would be arduous and complicated, yet yield no materially better educational result.

The review of the whole therefore is accomplished in two ways. First of all, we shall now reread each chapter from start to finish (this time without repeating the English translation). Second, we shall review the contents of each chapter, this time asking the question of how we may describe the *sequence* and flow of ideas, not merely interpreting each thought-unit (pericope) in an isolated way. We shall try to account for the grouping of materials chapter by chapter. In the next exercise we explain the order and structure of the entire set of six chapters.

So the work now is description of large-scale conglomerates, the review of the main propositions, the interpretation of how these several principal ideas are expressed in groups of pericopae.

ii. Mishnah Makhshirin Chapter One

כָּל מַשְׁקֶה שֶׁתְּחִלָּתוֹ לְרָצוֹן, אַף עַל פִּי שֶׁאֵין סוֹפוֹ לְרָצוֹן, אוֹ שֶׁסּוֹפוֹ לְרָצוֹן, אַף עַל פִּי שֶׁאֵין תְּחִלָּתוֹ לְרָצוֹן – הֲרֵי זֶה בְּכִי יֻתַּן. מַשְׁקִין טְמֵאִים מְטַמְּאִין לְרָצוֹן וְשֶׁלֹּא לְרָצוֹן. הַמַּרְעִיד אֶת הָאִילָן לְהַשִּׁיר מִמֶּנּוּ אֹכָלִין, אוֹ אֶת הַטֻּמְאָה – אֵינָן בְּכִי יֻתַּן. לְהַשִּׁיר מִמֶּנּוּ מַשְׁקִין – בֵּית שַׁמַּאי אוֹמְרִים: הַיּוֹצְאִין, וְאֶת שֶׁבּוֹ – בְּכִי יֻתַּן. בֵּית הִלֵּל אוֹמְרִים – הַיּוֹצְאִין בְּכִי יֻתַּן, וְאֶת שֶׁבּוֹ – אֵינָן בְּכִי יֻתַּן, מִפְּנֵי שֶׁהוּא מִתְכַּוֵּן שֶׁיֵּצְאוּ מִכֻּלּוֹ.

הַמַּרְעִיד אֶת הָאִילָן וְנָפַל עַל חֲבֵרוֹ, אוֹ סוֹכָה וְנָפְלָה עַל חֲבֶרְתָּהּ, וְתַחְתֵּיהֶן זְרָעִים אוֹ יְרָקוֹת הַמְחֻבָּרִין לַקַּרְקַע – בֵּית שַׁמַּאי אוֹמְרִים: בְּכִי יֻתַּן. בֵּית הִלֵּל אוֹמְרִים: אֵינָן בְּכִי יֻתַּן. אָמַר רַבִּי יְהוֹשֻׁעַ מִשּׁוּם אַבָּא יוֹסֵי חֲלִיקוֹפְרִי אִישׁ

טִבְעוֹן: תְּמַהּ עַצְמָךְ אִם יֵשׁ מַשְׁקֶה טָמֵא בַּתּוֹרָה עַד שֶׁיִּתְכַּוֵּן
וְיִתֵּן, שֶׁנֶּאֱמַר: 'וְכִי יֻתַּן מַיִם עַל זֶרַע'. הַנּוֹעֵר אֲגֻדָּה שֶׁלַּיָּרָק, וְיָרְדוּ מִצַּד הָעֶלְיוֹן לַתַּחְתּוֹן – בֵּית
שַׁמַּאי אוֹמְרִים: בְּכִי יֻתַּן. בֵּית הִלֵּל אוֹמְרִים: אֵינָם בְּכִי יֻתַּן.
אָמְרוּ בֵּית הִלֵּל לְבֵית שַׁמַּאי: וַהֲלֹא הַנּוֹעֵר אֶת הַקֶּלַח,
חוֹשְׁשִׁין אָנוּ שֶׁמָּא יָצְאוּ מִן הֶעָלֶה לֶעָלֶה? אָמְרוּ לָהֶן בֵּית
שַׁמַּאי: שֶׁהַקֶּלַח אֶחָד, וַאֲגֻדָּה קְלָחִים הַרְבֵּה. אָמְרוּ לָהֶם
בֵּית הִלֵּל: הֲרֵי הַמַּעֲלֶה שַׂק מָלֵא פֵּרוֹת וּנְתָנוֹ עַל גַּב הַנָּהָר,
חוֹשְׁשִׁין אָנוּ שֶׁמָּא יָרְדוּ מִצַּד הָעֶלְיוֹן לַתַּחְתּוֹן? אֲבָל אִם
הֶעֱלָה שְׁנַיִם וּנְתָנָן זֶה עַל גַּב זֶה – הַתַּחְתּוֹן בְּכִי יֻתַּן. וְרַבִּי יוֹסֵי
אוֹמֵר: הַתַּחְתּוֹן טָהוֹר.

הַמְמַחֵק אֶת הַכְּרֵישָׁה, וְהַסּוֹחֵט שְׂעָרוֹ בִּכְסוּתוֹ – רַבִּי יוֹסֵי
אוֹמֵר: הַיּוֹצְאִין – בְּכִי יֻתַּן, וְאֶת שֶׁבּוֹ – אֵינָן בְּכִי יֻתַּן, מִפְּנֵי
שֶׁהוּא מִתְכַּוֵּן שֶׁיֵּצְאוּ מִכֻּלּוֹ.

הַנּוֹפֵחַ בָּעֲדָשִׁים, לְבָדְקָן אִם יָפוֹת הֵן – רַבִּי שִׁמְעוֹן אוֹמֵר:
אֵינָן בְּכִי יֻתַּן, וַחֲכָמִים אוֹמְרִים: בְּכִי יֻתַּן. וְהָאוֹכֵל שֻׁמְשְׁמִין
בְּאֶצְבָּעוֹ, מַשְׁקִין שֶׁעַל יָדוֹ – רַבִּי שִׁמְעוֹן אוֹמֵר: אֵינָן בְּכִי
יֻתַּן. וַחֲכָמִים אוֹמְרִים: בְּכִי יֻתַּן. הַטּוֹמֵן פֵּרוֹתָיו בַּמַּיִם מִפְּנֵי
הַגַּנָּבִים – אֵינָן בְּכִי יֻתַּן. מַעֲשֶׂה בְּאַנְשֵׁי יְרוּשָׁלַם שֶׁטָּמְנוּ דְבֵלָתָן
בַּמַּיִם מִפְּנֵי הַסִּיקָרִין – וְטִהֲרוּ לָהֶן חֲכָמִים. הַנּוֹתֵן פֵּרוֹתָיו
בְּשִׁבֹּלֶת הַנָּהָר לַהֲבִיאָן עִמּוֹ – אֵינָן בְּכִי יֻתַּן.

The problem of the chapter is the effect of a person's intention or will on the status of liquids, itself a subtle matter. There are three major points in the chapter.

First, intention is temporally indivisible (M. 1:1). That is, if at one point I do want the liquid and, specifically, want it to fall on my produce, and if at a later point I change my mind, or vice versa, that is of no consequence. Once I give my approval to the use of the liquid, the matter is done. The liquid then gains, and never loses, the capacity to impart susceptibility to uncleanness and to render that on which it falls susceptible.

The second major point of the chapter is that intention itself may or may not be divisible (M. 1:2-4 + 5). If I want the liquid to fall in a given place, and some of the liquid does, and some does not, fall in that place, then the liquid that has not fallen where I want it may (by the Shammaites) or may not (by the Hillelites) be deemed capable of imparting susceptibility to uncleanness. The former hold that all of the liquid has been subject to my intention. In the view of the latter, only part of the liquid has actually conformed to my intention. Or if the liquid falls on an insusceptible object, for example, on vegetables attached to the ground ("unplucked vegetables"), the vegetables are not made susceptible to uncleanness. But the water that has fallen on them may or may not retain the capacity to impart susceptibility, so that, if plucked vegetables touch the water on unplucked vegetables, or if the unplucked vegetables while wet are uprooted and so made susceptible to susceptibility, they then are subject to the effects of the liquid.

This issue is subject to diverse conceptions of the Houses' positions. M. 1:2 holds that the Houses agree that if one shakes a tree to bring down fruit, water that falls with the fruit is not capable of imparting susceptibility to uncleanness. Why not? Because I did not shake the tree for the moisture thereon, but only for the fruit. What if I want the moisture, but only part of the moisture falls? Is the other part, that remaining in the tree, capable of imparting uncleanness? On this point the Houses are supposed to have differed, as I said, with the Shammaites holding that all of the water has been subject to my will or intention, and the Hillelites regarding the water that has not actually fallen as I wanted it to fall to be incapable of imparting susceptibility to uncleanness. To the Shammaites, intent is indivisible. To the Hillelites it is subject to its own nuance. This dispute looks suspiciously parallel to M. 1:1, which on the face of it states the Shammaite conception. But that is not a major problem.

What is difficult is the sequence of disputes flowing out of the agreement at M. 1:2A-C. The first is, as just now stated, on the intent to shake down liquids, not all of which fall. The second, at M. 1:3, is shaking a tree—without specified object of intent, that is, to bring down liquid or to bring down fruit—with that which falls from the tree landing on another tree or on a bush. The majority of MSS have a singular verb, which does not suggest that the subject of the sentence is liquids. But M. 1:2A speaks of food—pieces of fruit—in the plural. In any event the net effect is the same. The liquid that falls does not fall upon the ground but upon another tree and thence upon the ground. Accordingly, we have an intervening case. The statement of the dispute is further enriched with a secondary layer of problems, at M. 1:3J, which says that that which is shaken from tree to tree and thence to the ground lands on seeds or unplucked vegetables. At this point comes the issue, already stated, about whether or not the liquid that lands on insusceptible vegetables but thereafter touches vegetables that can be rendered susceptible to uncleanness then does impart susceptibility. Finally, Joshua cites Abba Yosé. The purpose of the saying, which stresses that liquid does not impart susceptibility unless someone intentionally places it on the appropriate substance, poses problems. A sign of the diverse potentialities of the pericope is that this saying is interpreted as explaining the position of both Houses, of one House only (the Hillelites'), or of neither House.

The third element in the tripartite Houses' dispute, M. 1:4, restates the matter, now in terms of shaking not a tree but a bunch of vegetables. The liquid flows from the top to the bottom of the vegetables. We are given the standard apodosis; the House of Shammai say, "It [the liquid that is shaken] falls under the law, If water be put," and the House of Hillel say, "It does not." But the debate that follows introduces conceptions, upon which both Houses are claimed to be in agreement, not stated in the basic dispute at all. The Hillelites' argument, opening the debate, is that the Shammaites agree that one who shakes a single stalk does not take into account the liquid's falling from leaf to leaf on the stalk. We have no datum in which the Shammaites make any such concession. The Shammaites distinguish the bunch of vegetables from the single stalk. Then the Hillelites introduce a quite separate case, again not given in M. or in T. If a person brings up a sack of vegetables from the river and puts them on the bank to let the water flow back into the river, that single sack is unaffected. That is, we do not take account of liquid flowing from the top to the bottom of the sack.

This is assumed to be the position of the Shammaites as well. Now they have to show what difference there is between the bunch of vegetables and the sack of vegetables, and they, of course, fall silent. M. 1:4T then has a law that appropriately should begin, *And they agree.* For the Hillelites have spoken of a single sack. The Hillelites are assumed, then, to agree (with the Shammaites) that in the case of two sacks, we do regard water from the upper to the lower sack as capable of activating the processes of contamination. Yosé at M. simply states that the lower sack is clean.

The third major point of the chapter, M. 1:6H-L, is stated with remarkable brevity. If I am forced to wet down my produce, for instance, to hide it in a well from thieves, that does not constitute intentional wetting down, even though my actual act of putting the fruit into water is deliberate. Likewise, even if the force of circumstance makes necessary the infusion of water into the produce, which, by consequence, is done with deliberation, that does not mean that the liquid has been intentionally applied to the produce. The illustrative case of the unstated principle is remarkable for its leniency. If in order to carry produce, one floats it down a stream, that is not intentional wetting down.

Formal traits require only brief comment. Tightly disciplined declarative sentences, as at M. 1:1, alternate with equally well constructed Houses' disputes, M. 1:2-4. One reason for the highly limited formulaic repertoire, of course, is the fixed apodosis, BKY YTN +/- *not.* Other language is available, TM' and THWR, which is even mixed with the former (e.g. at M. 1:1). The openly Ushan materials of M. 1:5-6 preserve the formulaic and disciplined style of the foregoing pericopae in the names of the Houses. The hand of the ultimate redactor is best discerned in the opening clauses of each and every unit of tradition after M. 1:1. He invariably makes use of the present participle, *He who . . . ,* and an apocopated apodosis, *it is subject to the law . . . ,* which refers not to the man who has shaken the tree or dried off the leeks or blown upon the sesame seeds, but to the liquid present in the tree or leeks or in his breath. The full consistency imposed by the penultimate redactor is best seen at M. 1:6H and L, *He who hides . . . , he who places . . . ,* for neither of these matters is of the narrowly casuistic nature of the foregoing. Both intend to give general rules. Yet they

conform to the pattern of the chapter, participle + apocopation.
The shift at M. 2:1 is unmistakable and proves that we are right in
noting the highly distinctive stylistic character of Chapter One.

iii. Mishnah Makhshirin Chapter Two

זֵעַת בָּתִּים, בּוֹרוֹת, שִׁיחִין, וּמְעָרוֹת – טְהוֹרָה. זֵעַת הָאָדָם –
טְהוֹרָה. שָׁתָה מַיִם טְמֵאִים וְהִזִּיעַ – זֵעָתוֹ טְהוֹרָה. בָּא בְמַיִם
שְׁאוּבִים וְהִזִּיעַ – זֵעָתוֹ טְמֵאָה. נִסְתַּפֵּג וְאַחַר כָּךְ הִזִּיעַ – זֵעָתוֹ
טְהוֹרָה.

מֶרְחָץ טְמֵאָה – זֵעָתָה טְמֵאָה; וּטְהוֹרָה – בְּכִי יֻתַּן. הַבְּרֵכָה
שֶׁבַּבַּיִת, הַבַּיִת מֵזִיעַ מֵחֲמָתָהּ: אִם טְמֵאָה – זֵעַת כָּל הַבַּיִת
שֶׁמֵּחֲמַת הַבְּרֵכָה, טְמֵאָה.

שְׁתֵּי בְרֵכוֹת, אַחַת טְהוֹרָה וְאַחַת טְמֵאָה, הַמֵּזִיעַ קָרוֹב
לַטְּמֵאָה – טָמֵא; קָרוֹב לַטְּהוֹרָה – טָהוֹר. מֶחֱצָה לְמֶחֱצָה –
טָמֵא. בַּרְזֶל טָמֵא שֶׁבְּלָלוֹ עִם בַּרְזֶל טָהוֹר: אִם רֹב מִן
הַטָּמֵא – טָמֵא; וְאִם רֹב מִן הַטָּהוֹר – טָהוֹר. מֶחֱצָה לְמֶחֱצָה –
טָמֵא. גִּסְטְרָיוֹת שֶׁיִּשְׂרָאֵל וְגוֹיִם מַטִּילִין לְתוֹכָן: אִם רֹב מִן
הַטָּמֵא – טָמֵא; וְאִם רֹב מִן הַטָּהוֹר – טָהוֹר. מֶחֱצָה לְמֶחֱצָה –
טָמֵא. מֵי שְׁפִיכוּת שֶׁיָּרְדוּ עֲלֵיהֶן מֵי גְשָׁמִים: אִם רֹב מִן
הַטָּמֵא – טָמֵא; וְאִם רֹב מִן הַטָּהוֹר – טָהוֹר. מֶחֱצָה לְמֶחֱצָה –
טָמֵא. אֵימָתַי? בִּזְמַן שֶׁקָּדְמוּ מֵי שְׁפִיכוּת, אֲבָל אִם קָדְמוּ מֵי
גְשָׁמִים, אֲפִלּוּ כָל שֶׁהֵן, לְמֵי שְׁפִיכוּת – טָמֵא.

הַטּוֹרֵף אֶת גַּגּוֹ, וְהַמְכַבֵּס אֶת כְּסוּתוֹ וְיָרְדוּ עֲלֵיהֶן גְּשָׁמִים: אִם
רֹב מִן הַטָּמֵא – טָמֵא; וְאִם רֹב מִן הַטָּהוֹר – טָהוֹר. מֶחֱצָה
לְמֶחֱצָה – טָמֵא. רַבִּי יְהוּדָה אוֹמֵר: אִם הוֹסִיפוּ לְנַטֵּף.

עִיר שֶׁיִּשְׂרָאֵל וְנָכְרִים דָּרִים בָּהּ, וְהָיָה בָהּ מֶרְחָץ מַרְחֶצֶת
בַּשַּׁבָּת: אִם רֹב נָכְרִים – רוֹחֵץ מִיָּד; וְאִם רֹב יִשְׂרָאֵל – יַמְתִּין
כְּדֵי שֶׁיֵּחַמּוּ הַחַמִּין. מֶחֱצָה לְמֶחֱצָה – יַמְתִּין כְּדֵי שֶׁיֵּחַמּוּ
הַחַמִּין. רַבִּי יְהוּדָה אוֹמֵר: בְּאַמְבָּטִי קְטַנָּה, אִם יֵשׁ בָּהּ
רָשׁוּת – רוֹחֵץ בָּהּ מִיָּד.

מָצָא בָּהּ יָרָק נִמְכָּר: אִם רֹב גּוֹיִם – לוֹקֵחַ מִיָּד; וְאִם רֹב יִשְׂרָאֵל – יַמְתִּין כְּדֵי שֶׁיָּבוֹא מִמָּקוֹם קָרוֹב. מֶחֱצָה לְמֶחֱצָה – יַמְתִּין כְּדֵי שֶׁיָּבוֹא מִמָּקוֹם קָרוֹב. וְאִם יֵשׁ בָּהּ רָשׁוּת – לוֹקֵחַ מִיָּד.

מָצָא בָּהּ תִּינוֹק מֻשְׁלָךְ: אִם רֹב גּוֹיִם – גּוֹי; וְאִם רֹב יִשְׂרָאֵל – יִשְׂרָאֵל. מֶחֱצָה לְמֶחֱצָה – יִשְׂרָאֵל. רַבִּי יְהוּדָה אוֹמֵר: הוֹלְכִין אַחַר רֹב הַמַּשְׁלִיכִין.

מָצָא בָּהּ מְצִיאָה: אִם רֹב גּוֹיִם – אֵינוֹ צָרִיךְ לְהַכְרִיז; וְאִם רֹב יִשְׂרָאֵל – צָרִיךְ לְהַכְרִיז. מֶחֱצָה לְמֶחֱצָה – צָרִיךְ לְהַכְרִיז. מָצָא בָּהּ פַּת – הוֹלְכִין אַחַר רֹב הַנַּחְתּוֹמִין. וְאִם הָיְתָה פַּת עִיסָה – הוֹלְכִים אַחַר רֹב אוֹכְלֵי פַּת עִיסָה. רַבִּי יְהוּדָה אוֹמֵר: אִם הָיְתָה פַּת קִיבָר – הוֹלְכִין אַחַר רֹב אוֹכְלֵי פַּת קִיבָר.

מָצָא בָּהּ בָּשָׂר – הוֹלְכִין אַחַר רֹב הַטַּבָּחִים. אִם הָיָה מְבֻשָּׁל – הוֹלְכִים אַחַר רֹב אוֹכְלֵי בָשָׂר מְבֻשָּׁל. הַמּוֹצֵא פֵרוֹת בַּדֶּרֶךְ: אִם רֹב מַכְנִיסִין לְבָתֵּיהֶן – פָּטוּר; וְלִמְכֹּר בַּשּׁוּק – חַיָּב. מֶחֱצָה לְמֶחֱצָה – דְּמַאי. אוֹצָר שֶׁיִּשְׂרָאֵל וְגוֹיִם מַטִּילִין לְתוֹכוֹ: אִם רֹב גּוֹיִם – וַדַּאי; וְאִם רֹב יִשְׂרָאֵל – דְּמַאי. מֶחֱצָה לְמֶחֱצָה – וַדַּאי; דִּבְרֵי רַבִּי מֵאִיר. וַחֲכָמִים אוֹמְרִים: אֲפִלּוּ כֻלָּם גּוֹיִם, וְיִשְׂרָאֵל אֶחָד מַטִּיל לְתוֹכוֹ – דְּמַאי.

פֵּרוֹת שְׁנִיָּה שֶׁרַבּוּ עַל שֶׁלַּשְּׁלִישִׁית, וְשֶׁלַּשְּׁלִישִׁית עַל שֶׁלָּרְבִיעִית, וְשֶׁלָּרְבִיעִית עַל שֶׁלַּחֲמִישִׁית, וְשֶׁלַּחֲמִישִׁית עַל שֶׁלַּשִּׁשִּׁית, וְשֶׁלַּשִּׁשִּׁית עַל שֶׁלַּשְּׁבִיעִית, וְשֶׁלַּשְּׁבִיעִית עַל שֶׁלְּמוֹצָאֵי שְׁבִיעִית – הוֹלְכִין אַחַר הָרֹב. מֶחֱצָה לְמֶחֱצָה – לְהַחְמִיר.

The entire chapter is a unitary construction, exhibiting traits of extremely careful workmanship, except for a small, interpolated pericope, M. 2:1B-E. The unit begins with the rule for the sweat of damp walls of houses and the like, M. 2:1A, which is contrasted with that of the bath-house, M. 2:2. If the water of the bath-house is clean, then the sweat of the walls is clean (but subject to the law, If water be put). If the water of the bath-house is unclean, then the sweat of the walls is unclean. This brings us to the pivotal rule, M. 2:2C-F. We have a pool in a house, thus combining M. 2:1A and M. 2:2A-B. If the walls sweat on account of the presence of the pool, then the sweat is taken into account. If the pool's water is unclean, so is the sweat of the walls that is caused by the pool, but not the sweat of the walls that is not caused by the pool. M. 2:3A-D now sets up the form to be followed through the remainder of the chapter. What if there are two pools in a house, one clean and one unclean? The wall that sweats nearer to the clean pool produces clean sweat, and that which sweats nearer to the unclean one produces unclean sweat. Accordingly, the opening construction is a smooth and logical progression of rules.

The rest of the chapter depends on the principle of M. 2:3A-D. We are given a series of cases, most of them irrelevant to Makhshirin, in which we have combinations of unclean and clean things, or mixtures of liquids, or mixed populations, or the like. In all cases we follow the majority, and, if matters are equal, we impose the stringent ruling of status. Counting M. 2:3A-D, there are fourteen such examples in all. The first group, M. 2:3-4, deal with liquids, excluding M. 2:3E-H, which is cited verbatim from M. Kel. 11:4. The other entries leave matters of liquids entirely. Glosses are inserted at exactly the same point in all glossed pericopae. All glosses, of course, are Ushan, and the construction as a whole must be located among Ushan circles, in particular Judah's and Meir's. When we come to M. 2:11, finally, we observe that the established form is grossly augmented with an immense protasis, but the apodosis is as tight and disciplined as the foregoing, a fine example of the revision of formal traits to mark the end of a major construction.

iv. Mishnah Makhshirin Chapter Three

פרק שלישי

שַׂק שֶׁהוּא מָלֵא פֵּרוֹת וּנְתָנוֹ עַל גַּב הַנָּהָר, אוֹ עַל פִּי הַבּוֹר,

אוֹ עַל מַעֲלוֹת הַמְּעָרָה, וְשָׁאֲבוּ: כָּל שֶׁשָּׁאֲבוּ – בְּכִי יֻתַּן. רַבִּי יְהוּדָה אוֹמֵר: כָּל שֶׁהוּא כְּנֶגֶד הַמַּיִם – בְּכִי יֻתַּן, וְכָל שֶׁאֵינוֹ כְּנֶגֶד הַמַּיִם – אֵינוֹ בְּכִי יֻתַּן.

חָבִית שֶׁהִיא מְלֵאָה פֵּרוֹת וּנְתוּנָה לְתוֹךְ הַמַּשְׁקִין, אוֹ מְלֵאָה מַשְׁקִין וּנְתוּנָה לְתוֹךְ הַפֵּרוֹת, וְשָׁאֲבוּ: כָּל שֶׁשָּׁאֲבוּ – בְּכִי יֻתַּן. בְּאֵלּוּ מַשְׁקִים אָמְרוּ? בַּמַּיִם, וּבַיַּיִן, וּבַחֹמֶץ. וּשְׁאָר כָּל הַמַּשְׁקִין – טְהוֹרִין. רַבִּי נְחֶמְיָה מְטַהֵר בַּקִּטְנִית, שֶׁאֵין הַקִּטְנִית שׁוֹאֶבֶת.

הָרוֹדֶה פַּת חַמָּה וּנְתָנָהּ עַל פִּי חָבִית שֶׁלַּיַּיִן – רַבִּי מֵאִיר מְטַמֵּא; וְרַבִּי יְהוּדָה מְטַהֵר. רַבִּי יוֹסֵי מְטַהֵר בְּשֶׁלַּחִטִּים, וּמְטַמֵּא בְּשֶׁלַּשְּׂעוֹרִים, מִפְּנֵי שֶׁהַשְּׂעוֹרִים שׁוֹאֲבוֹת.

הַמְרַבֵּץ אֶת בֵּיתוֹ וְנָתַן בּוֹ חִטִּים, וְטָנְנוּ: אִם מֵחֲמַת הַמַּיִם – בְּכִי יֻתַּן; וְאִם מֵחֲמַת הַסֶּלַע – אֵינָן בְּכִי יֻתַּן. הַמְכַבֵּס אֶת כְּסוּתוֹ בַּעֲרֵבָה, נָתַן בָּהּ חִטִּים, וְטָנְנוּ: אִם מֵחֲמַת הַמַּיִם – בְּכִי יֻתַּן; אִם מֵחֲמַת עַצְמָן – אֵינָן בְּכִי יֻתַּן. הַמְטַנֵּן בַּחוֹל, הֲרֵי זֶה בְּכִי יֻתַּן. מַעֲשֶׂה בְאַנְשֵׁי הַמָּחוֹז שֶׁהָיוּ מְטַנְּנִין בַּחוֹל, אָמְרוּ לָהֶם חֲכָמִים: אִם כָּךְ הֱיִיתֶם עוֹשִׂים, לֹא עֲשִׂיתֶם טַהֲרָה מִימֵיכֶם.

הַמְטַנֵּן בְּטִיט הַנֶּגוּב – רַבִּי שִׁמְעוֹן אוֹמֵר: אִם יֶשׁ בּוֹ מַשְׁקֶה טוֹפֵחַ – בְּכִי יֻתַּן; וְאִם לָאו – אֵינוֹ בְּכִי יֻתַּן. הַמְרַבֵּץ אֶת גָּרְנוֹ, אֵינוֹ חוֹשֵׁשׁ שֶׁמָּא נָתַן בָּהּ חִטִּים וְטָנְנוּ. הַמְלַקֵּט עֲשָׂבִים כְּשֶׁהַטַּל עֲלֵיהֶם, לְהָטֵן בָּהֶם חִטִּים – אֵינָן בְּכִי יֻתַּן. אִם נִתְכַּוֵּן לְכָךְ, הֲרֵי זֶה בְּכִי יֻתַּן. הַמּוֹלִיךְ חִטִּין לִטְחוֹן וְיָרְדוּ עֲלֵיהֶן גְּשָׁמִים: אִם שָׂמַח – בְּכִי יֻתַּן. רַבִּי יְהוּדָה אוֹמֵר: אִי אֶפְשָׁר שֶׁלֹּא לִשְׂמוֹחַ, אֶלָּא – אִם עָמַד.

הָיוּ זֵיתָיו נְתוּנִים בַּגַּג וְיָרְדוּ עֲלֵיהֶן גְּשָׁמִים: אִם שָׂמַח – בְּכִי יֻתַּן. רַבִּי יְהוּדָה אוֹמֵר: אִי אֶפְשָׁר שֶׁלֹּא לִשְׂמוֹחַ, אֶלָּא – אִם פָּקַק אֶת הַצִּנּוֹר, אוֹ אִם חִלְחֵל לְתוֹכָן.

הַחַמָּרִיו שֶׁהָיוּ עוֹבְרִים בַּנָּהָר וְנָפְלוּ שַׂקֵּיהֶם לַמַּיִם: אִם שָׂמְחוּ – בְּכִי יֻתַּן. רַבִּי יְהוּדָה אוֹמֵר: אִי אֶפְשָׁר שֶׁלֹּא לִשְׂמוֹחַ,

אֶלָּא – אִם הָפַכוּ. הָיוּ רַגְלָיו מְלֵאוֹת טִיט, וְכֵן רַגְלֵי בְהֶמְתּוֹ,
עָבַר בַּנָּהָר: אִם שָׂמַח – בְּכִי יֻתַּן. רַבִּי יְהוּדָה אוֹמֵר: אִי
אֶפְשָׁר שֶׁלֹּא לִשְׂמוֹחַ, אֶלָּא–אִם עָמַד וְהֵדִיחַ בָּאָדָם..וּבִבְהֵמָה
טְמֵאָה לְעוֹלָם טָמֵא.

הַמּוֹרִיד אֶת הַגַּלְגַּלִּים וְאֶת כְּלֵי הַבָּקָר בְּשָׁעַת הַקָּדִים לַמַּיִם,
בִּשְׁבִיל שֶׁיָּחוּצוּ, הֲרֵי זֶה בְּכִי יֻתַּן. הַמּוֹרִיד בְּהֵמָה לִשְׁתּוֹת:
הַמַּיִם הָעוֹלִים בְּפִיהָ – בְּכִי יֻתַּן; וּבְרַגְלֶיהָ – אֵינָן בְּכִי יֻתַּן.
אִם חָשַׁב שֶׁיְּדוֹחוּ רַגְלֶיהָ, אַף הָעוֹלִין בְּרַגְלֶיהָ – בְּכִי יֻתַּן.
בְּשָׁעַת הַיַּחַף וְהַדַּיִשׁ לְעוֹלָם טָמֵא. הוֹרִיד חֵרֵשׁ שׁוֹטֶה וְקָטָן,
אַף עַל פִּי שֶׁחוֹשֵׁב שֶׁיְּדוֹחוּ רַגְלֶיהָ – אֵינָן בְּכִי יֻתַּן, שֶׁיֵּשׁ לָהֶן
מַעֲשֶׂה, וְאֵין לָהֶן מַחֲשָׁבָה.

The present chapter supplies further refinements of the principle that water detached and used with approval imparts susceptibility to uncleanness. The secondary issues raised are as follows: first, whether or not various substances absorb liquid (M. 3:1, 2, 3); second, whether or not it is the person's intent that the liquid be absorbed—specifically, whether or not one wants grain to be wet down (M. 3:4, 5A-F); and third, whether or not intention is signified solely by consequent deed (M. 3:5G-I, 6, 7 + 8). The second set is basically Simeon's, the third Judah's. Simeon takes account of the traits of the water. Judah maintains that we reckon only with what a person actually does, which deed determines our interpretation of his primary intent.

The chapter's formal units are clearly marked off by diverse patterns in the basic sentence structure. M. 3:1 and 2 place emphasis on the *object which*-construction, with the expected apocopation at the apodosis. M. 3:3, 4A, D, and G, 3:5A, D, G, all commence with the participial substantive, *he-who-does-so-and-so*, with apocopated apodosis. M. 3:6 breaks the apocopation: *[If] his olives were . . . and it rained . . . if he was happy . . .* , that is, a fluent sentence entirely lacking in apocopation. But the pericope is integral to Judah's construction. M. 3:7 returns to the opening construction, *The ass-drivers who were . . . if . . . , [if] its*

feet were . . . , if . . . , that is to say, as at M. 3:6, nothing more
than complete sentences. M. 3:8 reverts to the *he-who*-construction
throughout A-E, then closes with the complete sentences in the
form of M. 3:6-7—a handsome amalgamation of both predominant
forms—concluding the chapter by drawing on each.

v. Mishnah Makhshirin Chapter Four

פרק רביעי

הַשּׁוֹחֶה לִשְׁתּוֹת, הַמַּיִם הָעוֹלִים בְּפִיו וּבִשְׂפָמוֹ – בְּכִי יֻתַּן.
בְּחָטְמוֹ, וּבְרֹאשׁוֹ, וּבִזְקָנוֹ – אֵינָן בְּכִי יֻתַּן. הַמְמַלֵּא בֶחָבִית,
הַמַּיִם הָעוֹלִים אַחֲרֶיהָ, וּבַחֶבֶל שֶׁהוּא מְכֻנָּן עַל צַוָּארָה,
וּבַחֶבֶל שֶׁהוּא לְצָרְכָהּ – הֲרֵי זֶה בְּכִי יֻתַּן. כַּמָּה הוּא צָרְכָּהּ?
רַבִּי שִׁמְעוֹן בֶּן אֶלְעָזָר אוֹמֵר: טֶפַח. נְתָנָהּ תַּחַת הַצִּנּוֹר – אֵינָן
בְּכִי יֻתַּן.

מִי שֶׁיָּרְדוּ עָלָיו גְּשָׁמִים, אֲפִלּוּ אַב הַטֻּמְאָה – אֵינָן בְּכִי יֻתַּן.
וְאִם נִעֵר – בְּכִי יֻתַּן. עָמַד תַּחַת הַצִּנּוֹר לְהָקֵר, אוֹ לִדּוֹחַ:
בַּטָּמֵא – טָמֵאן. וּבַטָּהוֹר – בְּכִי יֻתַּן.

הַכּוֹפֶה קְעָרָה עַל הַכֹּתֶל בִּשְׁבִיל שֶׁתִּדּוֹחַ, הֲרֵי זֶה בְּכִי יֻתַּן.
אִם בִּשְׁבִיל שֶׁלֹּא יִלְקֶה הַכֹּתֶל – אֵינָן בְּכִי יֻתַּן.

חָבִית שֶׁיָּרַד הַדֶּלֶף לְתוֹכָהּ – בֵּית שַׁמַּאי אוֹמְרִים: יִשָּׁבֵר.
בֵּית הִלֵּל אוֹמְרִים: יְעָרֶה. וּמוֹדִים שֶׁהוּא מוֹשִׁיט אֶת יָדוֹ
וְנוֹטֵל פֵּרוֹת מִתּוֹכָהּ, וְהֵם טְהוֹרִים.

עֲרֵבָה שֶׁיָּרַד הַדֶּלֶף לְתוֹכָהּ, הַנִּתָּזִין וְהַצִּפִּין – אֵינָן בְּכִי יֻתַּן.
נְטָלָהּ לְשָׁפְכָהּ – בֵּית שַׁמַּאי אוֹמְרִים: בְּכִי יֻתַּן. בֵּית הִלֵּל
אוֹמְרִים: אֵינָן בְּכִי יֻתַּן. הִנִּיחָהּ שֶׁיֵּרַד הַדֶּלֶף לְתוֹכָהּ, הַנִּתָּזִין
וְהַצִּפִּין – בֵּית שַׁמַּאי אוֹמְרִים: בְּכִי יֻתַּן. בֵּית הִלֵּל אוֹמְרִים:
אֵינָן בְּכִי יֻתַּן. נְטָלָהּ לְשָׁפְכָהּ – אֵלּוּ וָאֵלּוּ מוֹדִים שֶׁהֵן בְּכִי יֻתַּן.
הַמַּטְבִּיל אֶת הַכֵּלִים, וְהַמְכַבֵּס אֶת כְּסוּתוֹ בַּמְּעָרָה: הַמַּיִם
הָעוֹלִים בְּיָדָיו – בְּכִי יֻתַּן; בְּרַגְלָיו – אֵינָן בְּכִי יֻתַּן. רַבִּי
אֶלְעָזָר אוֹמֵר: אִם אִי אֶפְשָׁר לוֹ שֶׁיֵּרַד, אֶלָּא אִם כֵּן נִטַּנְּפוּ

רַגְלָיו, אַף הָעוֹלִיו בְּרַגְלָיו – בְּכִי יֻתַּן.

קֻפָּה שֶׁהִיא מְלֵאָה תְּרְמוֹסִין וּנְתָנָהּ לְתוֹךְ מִקְוֶה – מוֹשִׁיט יָדוֹ
וְנוֹטֵל תֻּרְמוֹסִין מִתּוֹכָהּ, וְהֵם טְהוֹרִים. הֶעֱלָם מִן הַמַּיִם:
הַנּוֹגְעִים בַּקֻּפָּה – טְמֵאִים, וּשְׁאָר כָּל הַתֻּרְמוֹסִים – טְהוֹרִים.
צִנּוֹן שֶׁבַּמְּעָרָה – נִדָּה מַדִּיחַתּוּ, וְהוּא טָהוֹר. הֶעֱלַתּוּ כָּל שֶׁהוּא
מִן הַמַּיִם – טָמֵא.

פֵּרוֹת שֶׁנָּפְלוּ לְתוֹךְ אַמַּת הַמַּיִם, פָּשַׁט מִי שֶׁהָיוּ יָדָיו טְמֵאוֹת
וּנְטָלָן – יָדָיו טְהוֹרוֹת, וְהַפֵּרוֹת טְהוֹרִים. וְאִם חָשַׁב שֶׁיִּדּוֹחוּ
יָדָיו – יָדָיו טְהוֹרוֹת, וְהַפֵּרוֹת בְּכִי יֻתַּן.

קְדֵרָה שֶׁהִיא מְלֵאָה מַיִם וּנְתוּנָה לְתוֹךְ הַמִּקְוֶה, וּפָשַׁט אַב
הַטֻּמְאָה אֶת יָדוֹ לְתוֹכָהּ – טְמֵאָה; מַגַּע טְמֵאוֹת – טְהוֹרָה.
וּשְׁאָר כָּל הַמַּשְׁקִין – טְמֵאִין, שֶׁאֵין הַמַּיִם מְטַהֲרִים אֶת שְׁאָר
הַמַּשְׁקִין.

הַמְמַלֵּא בַּקֵּילוֹן, עַד שְׁלֹשָׁה יָמִים – טְמֵאִין. רַבִּי עֲקִיבָא
אוֹמֵר: אִם נִגְבּוּ – מִיָּד טְהוֹרִים; וְאִם לֹא נִגְבּוּ, אֲפִלּוּ עַד
שְׁלֹשִׁים יוֹם – טְמֵאִים.

עֵצִים שֶׁנָּפְלוּ עֲלֵיהֶם מַשְׁקִין וְיָרְדוּ עֲלֵיהֶם גְּשָׁמִים, אִם רַבּוּ –
טְהוֹרִים. הוֹצִיאָם שֶׁיֵּרְדוּ עֲלֵיהֶם גְּשָׁמִים, אַף עַל פִּי שֶׁרַבּוּ –
טְמֵאִים. בָּלְעוּ מַשְׁקִים טְמֵאִים, אַף עַל פִּי שֶׁהוֹצִיאָם שֶׁיֵּרְדוּ
עֲלֵיהֶן גְּשָׁמִים – טְהוֹרִין. וְלֹא יַסִּיקֵם אֶלָּא בְיָדַיִם טְהוֹרוֹת
בִּלְבַד. רַבִּי שִׁמְעוֹן אוֹמֵר: אִם הָיוּ לַחִין וְהִסִּיקָן, וְרַבּוּ
הַמַּשְׁקִין הַיּוֹצְאִין מֵהֶן עַל הַמַּשְׁקִין שֶׁבָּלְעוּ – טְהוֹרִים.

This chapter takes up exactly at the point at which the former leaves off, with the principle that, whereas water that one wants does impart susceptibility to uncleanness, water not essential to the person's primary intent is not under the law, If water be put. M. 4:1 repeats the main point of M. 3:8. It is not surprising that the formulary pattern, *He who . . . , lo, it is under the law . . . ,* familiar at M. 3:8, recurs at M. 4:1 and thereafter. M. 4:2-3 persist in the same principle and pattern. If rain falls on someone, that does not impart susceptibility to uncleanness. But if the person

somehow responds to the rain, then the water does impart susceptibility to uncleanness. Obviously, if a person stands under a water-
spout to cool off, the water is wanted. If he is unclean, the water
is unclean. If he is clean, the water is under the law, If water be
put. The same distinction is made at M. 4:3 with reference to an
inanimate object.

M. 4:4-5 present a triplet of Houses' disputes. Their main principle is remarkably familiar. It is, as we see, none other than a
restatement of the dispute of M. 1:2-4. If I move water, does that
fact by itself mean that I have wanted, or now want, the water,
along the lines of M. 1:1 and the Shammaite position of M. 1:2?
Or does my disposition of the water—I pour it out—indicate that I
never wanted it at all (as Judah would insist)? At M. 4:4 the Houses
debate the status of a jug into which rain has dripped from the roof.
The jug contains pieces of fruit. I want to pour out the water so as to
reach the fruit, M. 4:4D suggests. What shall I do? The Shammaites
say I have to break the jug. That is the only way that I can indicate
I really do not want the water at all. If I pick up the jug and pour
out the water, I stir up the water, which renders the fruit susceptible. Not breaking the jar, I indicate that, for a brief moment, I
might want to keep the water, therefore I approve its present location, and M. 1:1 is invoked. The Hillelites say I simply pour out
the water. That action retrospectively indicates I never wanted the
water to begin with. The Houses agree that if I reach in and take
the fruit out, the fruit is unaffected by the water, for I have demon-
strated by deed that I do not want wet fruit.

At M. 4:5F-I, we have a trough that has collected water from
the roof. It was not placed there for that purpose. What is the status
of water that overflows or splashes out? Both parties agree it is
insusceptible. What about emptying the trough? When I do so,
as before, I indicate that I originally was satisfied to have it in its
original location—so say the Shammaites. The Hillelites rule as expected. If I deliberately leave the trough to collect the rain-drippings,
what is the status of water that splashes out or overflows? This is
precisely the issue of M. 1:2: water shaken out of the tree as against
water remaining in the tree after I shake the tree, here: splashed
water. Since the water did not reach and remain at the location
that I intended for it, the Hillelites regard it as water not in its

present location with approval. The Shammaites invoke a narrow construction of M. 1:1. Since at some point I wanted the water, wherever it is ultimately located, it has been subject to my approval. M. 4:5P-S go over the ground of M. 4:1-3, making exactly the same distinction.

M. 4:6 then repeats the point on which the Houses agree at M. 4:4D. But it wishes to make a further one as well. I have a basket full of lupines, placed in an immersion-pool. In line with M. 4:4, if I take the lupines out by hand, they are not deemed rendered susceptible by the water of the pool. What if I take the basket, including the lupines, out of the pool-water? The water on the sides of the baskets is detached with approval. Therefore the lupines touching the sides of the baskets are deemed susceptible to uncleanness. But the ones not touching the sides are not affected by water with approval and remain clean. M. 4:7 makes precisely this same point. If pieces of fruit fall in a water channel, I reach in even with dirty hands and the fruit remains insusceptible and clean. My hands are clean as well, having been washed in the pool. If my intent, in reaching into the water, was to wash off (thus also: purify) my hands, however, then the hands are clean (as before). But the fruit has been rendered susceptible to uncleanness.

M. 4:8 develops this matter, stressing that if there is an earthenware pot full of water lying in an immersion-pool, a person who is a Father of uncleanness reaches into the pot and renders it unclean. Why? Because a clay pot is made unclean through its air-space, and a Father of uncleanness can make the pot unclean. If it is someone in the first remove of uncleanness who reaches in, however, he does not contaminate the pot. M. 4:8E-F add a rather curious gloss, introducing an issue not present at M. 4:3A-D.

M. 4:9, continuing the established formulary pattern, deals with a wooden bucket of some kind, parallel to the clay pot of M. 4:8. How long is water deemed absorbed by the wood? Once I use the bucket, I clearly detach water with intent and approval. For three days moisture in the bucket is deemed susceptible to uncleanness on that account. 'Aqiba holds that if one dried off the bucket, whatever moisture remains is forthwith deemed clean. Why? Because, by drying off the bucket, I indicate that I do not want the water that has been detached. If it is not dried off, then even after thirty days, water in the bucket is deemed detached with approval. Whether 'Aqiba intends to gloss or to differ from the anonymous rule is under discussion.

M. 4:10A-E pose few problems, but M. 4:10F does. The former make the point that when insusceptible water forms the greater part over susceptible water in a mixture of both, the former imparts its traits upon the whole, just as we know from M. 2:3. Therefore if liquids are on pieces of wood, and rain falls on them, and if the rain is more than the liquids, then the wood is insusceptible to uncleanness. If, however, I put the wood outside, so intending that the rain fall on it, then the status of the rain is no different from the liquid. The wood under all circumstances is susceptible to uncleanness and unclean. At D we make the point that if the unclean liquids were absorbed into the wood, then, if rain falls, even with approval, on the wood, the wood remains clean, because the rain has not had contact with the absorbed liquid.

vi. Mishnah Makhshirin Chapter Five

פרק חמישי

מִי שֶׁטָּבַל בַּנָּהָר, וְהָיָה לְפָנָיו נָהָר אַחֵר וְעָבַר בּוֹ – טָהֲרוּ שְׁנִיִּים אֶת הָרִאשׁוֹנִים. דְּחָהוּ חֲבֵרוֹ לְשָׁכְרוֹ, וְכֵן לִבְהֶמְתּוֹ – טָהֲרוּ שְׁנִיִּים אֶת הָרִאשׁוֹנִים. וְאִם כִּמְשַׂחֵק עִמּוֹ, הֲרֵי זֶה בְּכִי יֻתַּן.

הַשָּׁט עַל פְּנֵי הַמַּיִם, הַנִּתָּזִיז – אֵינָן בְּכִי יֻתַּן. וְאִם נִתְכַּוֵּן לְהַתִּיז עַל חֲבֵרוֹ, הֲרֵי זֶה בְּכִי יֻתַּן. הָעוֹשֶׂה צִפּוֹר בַּמַּיִם, הַנִּתָּזִין וְאֶת שֶׁבָּהּ – אֵינָן בְּכִי יֻתַּן.

פֵּרוֹת שֶׁיָּרַד הַדֶּלֶף לְתוֹכָן וּבְלָלָן שֶׁיְּגוּבוּ – רַבִּי שִׁמְעוֹן אוֹמֵר: בְּכִי יֻתַּן. וַחֲכָמִים אוֹמְרִים: אֵינָן בְּכִי יֻתַּן.

הַמּוֹדֵד אֶת הַבּוֹר בֵּין לְעָמְקוֹ בֵּין לְרָחְבּוֹ, הֲרֵי זֶה בְּכִי יֻתַּן; דִּבְרֵי רַבִּי טַרְפוֹן. רַבִּי עֲקִיבָא אוֹמֵר: לְעָמְקוֹ – בְּכִי יֻתַּן, וּלְרָחְבּוֹ – אֵינוֹ בְּכִי יֻתַּן.

פָּשַׁט יָדוֹ, אוֹ רַגְלוֹ, אוֹ קָנֶה לַבּוֹר, לֵידַע אִם יֶשׁ בּוֹ מַיִם–אֵינָן

בְּכִי יֻתַּן; לֵידַע כַּמָּה מַיִם יֵשׁ בּוֹ, הֲרֵי זֶה בְּכִי יֻתַּן. זָרַק אֶת
הָאֶבֶן לַבּוֹר, לֵידַע אִם יֶשׁ בּוֹ מַיִם: הַנִּתָּזִין—אֵינָן בְּכִי יֻתַּן,
וְאֶת שֶׁבָּאֶבֶן – טְהוֹרִים.
הַחוֹבֵט עַל הַשֶּׁלַח: חוּץ לַמַּיִם – בְּכִי יֻתַּן; לְתוֹךְ הַמַּיִם –
אֵינָן בְּכִי יֻתַּן. רַבִּי יוֹסֵי אוֹמֵר: אַף לְתוֹךְ הַמַּיִם – בְּכִי יֻתַּן,
מִפְּנֵי שֶׁהוּא מִתְכַּוֵּן שֶׁיֵּצְאוּ עִם הַצּוֹאָה.
הַמַּיִם הָעוֹלִין בַּסְּפִינָה, וּבָעֵקֶל, וּבַמְּשׁוֹטוֹת – אֵינָן בְּכִי יֻתַּן.
בַּמְּצוֹדוֹת, וּבָרְשָׁתוֹת, וּבַמִּכְמָרוֹת – אֵינָן בְּכִי יֻתַּן. וְאִם
נִעֵר – בְּכִי יֻתַּן. הַמּוֹלִיךְ אֶת הַסְּפִינָה לַיָּם הַגָּדוֹל, לְצָרְפָהּ,
הַמּוֹצִיא מַסְמֵר לַגְּשָׁמִים, לְצָרְפוֹ, הַמַּנִּיחַ אֶת הָאוּד בַּגְּשָׁמִים,
לְכַבּוֹתוֹ – הֲרֵי זֶה בְּכִי יֻתַּן.
קַסְיָא שֶׁלַּשֻּׁלְחָנוֹת, וְהַשִּׁיפָא שֶׁלַּלְּבֵנִים – אֵינָן בְּכִי יֻתַּן. וְאִם
נִעֵר – בְּכִי יֻתַּן.
כָּל הַנִּצּוֹק – טָהוֹר, חוּץ מִדְּבַשׁ הַזִּיפִין, וְהַצַּפַּחַת. בֵּית שַׁמַּאי
אוֹמְרִים: אַף הַמִּקְפָּה שֶׁלַּגְּרִיסִין, וְשֶׁלַּפּוֹל, מִפְּנֵי שֶׁהִיא
סוֹלֶדֶת לְאַחֲרֶיהָ.
הַמְעָרֶה מֵחַם לְחַם, וּמִצּוֹנֵן לְצוֹנֵן, וּמֵחַם לְצוֹנֵן – טָהוֹר.
מִצּוֹנֵן לְחַם – טָמֵא. רַבִּי שִׁמְעוֹן אוֹמֵר: אַף הַמְעָרֶה מֵחַם
לְחַם, וְכֹחוֹ שֶׁלַּתַּחְתּוֹן יָפֶה מִשֶּׁלָּעֶלְיוֹן – טָמֵא.
הָאִשָּׁה שֶׁהָיוּ יָדֶיהָ טְהוֹרוֹת, וּמְגִיסָה בִּקְדֵרָה טְמֵאָה: אִם
הִזִּיעוּ יָדֶיהָ – טְמֵאוֹת. הָיוּ יָדֶיהָ טְמֵאוֹת, וּמְגִיסָה בִּקְדֵרָה
טְהוֹרָה: אִם הִזִּיעוּ יָדֶיהָ – הַקְּדֵרָה טְמֵאָה. רַבִּי יוֹסֵי אוֹמֵר:
אִם נָטְפוּ. הַשּׁוֹקֵל עֲנָבִים בְּכַף מֹאזְנַיִם – הַיַּיִן שֶׁבַּכַּף טָהוֹר,
עַד שֶׁיְּעָרֶה לְתוֹךְ הַכֶּלִי. הֲרֵי זֶה דוֹמֶה לְסַלֵּי זֵיתִים וַעֲנָבִים
כְּשֶׁהֵן מְנַטְּפִין.

The present chapter is in two parts, M. 5:1-8, which go over the
ground of Chapter 4, and M. 5:9-11, which raise an issue familiar
from M. Toh. 8:8-9 and have nothing to do with our tractate. The
important point in the former set is that liquid that is detached
with approval is capable of imparting susceptibility to uncleanness,

but that which is not essential or which is incidental to one's purpose is not. Accordingly, at M. 5:1, if one immerses in one river and then happens to pass through a second, the water of the former, which does impart susceptibility to uncleanness, is washed away or annulled by the water of the second, which one did not detach with approval (in Maimonides' terms) and which in no way is subject to wish or intention. Obviously, M. 5:1 adds, if someone pushed the man into the water after immersion in a river, the water of the second immersion washes away that of the first, and the water on the man now is not susceptible to uncleanness. M. 5:2 carries forward the matter of swimming, asking about water that splashes. That is incidental and is not detached with approval. If one splashes someone else, of course, the water splashed is able to impart susceptibility to uncleanness. M. 5:2 further refers to making a "bird" in the water, which, in line with M. Miq. 10:4, may be a bubble, or may be some sort of float or duck ("rubber duckie") (T. refers to a chicken in this context) used for assisting a swimmer or as a bubblepipe or some sort of a toy in the water. Water splashed by the bird or found outside it is incidental to the utilization of the bird and is not detached with approval.

M. 5:3 brings us back to familiar territory, namely, the disputes of the Houses, in particular M. 4:4-5. If rain-drippings fall onto fruit and one mixes the fruit together to dry it off more rapidly, Simeon says that the formerly dry fruit is now rendered susceptible to uncleanness, since liquid is put on it. Sages maintain that since the purpose is to hasten the evaporation of the water, the ultimate end is determinative. The water is incapable of imparting uncleanness to the formerly dry fruit, since the purpose is to cause it all to evaporate.

M. 5:4 again introduces a familiar issue, that of M. 4:1, explicitly imposed upon the interpretation of the matter by T. If one measures a cistern, whether its breadth or its depth, the water that comes up on the measuring rod is subject to the law, If water be put. This is Tarfon's view. So far as he is concerned, the purpose is fulfilled, the water detached with approval. 'Aqiba, like the Hillelites, imposes a strict construction of the law. If one dips the stick into the water to find the depth of the cistern, then he does detach the water of the cistern with approval. But if he measures the cistern breadthwise, he does not need to stick the measuring-rod into the water. Water that happens to come up on the stick therefore is not subject to the rule, If water be put. M. 5:5 goes over exactly this same rule, primarily from 'Aqiba's perspective, although Tarfon may certainly try to show that M. 5:5 is in conformity with his principle at M. 5:4.

M. 5:6-8 contain nothing new. If one beats on a pelt, and the pelt is outside of the water, his intent is certainly to dry the pelt. Therefore water that splashes out of the pelt, conforming as it does to his intent, is detached with approval. But if the pelt is beaten while it is in the water, then he has no hope of deliberately removing the water. What splashes out is not subject to the law, If water be put. Yosé differs. Even if one beats the pelt in the water, his intent is to clean the pelt. He wants the water to carry off the dirt, and therefore the water is detached with approval. At M. 5:7 we come to various parts of the ship and the status of water detached thereby. Water that comes up on the oars or bilge or on nets is not detached with approval. If then one shakes it off, in line with M. 4:2 and the Shammaites of M. 1:2-4, it is detached with approval. The use of rain-water is reintroduced in the same pericope. If one makes use of rain-water, e.g., to extinguish the fire of a brand or to refine molten nails, the water is subject to the law, If water be put. Water found on the covers of tables or bricks, M. 5:8, obviously is not wanted, unless shaken off.

The problem of M. 5:9-11 is the status of a column or a jet of water. Does uncleanness rise from the bottom of such a column to the top? If one pours liquid from a clean utensil into an unclean utensil, is the former made unclean by connection through the jet of liquid to the latter? No, it is not. (Exceptions to this rule involve thick and greasy liquids that tend to flow back upon the jet.) At M. 5:10 we have a further, interesting issue. What is the status of vapor or steam? If hot water is poured onto hot, cold onto cold, or hot onto cold, the former rule applies. That is, there no connection by means of the jet. But if cold water is poured into hot, then there is steam or vapor, and this does contaminate the upper source of the liquid. Simeon says that even when hot is pushed onto hot, if the lower water is hotter than the upper, the same effect applies. M. 5:11 then in part illustrates his position, with an interesting case. We have a woman with clean hands, stirring a pot whose contents are unclean. If the woman's hands perspired, they are unclean. That is, the unclean vapor affects the hands. Then, along the lines of Simeon's argument at M. 5:10, at M. 5:11E-H, we have perspiring hands, which are unclean. The pot is clean—but it is hot, thus, as Simeon says, hot and hot. If the woman's hands perspire, the pot is unclean. Yosé rejects this entire line of argument. In his view, we do not take account of the effects of steam or vapor. Only if the hands actually perspired and drops of sweat fall into the pot is the pot unclean. Since we have dealt with matters of interest specifically to M. Tohorot 8:8-9, we proceed, at the end, with attention to the rule of M. Toh. 9:1ff. Moisture of grapes or olives in a basket that will not retain moisture does not impart susceptibility to uncleanness. Why not? Because the liquid simply is not wanted but is left in a basket that will let it flow out onto the ground.

vii. Mishnah Makhshirin Chapter Six

פרק שישי

הַמַּעֲלֶה פֵרוֹתָיו לַגַּג מִפְּנֵי הַכְּנִימָה, וְיָרַד עֲלֵיהֶם טַל – אֵינָם בְּכִי יֻתַּן. אִם נִתְכַּוֵּן לְכָךְ, הֲרֵי זֶה בְּכִי יֻתַּן. הֶעֱלָן חֵרֵשׁ שׁוֹטֶה וְקָטָן, אַף עַל פִּי שֶׁחִשֵּׁב שֶׁיֵּרַד עֲלֵיהֶן הַטַּל – אֵינָן בְּכִי יֻתַּן; שֶׁיֵּשׁ לָהֶן מַעֲשֶׂה, וְאֵין לָהֶן מַחֲשָׁבָה.

הַמַּעֲלֶה אֶת הָאֲגֻדּוֹת, וְאֶת הַקְּצִיעוֹת, וְאֶת הַשּׁוּם לַגַּג, בִּשְׁבִיל שֶׁיַּמְתִּינוּ – אֵינָן בְּכִי יֻתַּן. כָּל הָאֲגֻדּוֹת שֶׁלְּבֵית הַשְּׁוָקִים – טְמֵאִין. רַבִּי יְהוּדָה מְטַהֵר בַּלַּחִים. אָמַר רַבִּי מֵאִיר: וְכִי מִפְּנֵי מַה טָמְאוּ? אֶלָּא מִפְּנֵי מַשְׁקֵה הַפֶּה! כָּל הַקְּמָחִין, וְהַסְּלָתוֹת שֶׁלְּבֵית הַשְּׁוָקִים – טְמֵאִים. הַחִילְקָה, הַטְּרָגִיס, וְהַטִּסְנִי – טְמֵאִים בְּכָל מָקוֹם.

כָּל הַבֵּיצִים בְּחֶזְקַת טַהֲרָה, חוּץ מִשֶּׁלְּמוֹכְרֵי מַשְׁקֶה. וְאִם הָיוּ מוֹכְרִין עִמָּהֶן פֵּרוֹת יְבֵשִׁים – טְהוֹרוֹת. כָּל הַדָּגִים בְּחֶזְקַת טֻמְאָה. רַבִּי יְהוּדָה אוֹמֵר: חֲתִיכַת אִילְתִית וְדָג הַמִּצְרִי הַבָּא בַקֻּפָּה, וְקוּלְיָס הָאִסְפָּנִין – הֲרֵי אֵלּוּ בְּחֶזְקַת טַהֲרָה. כָּל הַצִּיר בְּחֶזְקַת טֻמְאָה. וְעַל כֻּלָּם עַם הָאָרֶץ נֶאֱמָן לוֹמַר:

טְהוֹרִים הֵן, חוּץ מִשֶּׁלַּדָּגָה, מִפְּנֵי שֶׁהֵן מַפְקִידִין אוֹתָהּ אֵצֶל
עַם הָאָרֶץ. רַבִּי אֱלִיעֶזֶר בֶּן יַעֲקֹב אוֹמֵר: צִיר טָהוֹר שֶׁנָּפַל
לְתוֹכוֹ מַיִם כָּל שֶׁהֵז – טָמֵא.

שִׁבְעָה מַשְׁקִיז הֵן: הַטַּל, וְהַמַּיִם, הַיַּיִן, וְהַשֶּׁמֶז, וְהַדָּם, וְהֶחָלָב,
וּדְבַשׁ דְּבוֹרִים. דְּבַשׁ צְרָעִים – טָהוֹר, וּמֻתָּר בַּאֲכִילָה.

תּוֹלְדוֹת לַמַּיִם: הַיּוֹצְאִיז מִן הָעַיִז, מִן הָאֹזֶז, מִן הַחֹטֶם, מִן
הַפֶּה, מֵי רַגְלַיִם, בֵּיז גְּדוֹלִים בֵּיז קְטַנִּים, לְדַעְתּוֹ וְשֶׁלֹּא
לְדַעְתּוֹ. תּוֹלְדוֹת לַדָּם: דַּם שְׁחִיטָה בַּבְּהֵמָה וּבַחַיָּה וּבָעוֹפוֹת
הַטְּהוֹרִים, וְדַם הַקָּזָה לִשְׁתִיָּה. מֵי חָלָב – כֶּחָלָב, וְהַמֹּחַל –
כַּשֶּׁמֶז, שֶׁאֵיז הַמֹּחַל יוֹצֵא מִידֵי שֶׁמֶז; דִּבְרֵי רַבִּי שִׁמְעוֹז. רַבִּי
מֵאִיר אוֹמֵר: אַף עַל פִּי שֶׁאֵיז עִמּוֹ שֶׁמֶז. דַּם הַשֶּׁרֶץ – כִּבְשָׂרוֹ,
מְטַמֵּא, וְאֵינוֹ מַכְשִׁיר; וְאֵיז לָנוּ כַּיּוֹצֵא בוֹ.

אֵלּוּ מְטַמְּאִיז וּמַכְשִׁירִיז: זוֹבוֹ שֶׁלַּזָּב, וְרֻקּוֹ, וְשִׁכְבַת זַרְעוֹ,
וּמֵימֵי רַגְלָיו, וּרְבִיעִית מִז הַמֵּת, וְדַם הַנִּדָּה. רַבִּי אֱלִיעֶזֶר
אוֹמֵר: שִׁכְבַת זֶרַע אֵינָהּ מַכְשֶׁרֶת. רַבִּי אֶלְעָזָר בֶּז עֲזַרְיָה
אוֹמֵר: דַּם הַנִּדָּה אֵינוֹ מַכְשִׁיר. רַבִּי שִׁמְעוֹז אוֹמֵר: דַּם הַמֵּת
אֵינוֹ מַכְשִׁיר. וְאִם נָפַל עַל הַדַּלַּעַת – גּוֹרְדָהּ, וְהִיא טְהוֹרָה.
אֵלּוּ לֹא מְטַמְּאִיז וְלֹא מַכְשִׁירִיז: הַזֵּעָה, וְהַלֵּחָה סְרוּחָה,
וְהָרְאִי, וְהַדָּם הַיּוֹצֵא עִמָּהֶם, וּמַשְׁקֵה בֶּז שְׁמוֹנָה. רַבִּי יוֹסֵי
אוֹמֵר: חוּץ מִדָּמוֹ. וְהַשּׁוֹתֶה מֵי טְבֶרְיָה, אַף עַל פִּי שֶׁיּוֹצְאִיז
נְקִיִּים, דַּם שְׁחִיטָה בַּבְּהֵמָה וּבַחַיָּה וּבָעוֹפוֹת הַטְּמֵאִים, וְדַם
הַקָּזָה לִרְפוּאָה. רַבִּי אֶלְעָזָר מְטַמֵּא בָּאֵלּוּ. רַבִּי שִׁמְעוֹז בֶּז
אֶלְעָזָר אוֹמֵר: חֲלֵב הַזָּכָר – טָהוֹר.

חֲלֵב הָאִשָּׁה מְטַמֵּא לְרָצוֹז וְשֶׁלֹּא לְרָצוֹז, וַחֲלֵב הַבְּהֵמָה אֵינוֹ
מְטַמֵּא אֶלָּא לְרָצוֹז. אָמַר רַבִּי עֲקִיבָא: קַל וָחֹמֶר הַדְּבָרִים:
מָה אִם חֲלֵב הָאִשָּׁה שֶׁאֵינוֹ מְיֻחָד אֶלָּא לַקְּטַנִּים, מְטַמֵּא
לְרָצוֹז וְשֶׁלֹּא לְרָצוֹז, חֲלֵב הַבְּהֵמָה שֶׁהוּא מְיֻחָד לַקְּטַנִּים
וְלַגְּדוֹלִים, אֵינוֹ דִיז שֶׁיְּטַמֵּא לְרָצוֹז וְשֶׁלֹּא לְרָצוֹז? אָמְרוּ לוֹ:
לֹא, אִם טִמֵּא חֲלֵב הָאִשָּׁה שֶׁלֹּא לְרָצוֹז, שֶׁדַּם מַגְּפָתָהּ טָמֵא,
יְטַמֵּא חֲלֵב הַבְּהֵמָה שֶׁלֹּא לְרָצוֹז, שֶׁדַּם מַגְּפָתָהּ טָהוֹר? אָמַר

לָהֶם: מַחְמִיר אֲנִי בְּחָלָב מִבַּדָּם, שֶׁהַחוֹלֵב לִרְפוּאָה, טָמֵא,
וְהַמַּקִּיז לִרְפוּאָה, טָהוֹר. אָמְרוּ לוֹ: סַלֵּי זֵיתִים וַעֲנָבִים יוֹכִיחוּ,
שֶׁהַמַּשְׁקִים הַיּוֹצְאִין מֵהֶן לְרָצוֹן, טְמֵאִים, וְשֶׁלֹּא לְרָצוֹן,
טְהוֹרִים. אָמַר לָהֶן: לֹא, אִם אֲמַרְתֶּם בְּסַלֵּי זֵיתִים וַעֲנָבִים,
שֶׁתְּחִלָּתָן אֹכֶל וְסוֹפָן מַשְׁקֶה, תֹּאמְרוּ בְחָלָב שֶׁתְּחִלָּתוֹ וְסוֹפוֹ
מַשְׁקֶה? עַד כָּאן הָיְתָה תְשׁוּבָה. אָמַר רַבִּי שִׁמְעוֹן: מִכָּאן
וְאֵילָךְ הָיִינוּ מְשִׁיבִיו לְפָנָיו: מֵי גְשָׁמִים יוֹכִיחוּ, שֶׁתְּחִלָּתָן
וְסוֹפָן מַשְׁקֶה, וְאֵינָן מְטַמְּאִין אֶלָּא לְרָצוֹן. אָמַר לָנוּ: לֹא,
אִם אֲמַרְתֶּם בְּמֵי גְשָׁמִים שֶׁאֵין רֻבָּן לְאָדָם אֶלָּא לָאֲרָצוֹת
וְלָאִילָנוֹת, וְרֹב הֶחָלָב לָאָדָם.

The chapter is in three parts, each marked off from the others
by a dramatic shift in formulary pattern. M. 6:1-2A-C complete
the interests of the foregoing chapters and also carry forward their
pronounced preference for apocopation. The point is that if one
puts produce on the roof not intending it to be wet down, then
dew is not deemed to render the produce susceptible to uncleanness. The point is virtually identical to that, in connection with
dew, at M. 3:5, and the conclusion, on the capacity of those without ability to speak or to give testimony to effect an action but
not to impose their will, M. 6:1E-G, is verbatim at M. 3:8. The
repetition of the rule, M. 6:2A-C, poses no surprises.

The next unit, M. 6:2D-H, expresses in simple declarative sentences the rule on the presumed status of various sorts of food.
Vegetables situated in the market place are assumed to be unclean.
In this instance, it is generally taken for granted that *unclean*
means both *susceptible to uncleanness,* because of liquid put on
the vegetables to keep them fresh, and *actually unclean,* because
of the contaminating effects of *Zabs* and others who have drooled
on or touched the vegetables. The same sort of declarative sentences,
built on the fluent form, *All . . . in . . . are unclean/clean,*
recurs at M. 6:2D, G, H, and M. 6:3A, D, F, six in all. If the set
began as a single, highly disciplined unit of formally coherent statements, however, it has been broken up by many and diverse glosses
and interpolations.

M. 6:4-7, with a lovely autonomous appendix at M. 6:8, shift the formulary pattern again, now to a series of lists, with a remarkably complex formal history. M. 6:4 announces *There are seven liquids* [to which the law, If water be put, applies]. M. 6:5 takes up the items in the foregoing, giving subspecies of water and of blood, and some further augmentation to the original list. Whereas M. 6:5 seems to intend to develop M. 6:4 it ignores the order of items in M. 6:4, and the glosses are introduced in no clear order. M. 6:6A and M. 6:7A are clearly correlated:

> M. 6:6A: These impart uncleanness and impart suscepti-
> bility to uncleanness.
> M. 6:7A: these do not contract uncleanness *and do not
> impart susceptibility to uncleanness.*

The italicized words clearly do not augment the meaning of the sentence in which they occur, since liquid that cannot contract uncleanness also is not going to have the capacity to impart susceptibility to uncleanness. They therefore underline the intention of giving balanced lists. But the items in each, M. 6:6B-D and M. 6:7J-O, exhibit no contrapuntal or even conceptual relationship to one another. M. 6:7, moreover, turns out on closer examination to relate most clearly to M. 6:5. My guess is that the three lists begin in groups of four items, as specified above, pp. 83-84, and only later on were given both "appropriate" superscriptions, not to mention substantial interpolated materials.

M. 6:4 and M. 6:7 take for granted that blood of slaughtering of cattle, beasts, and fowl that are clean, and blood let out from the veins for drink, are subspecies of blood and impart susceptibility to uncleanness. Accepting that view, M. 6:5 declares that blood of slaughtering of cattle, beast, and fowl that are unclean and blood deriving from bloodletting are clean. M. 6:8 is located where it is because 'Aqiba takes these data for granted. His case is incomprehensible without them. But the case has nothing to do with the matter of which liquids impart or do not impart uncleanness or susceptibility to uncleanness. The issue is whether cow's milk imparts uncleanness whether or not it is detached with approval. The sages' anonymous rule, A, declares that woman's milk imparts uncleanness both with and without approval, but cow's milk imparts susceptibility only when detached with approval. 'Aqiba should say, "Even cow's milk: without approval." Instead he launches into a defense of that proposition. In the course of his argument, he alludes to the rules just now mentioned. But he cites them in an unexpected form, not as parts of a list, but in the *he who*-form: "He who draws milk for healing—it is unclean, and he who draws blood for healing—it is clean." Accordingly, the rules in our lists circulated in forms other than those before us. This is, furthermore, strongly suggested by the diverse formulary patterns applied at M. 6:5 in particular, some of which entirely ignore the established pattern, the list.

viii. Conclusion

When we laboriously worked our way through the tractate, pericope by pericope, we may have found it difficult to see the large, distinct groups of problems, focused on underlying conceptions or principles, carefully organized and distinctively shaped. Our survey of the sub-divisions of the tractate laid out by the copyists and early printers gives us a clear notion that the tractate indeed is topically organized. The framers take up a theme and dissect it along the lines dictated by the logic of that theme, fully exposing and exploring its generative problematic. They then pursue each of the segments of the problem in a fairly systematic and orderly way. That fact is now clear from our survey of what we have called "the groves." But, as I said earlier, it hardly pays to ask the medieval copyists to tell us what was in the mind of the tractate's framers, a thousand years earlier than the earliest manuscript evidence showing copyists' sub-divisions of the tractate. Accordingly, we have to find our own way back into the minds of the original framers of the tractate. This we shall now do by dissecting the tractate according to the internal evidence of conceptual or topical groupings, rather than the external evidence of chapters. To this point it is clear that there are such logical thematic groupings. What they are and how they may be discerned are the subjects of the next chapter.

Up to this point we are able to see that the Mishnah-tractate before us is not merely a collection of rules. It is not precisely a "law-code." For a law-code should organize the present laws. But that is not precisely what this tractate does—even though the tractate does do something like that (!). When we consider the long stretches of discourse on what is essentially a single theme, when we realize that we have numerous cases that make one point, we have to ask about that point. We go in search for the reasons people ask the questions they do about the topic under discussion—those questions, not some other questions.

What is it that defines the particular range or set of questions before us? What sets the exegetical agendum on susceptibility of wet wheat? It is, in fact, an underlying inquiry, a deeper problem that generates all of the concrete cases and that unites them into a single philosophical problem or proposition. But how do we find that "generative problematic"? The answer—in method and substance, the "how" and the "what"—is given in the next chapter, which explains the way we locate the road into the heart of the tractate. One thing is clear: The tractate is not simply a collection of facts about a topic. It is framed to turn facts into an essay. It is so shaped as to make a point (or a few simple points).

When earlier we reflected on the achievement of Mishnah's philosophers and framers, we noticed that their principal accomplishment is to make us want to know what they have to say to begin with, to allow us to enter into, even to participate, in their conversation. Thus far we have only come to the fringes of their discourse. We can make sense of the individual units of the tractate, and we can see how these units fit together into larger propositions or sustained accounts of an aspect of a problem. But where is the center, the heart? That is what we seek in the next chapter.

CHAPTER 6

From Groves to Forest: Discerning the Topical Structure of a Tractate

i. Introduction

Mishnah expresses its ideas in tiny pieces, case by case, problem by problem. Yet, as already is clear, the tractate before us also works on a particular topic and is not merely a mass of facts—discrete ideas and rules about diverse matters. Furthermore, the topic is treated systematically and in an orderly way. The tractate is organized around the requirements of the logical exposition of the stated theme. That much is proved by the character of the chapters that we have just reviewed. Now let us ask whether Mishnah has a particular *interest* in the topic under discussion—a set of recurring questions, problems, considerations—and, if so, how we may locate and define what that unifying interest is.

The topic by itself, after all, is a simple one, namely, the effect of liquids on dry foodstuffs. The main point may be stated briefly or at length. But it remains a single point, that what is dry is insusceptible to uncleanness, and what has been made wet is susceptible. It obviously is possible to illustrate that simple fact any number of times. But these illustrations, in the end, will say no more than a simple statement of the fact expresses. Now it is quite clear that our tractate wishes to say much more than a single fact, repeated many times in a multitude of variations. Even our simple review of the chapters indicates that the tractate takes up a sequence of problems and exposes its ideas on a number of successive topics.

When we have analyzed the topics among which the chapters are divided and discerned the reasons for the sequence in which we take up these subjects, we shall have a much clearer grasp of the tractate as a whole. At that point, we shall want to find out whether the tractate addresses itself to a topic, or whether, in connection with that topic, it wishes to ask a very specific *question.* As I already have stressed, the framers of the tractate may carry their topic in any number of directions. If they choose for sustained analysis one among many possible aspects of their theme, then that choice should precipitate inquiry on our part: Why have the sages of this tractate chosen this special aspect of the topic? What is it that they find particularly interesting or engaging in that aspect? When we are able to answer these questions, we may then make some sense of how the framers of the tractate came to ask the questions they did. We shall discover what generates and precipitates this range of problems laid forth for analysis and solution—this range, and not some other. The principle of selection and exegesis is the besought insight.

What expresses the present range of questions is the phrase "generative problematic." This phrase refers to the aspect of a topic that the thinkers behind the tractate find difficult and a source of troubled reflection, the "problematic." This "problematic" stands behind and provokes the kinds of questions encapsulated in the specific exercises of a tractate (or, in the central and critical exercises thereof), that is, that problem which generates the intellectual character of the tractate and the agendum expressed within the tractate. This search for a tractate's generative problematic, when successful, yields the possibility of stating precisely that matter about which the tractate wishes to express an opinion, simply, "what the tractate is about."

When we uncover the generative problematic of a tractate, we can make sense of why the tractate unfolds in the way it does and not some other. We accomplish the final act of exegesis that lays the tractate open for an entirely different set of exercises, historical ones. For, to state matters negatively, until we make sense of the parts and the whole, we cannot explain what is in our hands and how it works. We thus have no way to make use of the tractate as a cultural document, as an artifact of mind and society. All we have is a set of facts about the tractate or facts stated by the tractate. The former do not say anything beyond themselves—and who wants to hear about whether water on a rope imparts susceptibility to cultic uncleanness to some dry barley nearby! The latter do not tell us much if anything about the world in which the tractate took shape, let alone the judgment on that world expressed through the framing of the tractate. So what is now at hand is building that necessary bridge between the exegesis of the parts of the document, accomplished in parts I and III (Chapter V), and the exegesis of the document as a whole, begun here.

The way in which to accomplish that exegesis is to compose an outline of the tractate and, through the organizing medium of such an outline, to look for the chief interests of the tractate. Once we see the natural lines of division within the tractate, we further ask how the several themes or topics are put together, in what order, according to what logical scheme. Finally, we shall reflect on these facts, to come to a statement of the tractate's generative problematic. If we are able to discern a set of recurrent concerns and deeply imbedded logical tensions, stating them expresses that precipitating question. If we find out why the tractate's framers ask the questions before us, engage in the exercise laid out here, we shall find ourselves at the tractate's deepest layers of meaning. From there, the only way is outward, beyond the tractate's limits, toward that social and material world to which the tractate, in the second century, addressed its statements of meaning. It is that world which so captured the imagination of the framers and philosophers of the tractate as to raise those questions answered in a compelling way in this sequence of exercises.

For this last go-around, covering the tractate as a whole, I reproduce Makhshirin as it is given in the Kaufmann manuscript (pp. 549-55). This manuscript is universally regarded as the best available; it is complete for Mishnah. Since most of the better manuscript-evidences for Mishnah now have been reproduced and are in libraries throughout the English-speaking world, students should acquire the habit of checking manuscripts against the printed versions of Mishnah, however excellent these may be (as in the case of Albeck-Yalon). The extant manuscript evidence is essential and now accessible. A small exercise in the problems of variant readings, in connection with M. Makhshirin 1:2-4, already has indicated something of what is to be expected and of why this is important (and also, unimportant).

וסליק מסכת
נדה

מכשירין פירק א

כל משקה שתחילתו לרצון אף על
פי שאין סופו לרצון או שסופו לרצון
אף על פי שאין תחילתו לרצון הרי זה
בכי יותן משקין טמאין מטמאין לרצון
ושלא לרצון ב המעמיד את
האילן הישיר ממנו אלין אור את
הטומאה אינן בכי יותן הישיר ממנה
מישקין בית שמיי אומ הייצאין ואת
שבו בכי יותן בית הלל אומ היוצאין
בכי יותן ראות שבו אינן בכי יותן מפני
שהוא מיתכוין שייצאו מכולו ג
המעמיד על האילן ונפל על חבירין
אוסוכהו ונפלה על חבירה ותחומדין
ורמין או ירקות מחוברין לקרקע
בית שמיי אומ בכי יותן בית הלל אומ
אינן בכי יותן אמר ר׳ יהושע משם
אבה יוסה חליקופרי איש טיבעון
תמה עצמך אם יש משקה טמא
בתורה עד שיתכוין ויתן שני וכי
יתן מים על זרע ונפל מכל ד
הנוער אגודה שלירק וירדו מעד
העליון לתחתון בית שמיי אומ בכי יותן
ובית הלל אומ אינן בכי יותן אמר בית
הלל לבית שמיי והרי הנוער את הקלח
חוששין אנו שמא ויצאומין מעלה
לעלה אמרו להס בית שמיי שהקלח

אמר רבן גמליה לחכמים הרבה אמרו להם
בית הלל הרי המעלה סך כלאפירות
ועמדו על גב הנהר חושטין אנו שמא
ירדן מלעד העליון לתחתון אלא אם
הלכה שמים ועמדו זה על גל זה והתחתון
פב יתך ר׳ יוסה אומ חמיאנין טהורי
ה המעמיד את הברי שה והסוחט
שערו בבסמטר ר יוסה אומ הידעאן
בל״ין ואת שבו אין בל״ין מפני
שהוא מתכוין שיראו ומבל׳ ו
הנופה בעדשין לבודהן אספחתהן
ר שמעון אומ אינם בל״ין וחב אומ
בל״יתן האוכל שמשמין באיצבעי ם
משיקין שעליידי ן ר שמעון
אם אינם בל״ין וחב׳ אומ בל״יתן
הטומק פירותיו במים מפני הגנבים
אינו בל״ין מעשה באנשי ירושלה
שטמינו את דבילתן במים מפני הסיקרין
וטיהרו לחן חכמ הנותן את פירותיו
לשיבולת הנהר להביאן עימו אינן בל׳
יתן פ ב הל ו
וישעת בעים בורות שיחזן ומערות
טהורה וריעת אלם טהורה שוהמים
טמאים והרוע ויעתו טהורה פא
במים שאובין והזרע ויעתו טמאה
ניסתפג ואחר כך הזרע ויעתו טהורה
ר מרחיץ טולאה ריעתו טמאה
וכרוזויה בל׳ יתן הברידלז שכלבית
ובית מדרע מדוש תמה ואם טמאה ריעת

כל הבית שֶׁמְּרֻסָּה הַפְּרִיסָּה וּמְשָׂוֹד
ג. שְׁנֵי בְרֵיכוֹת אַחַת טְוֹמְאָה וְאַחַת
טְהוֹרָה הַמֵּדִיעַ קָרֹב לַטּוֹמְאָה טְמֵא
קָרֹב לַטּוֹב פָּרָה טָהוֹר מֶחֱיָה לְשׁוּמָּן
טְמֵא מֶחֱרְל טָמֵא שֶׁבֵּלֹּו יַשׁ בָּרֹךְ לַטָּהוֹר
אֹרֹב מִן הַטָּהוֹר טָהוֹר מֶחֱיָה הַלְמֶחֱיָה
טְמֵא וּבַּמְרִיוֹת שֶׁרֹשְׂרָאֵל וַעֲלִיס מְטּוֹלִים

לְתוֹכָן אֹם רֹב מִן הַטָּהוֹר טָהוֹר מֶחֱיָה
לְמֶחֱיָה מִי שֶׁפָּכוֹת שֶׁיֵּרְדוּ עֲלֵיהֶן מֵי
גֶשָׁמִים אֹם רֹב מִן הַטָּמֵא טָמֵא וְאֹם
רֹב מִן הַטָּהוֹר טָהוֹר מֶחֱיָה הַלְמֶחֱיָה
טְמֵא אֹמַּתֵי בִזְּמַן שֶׁקָּדְמוּ מֵי שְׁפִּיכוֹת
אֲבָל אָם קָדְמוּ מֵי גֶשָׁמִים אֲפִילוּ כָּל שֶׁהֵן
מִי שְׁפִיכוֹת טָמֵא   ד. הַטּוֹעַן אֶת
גַּגּוֹ וְחַד מְכַבֵּס אֶת כְּסוּתוֹ וְיָרְדוּ עֲלֵיהֶן
גֶשָׁמִים אֹם רֹב מִן הַטָּמֵא טָמֵא וְאֹם
רֹב מִן הַטָּהוֹר טָהוֹר מֶחֱיָה הַלְמֶחֱיָה
טְמֵא מִי יְהוּדָה אֹמֵר אֹם אֹם זֶה סָפֵק לְמַעַט
ה. עֵיר שֶׁרֹשְׂרָאֵל וְגוֹיִם דָּרִיס בְּתוֹכָהּ
וְהָיְתָה בָּהּ מִרְחֵץ מִרְחֵצֵת בְּשַׁבַּת אֹם
רֹב גּוֹיִס רוֹחֵץ בָּהּ מִיָּד אֹם רֹב יִשְׂרָאֵל
יַמְתִּין כְּדֵי שֶׁיֵּחַמּוּ מֶחֱיָה לְמֶחֱיָה
יַמְתִּין כְּדֵי פָּט וְיֵחַמּוּ הַחַמִּיס לִ יְהוּדָה
אֹם בָּאַמְּבַטִי קְטַנָּה אֹם יַשׁ בָּהּ רָשׁוּת
רוֹחֵץ מִיָּד   ו. מָצָא בָּהּ יָרֶק נִמְכָּר

אֹס רֹב גּוֹיִס לוֹקֵחַ מִיָּד אֹם לְשֶׁרֹ יַמְתִּין
כְּדֵי שֶׁיָּבֹא מִמָּקוֹם קָרֹב מֶחֱיָה לְשׁוּמָּה
יַמְתִּין כְּדֵי שֶׁיָּבֹא מִמָּקוֹם קָרֹב קַרֹבָּאם
וְאֹם בְּשַׁרֵשֶׁת לוֹקֵחַ מִיָּד ז. מָצָא בָּהּ

תינוק מוטל אם רוב נכרים פי אם רוב
ישראל ישראל מחצה למחצה ישראל
ריהודה או הלכים אחר רוב המשליכים
ח מצא בה מציעה האם רוב נכרים אינו
צריך להכריז מחצה למחצה צריך
להכריז מצאנה פת הולכין אחר רוב
העכו"ם ואם היתה פת עיפה הולכין
אחר רוב או כלי פת עיסה אחר יהודה
או אם היתה פת קבר הולכין אחר
רוב או כלי פת קברי ט מצא בה
בשר הולכין אחר רוב הטבחין אם
היו מבשל הולכין אחר רוב או כלי בשר
י המוציא פירות בדרך אם רובם
מבנסים לבתיהם פטור למכור בשוק
חייב מחצה למחצה דמיי אוצר מירש
ולקח מטולים לוכו אם רוב נכרים ודאי
אם רוב ישראל דמיי מחצה למחצה
ורב דייבר מאיר וחבם צמא אפילו כלו
מירש שראל אשר מטיל לוכו דמיי
לא פירות שניה שרבכי על השביעית
ושל שלישית על רביעית שלחמישית
על של שישית שלשישית על של שביעית
ושל שביעית על שלמוצאי שביעית
הולכין אחר רוב מחצה למחצה להזה
להחמיר פר ג הל יא
שוק שהוא כלא פירות ומקם צל גגת העמר
או עלפי חבד או על מעלית המערה
רש אומ כל פשאט בביתך יהדו
אומ בכל כל שהוא כנגד המיס בליבן

ושאינו כנגד המים אינן כלי יין ב

חבית שהוא מליאה פירות ונתונה

לתוך המשקין או מליאה משקין

ונתונה לתוך הפירות ושאבו כל שישראל

כלי יין טמאו משקין אמרו במים

ובין בחומץ ושאר כל המשקין טהורין

ר נחמיה מטהר בקיטונית שאון הקיאומת

שואבת ג ר יהודה פת חמה ותנה

על פי חבית של יין ר מאיר מטמא ר

יהודה מטהר ר יוסה מטהר בשל חיטין

מטמא בשל שעורין מפני שהשעורין

שואבד ר המרבץ את ביתו וטבמו

חיטיה וטננו אם מחמת מים כלי יין

אם מחמת הסלע אינן כלי יין המכבס

את כסותו בעריבה ותנן בה חיטיס

וטננו אם מחמת מים כלי יין אם

מחמת עצמה אינן כלי יין המטון

בחול חדי זה כלי יין מעשה באנשי

המחוז שהיו מטינין בחול אמרו להן

חכמים אם כך הייתם עושים לא עשיתם

טהרה מימיכם ה המטין בטיט

ונגבו שמען או אם רשבו משקה

טולפח כלי יין ואם לאו אינן כלי יין

המרבץ את גרנו אינו חושש שמא

מן בחיטים וטננו ו המלקט

עשבים כשהטל עליהן להטון בהן

חישיר אינן כלי יין אם נתבווץ לכן

הריבבי יטן המוליך וחיטיך לאוזן

חידרו עליהם כתומים אם שמ כלי יין

ר יהודה אומ אפשר שלא לשמוד
אלא אם עמד היו ויתיר מתומ בבגל
וירדו עליהם גשמים אם שמח בבי
יתן ר יהודה אומ איפשר שלא לשמוח
אלא אם פקק את העינור או אכ חלח
לתוכן ו ההמרים שהיו עוברים
בנהר ונפלו עיקריהם למים אם שמח
בכי יתן ר יהודה אומ אי אפשר שלא
לשמוח אלא אם הפכו היו רגליו
מליאות טיט וכן רגליבה מיתון ועבר
במגרר אם שמח בכי יתן ר יהודה אם
איפשר שלא לשמוח אלא אם עמד
והדיח באדם ובבהמה טמאה לעולם
טמא ח המוריד את הגלבין
ואת כלי הבקר בשעת הקדים למים
בשביל שיחוזכו והדי והבכי יתן
זו הורד בהמה לשתות המים העו
העורים בפיה בכי יתן וכבגליה אינן
בכי יתן אם חשב שיר וחזר רגליה
את העולין בגליה בכי יתן ובשעת
היחח והדיניש לעולל טמא הוריה
חרש שוטה וקטן אף על פי שחשב
שירוחזו רגליה אינן בכי יתן שיש
להן מעשה ואין להן מחשבה
פר ד ה ז ח
השוחח לשתות המים העולים בפיו
ובשפמו בכי יתן בחורמו וברא אשד
ובקנו אינן בכי יתן המלא בחבית
המים העולים אחריה ובחבל שהוא

מכנן על עראה ובהל שהוא לעימה
הריוה בלי יתן ולמה הוא עימוה
ר שמעון בן אלעזר או טפח ותנה
תחת הציעור איוה בלי יתן ב
מי שירד עליו וגשמים אפילו אב
העומאוה אינן בלי יתן ואס נער
בלי יתן עומומוחה היצימר להקר
או ליד וח בטמא טמאין ובטהור
בלי יתן ג ולכופה הערה לתיתל
בשליל שותרימח הרי זה הבלי יתן אם
בשליל שלא ילקה הכותב אינן בלי
יתן ד ולבית שיריד מדלף ולוזה
בית שמיר אומ ושבר לבית הלל אומ
יעמוה מודין שהוא מושיט ידו ומטל
פירות מתוכה והן מרהורין ה
ערוכה שירד מדלא ולתוכה הנותנין
והעפין אינן בלי יתן ועלה לטופס
בית שמיר אומ בלי יתן לבית הלל אומ
אינן בלי יתן ו ורמיחה שירד
הדלא לתוכה הנותנין והעפין בית
שמיר אומ בלי יתן לבית הלל אומ אינן
בלי יתן נטלה לטופכד אילו ואילו
מודים שהן בלי יתן ו המטביל
את הכלי והמלבס את מסומו במעיה
המיים העולים בידיו בלי יתן ומבלי
אינן בלי יתן ר אלעזר אום אפשר
לו שירד אלא אם כן נישטופו רגליו
אות העולים ברגליו בלי יתן ח
קופה שהוא מלאה תרמוסין ומעוה

לתוך המים מטשוטטידן ומטלתטורמוסין
מתוכה והן טהורין הרטב מן המים
העוגמיס בקופה טמאין ושאר כל הט
המשרמסין טהורין יגרו שהטמיה כל
פירה מריותה נהא וטהור הל טו כל
שהוא מן המיס טמא . ט פירות
טעפלו לתוך אמת המיס ופשט מי
שהיו ידיו טמאות ופטלן ידיו טהורות
והפירות טהורין אם חשב שידוחו
ידיו טהורות והפירות הם בכי יתן
יי הרירה שהיראו מלאהד מיס ומתמה
לתוך המחרה ופשט טל הכתומצאה אות
חרולתוכה טמאה מפגן טמאות טהורה
ושאר כל המשוקין טמאה שאין המיס
מטהרין אות שטר המשקין יא
המלא בקילון עד שלשה ימיס טמאין
רעקיקה אומ אם נגבו מיד טהורין אם
לא נגבו אפילו עד שלושיס יום טמאין
יב ימיס שנטפלו עליהן משקין וירדו
עליהן גשמים אם רבו טהורין הרימאן
שירד מליהן גשמיס את עלפי שרבו
טמאין כלעו משקה טמאין את עלפי
שהרימאן שירדה עליהן גשמיס טהורים
ולאיסיקם אלא בדריס טהורות מלבד
ר שמעון אימ אם הירלחים וחסיקן
רבו משקין הירימאן מהן על המשקיס
שבלע טהורין פרה יל יב
מי שטבלבנהר והרה לפניו נהר אוהר
ועמר בו וחוזרו שנייה את הירא שומיה

רידיו וחביר ולשוכרו וכן לבהמיו עיקר
טונים את הראשונים אם כמשוייק
עממו חרי זה בכי יען ב׳ השט על פני
המיס הנמתין איוכן איטן בכי יען ואם
מתכוין להיד על חביר הרי זה בכי יען
העושה צפור במיס הנוחין ארת
שנה אינכו בכי יען ג׳ פירות שמיד
הדלת להוכן ובלן שי יגבו ר איוכ איטן
בכי יען ד׳ המורד את הבור בין
לעמיד בין לרחבו הרי זה בכי יען דל
רטירפון ר׳ עקיבה אומ ל עומיקו בכי יען
לרחבו איטן בכי יען ה׳ פטו רזאו
רגלו או קנה לבור לידע אס ישבו מיס
אינן בכי יען לידע מקה מיס יש בו
הרי זה בכי יען ורק את האבן לבור
לידע אס יש בו מיס הנוחין איטן
בכי יען ראת שבאבן חזירין ו׳
הווכט על השלחורו למים בכי יען
וכתוך המים איטן בכי יען ר יוסה אומ
את בתוך המים בכי יען מפני שהוא
מתכוין שי רצאו עם המאה ז׳ המים
העולים בספינה ובעוק ובמשוטות
אינן בכי יען במצמורת וברשתורת
ובמכמורת איטן בכי יען אם נער בכי
יען המוליך את הספינה ליס הנדול

לימרפה המוציא מסמיר בבשמיס
ליערפו המעיזו את הקראור בבשמיס
לכבותן הרי זה כמיין ח קסייה
שלשל הזנות וכן שיפה של לימיס
אימ בב יתן ואם מעל בלי יתן ט
כל הנעמק עוהור חורץ מדב שלפוס
ותפחת הרביב בית שמד אומ אח מיקפה
שלבריסה שלפול לפני שהיא סולח
לאחריס ל המקטן מיהס לימס
ומעיכל למן מיהם ליען צהור
ומעונן לחם טמאר שימעון אומ
אח המקערה מיחכ לחס וכוחזו של
תחתו גיפה משל עליון טמאו יא
האשה שהיא ירדין טהורות מעשה
בקדירה טמאה אם הדיעו ידין ט
טמאות וגועסה בקדירה טהורה
אם הדיעו ידין בקדירה טמא הר
יוסה צום אם נתפו שול על עדביס
בבת מאוניה המן שהבת עהור
ינד שיעערה לתוך הכלי הרי זה דומה
לכלי וחיתיס ועודביס טהן מעשפיס
פר ו הל יא
ומעלה פירוקין לגג מפני הכמשה
מרד עליהן טל אימ בלי יתן ואם
מתכמן לכן הרי ואם בלי יתן הגל

חרש שוטה וקטן אעפ״י שהחשב
שיעד עליהן צריך אין בדבריהן שיעשה
מעשה ואין להן מחשבה במעילה
אתה אומ׳ צרות אתם עצרים ואת הפ׳...
לענג בשביל שיעמדי׳ מאין בריהן דל
ואם צרות שלבית המחוריא נאמין ל...
והנה זה מצחר בעוים צמראית וכ...
מפני מה טימם אלא מפני משקה
הפה כלהן שהיה והפצולות שלבליתא
השווקין טמאין הני שהם שרונים
והטרסקני עמאין ובל מיזם ב... כל
הבצים בחזקת טהרה חוץ משהמכ...
משקה אם היו מוליכי׳ עמהן פירות
ובשים סחורות להדבו וחזרו...
ומשאו ר יהודא צמראל...ל אחלות
ורב המערי הפא לקפ ה קלן ...ס...
ראסספן חרי איל בזו ושל סחור...
ולה הצר בזחקת סמיא ובלכ... שיס
האיר בעיכן לב טהר...ן הזרים ק...
הבה מפני שיפקרי דין אושתאל שם
הארץ ר אליעו כן וכב ...ר ...
שנפל לתוכו ים כלשק טמא ...
שלבעה משקין הן הטל והעים והשמן
והדם היהלב יקבש ...ל מיר ...ר צויח...
צהור וימומר באלישד ד תולדות
לפים ..צא מהחצן מן האוזן ובע...
החוטס מן הפה מירדליס בן בלוה
בין קטנים לדעמו ושל ולדמו ...ל..ה
לדם דם שחוטה ד..... וב.מ..ה

וכעולם נחמדיך יותר הרבה הדא לשלימיה
מיי אהלב בפול הממיל בשהן גסראין
מוכללבאהרחיצין רבי שמעון ר
מאיד אומר של פרסאין בו שמן יהב
הטרין כל שירו מטמאין רצוע מכשיר
ואין חושרין ראב כן ר אילו מטמעין
גמכשירין חבו שלוב נרוקן רטובת
זרעו ומי מי רצפו רדליעית מן דמת
ודב הממור ר אלימר אם שבת ורע
אימה מכשרת ר אלימר בן עזריה דו
דס הממור שמירות אם וסהמת איני
מכשיר ראס מפיך רצות מדה והיא
טהורה א אילו מטמין ולא מכשירין
הריצ וחלחו סרוחה והראי ודם
היולדא עיימן עישהו טמאה ר
וכסה צומ חורי מערמו תטיחודמי
עבירמיה אפצ פי רנאין נקיים ח
צב שוורצה בבהנה בוזהול עופות
הטראין רבהקו לפואה ר לעוד אר
מטמא באלי שמימן בן אלעוד אמ
חלב הבכ טהודי ט חלב הא שה
מעמאלרמון ולא לרמון וחלב תעמים
אימימעמא אלא לריטן צמך עינצה
קל וחומר הדבריץ מהאב ולב האשה
טאים מימחד אלא לקטמיס מטמא
לרמן ולא למין ולב הבהמה שהוא
מיחוד לקטרס ולגדוליס איני ריך
שימעמא להמן ושלא לרמן אמירלו
לאטופעא וחלב האשה שלא לרמן
שירה מגבפתה עמא ועמא וחלב הבהמה
בטהרה שלא לרמין שרה מגבפתה

Let us now turn to the outline of the tractate, so that, by describing and briefly stating the sequence of topics and principles, by induction we may uncover and then explain the ultimate redactor's conception of the appropriate organization of the tractate as a whole. In the present outline, our principal interest is in the major conceptual units within which the tractate takes shape. The internal organization of the intermediate units is not subject to discussion, because we have covered that topic in the preceding chapter.

I. *Intention: Divisible or Indivisible* 1:1-6

1:1 A-C: Liquid wanted at outset but not at the end or *vice versa* is under the law, If water be put.

1:1D: Unclean liquids impart uncleanness whether or not wanted.

1:2-4: He who shakes tree to bring down fruit—it [water that falls] is not under the law, If water be put. If he shakes tree to bring down liquids, what falls and what remains in tree are under the law, If water be put, so the House of Shammai. House of Hillel: Those that fall are under the law, If water be put. Those in tree are not, because he intends that all the water fall. + Two further disputes, debate. M. 1:3M Joshua in the name of Abba Yosé Holi Qofri of Tibe'on: Be surprised if liquid is unclean before a person intends to apply it.

1:5: He who rubs leek—Yosé: Those that exude are under the law, If water be put, and those that remain are not, because he intends that all the water fall.

1:6A-C: He who blows on lentils . . . , Simeon: They [drops of moisture in breath] are not under the law, If water be put. Sages: They are. D-G: Rerun: He who eats sesame with [wet] finger—liquids that are on the hand + Simeon, sages.

1:6H-L: He who hides fruit in water because of thieves—they are not under the law, If water be put. + Ma'aseh—Water applied under constraint is not applied intentionally.

II. *Liquids Capable of Imparting Susceptibility and How They Do So. 2:1-5:11*

A. *Liquids capable of imparting susceptibility to uncleanness mixed with liquids not capable of doing so. 2:1-11*

2:1A-B (+ C-E): Sweat of houses, etc., is clean. Sweat of man is unclean.

2:2: [If water of] bath-house is unclean, its sweat is unclean, and *vice versa*. Pool in house—water sweats on its account—if pool is unclean, sweat of whole house if unclean, and *vice versa*.

2:3A-D: Two pools, one clean, one unclean—wall nearer unclean is unclean, nearer clean, clean. Half and half—unclean.

—The whole set, 2:1A, 2:2-2:3D, is aimed at the final rule. The antecedent units simply supply the facts that permit the conclusion, *half and half.*

2:3E-T, 2:4-11: Thirteen more constructions along the same lines, in the same form. None relevant to Makhshirin.

B. *The role of intention. (I) Determining whether or not water imparts susceptibility to uncleanness.* 3:1-3

3:1: Sack of fruit by river—all fruit [that absorbs water] is under the law, If water be put. Judah: Whatever is over against water is under the law, etc. And what is not over against water is not. [Judah: Deed indicates prior intention.]

3.2: Jar full of fruit, set in liquids—fruit absorbed water— whatever is absorbed is under law, If water be put.

3:3: He who took hot bread and put it over wine-jar—Meir: Susceptible. Judah: Insusceptible. Yosé: Clean if bread is wheat (which does not absorb) and unclean if it is barley (which does).

C. *The role of intention. (II): Water used for one purpose— status as to a secondary purpose* 3:4-5:8

3:4: He who sprinkles a house [to wet down dust on the floor] and afterward put wheat into it and wheat grew damp—if it is on account of the water, it is subject to the law, If water be put, and if because of [the wheat of] the floor, it is not. + Further exemplification.

—Water used for one purpose *can* impart susceptibility in connection with a second *unrelated* purpose.

3:5A-F: He who dampens wheat with dry clay—Simeon: If there is dripping moisture, it is under the law, etc., and if not, it is not under the law, If water be put.

—It is not the man's intention to wet down the wheat.

3:5G-I, 3:6, 3:7: He who brings grain to the mill and (en route) rain fell on it—if he was happy, it is under the law, If water be put. Judah: He cannot avoid being happy. But if he stood still, it is under the law, etc. + Further examples.

—Deed defines intention or prior attitude.

3:8: He who wets wagon wheels etc. to swell out cracks—it is under the law, If water be put. He who brings ox to drink—water on mouth is under the law, etc., and water on hooves is not under the law, etc.

4:1: He who kneels down to drink—water on mouth is subject to law, etc., and water on nose and hair is not. He who draws water with a jug—water on outer parts is under the law, etc. And water on rope not needed in using jug is not.

4:2: He on whom rain fell—it is not under law, If water be put. And if he shook off rain, it is under the law, If water be put.

—Water is where it is with his approval.

4:3: He who puts a dish on end against the wall to rinse it off—it is under the law, If water be put. If he did so to protect the wall, it is not.

4:4-5/0: Jug into which water dripped from the roof—House of Shammai: It is broken. House of Hillel: It is emptied out. (Three disputes).

—The point is that if the man disposes of the water, in the Shammaites' view, he did not object to its original location. In the Hillelites' conception, his ultimate disposition of the water indicates he never wanted it (= Judah, Yosé b. R. Judah).

4:5P-S: He who dunks utensil—water on hands is under law, If water be put. Water on feet is not.

4:6: Basket of lupines in pool—one takes out fruit and it is insusceptible (= M. 4:4's agreement), etc.

4:7: Fruit in stream—one with unclean hands takes it out—hands are clean, fruit is insusceptible. If he intended to wash hands, hands are clean, but fruit is susceptible.

4:8: Clay dish full of water, placed in pool—Father of uncleanness put hand into dish['s airspace] —it is unclean, etc.

4:9: He who draws water with a swape-pipe—up to three days, water left therein imparts susceptibility. 'Aqiba: If dried out, it is insusceptible forthwith, and if not, it imparts susceptibility for a whole month.

—As with Judah, deed is determinative.

4:10: Pieces of wood on which liquid and rain fell—if rain was more than liquid, wood is insusceptible, etc.

5:1: He who immersed in a river and there was another before him, which he crossed—the water of the second purifies the first, etc.

5:2: He who swam in the water—water that splashed is not under the law, If water be put. If he did so intentionally, it is under the law, If water be put.

5:3: Pieces of fruit wet by water from roof—if one mixed wet with dry fruit [to accelerate evaporation] —Simeon: It is under the law, If water be put. Sages: It is not.

5:4: He who measures cistern, whether for depth or breadth—water on rod is under the law, If water be put, so Tarfon. 'Aqiba: Breadth—not depth—is.

5:5: [If] one stuck hand etc. into cistern to know whether there is water in it—water on hand is not under the law, If water be put. If he did so to find out how much water is in it, it is, etc.

5:6: He who beat pelt—outside the water—what splashes is subject to law, If water be put. If he beat the pelt inside the water, it is not. *Versus* Yosé.

5:7: Water that comes up on hull on ship, etc., on snares, etc., is not subject to law, If water be put. If he shook them, it is.

5:8: Covering for tables, etc.,—water on it is not under the law, If water be put. If he shook it, it is.

D. Appendix: *Stream as Connector* 5:9-11I

5:9: Any unbroken stream is clean, except thick honey.

5:10: He who empties hot [clean water] into hot [unclean], cold into cold, hot into cold—it is clean. Cold into hot—unclean. Simeon: Also hot into hot.

5:11A-I: Woman whose hands were clean, stirred pot—if hands sweated, they are unclean, etc. Yosé: Only if they dripped.

III. *Liquids* Not *Capable of Imparting Susceptibility. Liquids Not Used Intentionally Are Insusceptible* 5:11J-M, 6:1-3

5:11J-M: He who weighs grapes in a cup of a balance—wine in cup (left after weighing) is clean.

6:1: He who brings fruit to roof because of maggots, and dew fell on them—it is not under the law, If water be put. If he intended dew to wet them, they are.

6:2: He who brings bundles of vegetables, etc.—as above.

6:3: Eggs (in market) are assumed to be clean, except those of liquid-sellers, etc.

IV. *Liquids Defined: Those That Impart Susceptibility to Uncleanness* 6:4-8

6:4: Seven liquids impart susceptibility.

6:5: Development of foregoing.

6:6: These impart uncleanness and susceptibility to uncleanness.

6:7: These do not impart uncleanness or susceptibility to uncleanness.

6:8: Milk of woman imparts uncleanness whether or not with approval, and cow's milk only with approval. Said R. 'Aqiba + debate.

There is a clear sequence of themes or ideas. Unit I, for example, leads us to expect that its successor logically must deal with the topic of Unit II. Unit II.B bears a clear relationship to the materials before it. Unit II.D, to be sure, is clearly out of place and indeed has no self-evident location in our tractate, to which it is irrelevant. Unit III takes up the theme of Unit II.C. Unit II is much larger than the other, equivalent divisions, forming the bulk and center of the entire tractate. The unifying theme of that major unit is the distinctions of various kinds, and by diverse criteria, between water that is purposefully used and that imparts susceptibility to uncleanness, and water that is not purposefully used, or not primary and essential in the accomplishment of one's intention, and that therefore does not impart susceptibility to uncleanness. Have we correctly assigned to Unit II all of its constituent elements? It seems to me difficult to point to more than M. 4:8, possibly also M. 4:9, as not wholly within the limits of the stated theme, and the theme is blatant in all the distinct units. Indeed, the unit is noteworthy for its repetitiousness.

If, then, we were to ask the redactor of the tractate why he has laid things out as he has, how would he explain his results? I think he would tell us he chose Unit II for his center. This is the large and sustained essay on the nature and effect of intention—a worthy centerpiece indeed. Next he added Unit IV on liquids that impart susceptibility to uncleanness, a catalogue. The Unit I finds its way to the head of the sequence, announcing as it does the main theme of the whole, the issue of intention. In sum, he will claim to have given us a structure that opens with a splendid prologue, specifying the problematic of the tractate. There is no way of improving on M. 1:1A-C (+ M. 1:2-4) in this regard (even though, as we observe, it is not wholly *a propos* in the interpretation of all viewpoints supposedly subject to the rule). The Houses' disputes of M. 1:2-4, with their appended materials, M. 1:5-6, thus complete the prologue.

As noted, the prologue is also substantive and central to the tractate as a whole, and I think that is intentional. Then we have a large unit put together primarily because of formal, rather than substantive, redactional principles, which, at other tractates, e.g., Kelim, Ohalot, Negaim, Parah, Miqvaot, Baba Qamma, Shebuot, and Tohorot, we should have expected to find at the outset, as the opening statement. That is to say, the usual prologue, II.A, is a unit developed along wholly formalized lines, complete unto itself, and is in point of fact secondary to the main interests of the tractate. Then the redactor brings us to the complex of cogent and internally closely interrelated materials, M. 3:1-5:8, 5:11J-M, and 6:1-3. These, the justly proud redactor will tell us, then are concluded by a reversion to the theme of what is now the secondary prologue, Chapter Two, that is, liquids that do or do not impart susceptibility to uncleanness.

The ultimate redactor, to be sure, may wonder as we do about the place of materials drawn from M. Tohorot, that is, Unit III. If the materials are purposefully placed where they are, then the purpose should be to provide a concluding appendix. This means that both Unit III and Unit IV are meant as a reprise, in the context of Makhshirin, of grand themes of M. Tohorot, that is, M. 5:9-11, (with M. 6:1-2), bringing us back to M. Toh. 8:8-9, and, for the case of the fruit on the roof, perhaps M. Toh. 9:6. Since the main point for both tractates—Tohorot and Makhshirin—is that liquid that is wanted is susceptible to becoming unclean (Tohorot) or capable of imparting uncleanness (Makhshirin), the point is obvious and appropriate. Had matters been formulated somewhat differently, we should have regarded II.D as integral to III and the whole as aiming at IV. As it is, II.D forms a brilliant exposé of the links between two distinct but related tractates. This fact gives us only a hint as to the true genius of Mishnah's overall redaction. But that is yet another set of problems, I mean, explaining the order and system of Mishnah as a whole, an exquisitely redacted and carefully formulated document of literature and philosophy.

iii. Conclusion

We may now state the topic of the tractate as well as its generative problematic. (1) The *topic* is the character of liquids which to dry produce impart susceptibility to uncleanness. (2) The *problematic* is the effect of one's purpose, will, intention, or plan (however one expresses it) on the capacity of liquid to impart susceptibility to uncleanness.

This is "what the tractate is about," indicated by the character of the shank of the tractate—Unit II—as well as by the prologue, Unit I. So at the very outset (I) the framers of the tractate have announced both their topic and what they wish to know about that topic. They then proceed to present a discourse about their topic that is generated by a very particular matter, relevant, but not intrinsic, to that topic. So the precipitant, the excuse for the tractate is the matter of liquid's wetting down dry produce and rendering it susceptible to the uncleanness imparted by, e.g., a dead creeping thing. But the real purpose of the tractate is to reflect upon the nature and metaphysical effects of the human will. The tractate brings together diverse philosophies of intention (and confirmatory deed) and its power over the workings of the supernatural, above all concerning how we assess and interpret what a person wants to do by reference to what, in fact, he actually has done.

To conclude, I shall set forth the diverse positions taken by the authorities of the tractate on the issues expressed that are provoked by the tractate's generative problematic. Once we have accomplished this last task, we shall know whatever we are ever going to know about the ideas of the tractate, how they are precipitated and then expressed, put together, and organized, into a coherent and remarkably fluent document. This is the final stage in our methodological repertoire: exposing the heart of the matter.

If we begin with the fundamental principle behind the tractate, this: it is (1) that which is given in the name of Abba Yosé-Joshua (M. 1:3M): Water imparts susceptibility to uncleanness only when it is applied to produce intentionally or deliberately. This yields a secondary and derivative rule: (2) 'Aqiba's distinction at M. 4:9 and M. 5:4: Water intrinsic to one's purpose is detached with approval, but that which is not essential in accomplishing one's primary purpose is not under the law, If water be put. What 'Aqiba has done is to carry to its logical next stage the generative principle. If water applied with approval can impart susceptibility to uncleanness, then, it follows, only *that part* of the detached and applied water essential to one's intention is subject to the law, If water be put. Items in the name of second-century authorities that develop 'Aqiba's improvement of Abba Yosé's principle raise an interesting question: (3) What is the relationship between intention and action? Does intention to do something govern the decision in a case, even though one's action has produced a different effect? For example, if I intend to wet down only part of an object, or make use of only part of a body of water, but then wet down the whole or dispose of the whole, is the whole deemed susceptible? Does my consequent action revise the original effects of my intention? Judah and his son, Yosé, take up the position that ultimate deed or result is definitive of intention. What happens is retrospectively deemed to decide what I wanted to happen (see M. 3:5-7). Other Ushans, Yosé in particular (see M. 1:5), maintain the view that, while consequence plays a role in the determination of intention, it is not exclusive and definitive. What I wanted to make happen affects the assessment of what actually has happened.

1. Judah has the realistic notion that a person changes his mind, and therefore we adjudge a case solely by what he does and not by what he says he will do, intends, or has intended, to do. If we turn Judah's statement around, we come up with the conception predominant throughout his rulings: *A case is judged in terms solely of what the person does.* If he puts on water, that water in particular that he has deliberately applied imparts susceptibility to uncleanness. If he removes water, only that water he actually removes imparts susceptibility to uncleanness, but water that he intends to remove but that is not actually removed is not deemed subject to the person's original intention. And, it is fair to add, we know it is not subject to the original intention, because the person's action has not accomplished the original intention or has placed limits upon the original intention. What is done is wholly determinative of what is originally intended, and that is the case whether the result is that the water is deemed capable or incapable of imparting susceptibility to uncleanness.

2. Yosé at M. 1:5 expresses a contrary view. Water that has been wiped off is detached with approval. But water that has remained on the leek has not conformed to the man's intention, and that intention is shown by what the man has actually done. Accordingly,

the water remaining on the leek is not subject to the law, If water be put.

3. Simeon's point at M. 1:6 is that the liquid in the breath or left on the palm of the hand is not wanted and not necessary to the accomplishment of one's purpose. Simeon's main point is that liquid not essential in accomplishing one's purpose is not taken into account and does not come under the law, If water be put. Why not? Because water is held to be applied with approval *only* when it serves a specific purpose. That water which is incidental has not been subjected to the man's wishes and therefore does not impart susceptibility to uncleanness.

Simeon and Yosé deem water to have been detached and applied with approval only when it serves a person's essential purpose, and water that is not necessary in accomplishing that purpose is not deemed subject to the law, If water be put. That is why Simeon rules as he does. Yosé states a different aspect of the same conception. Water that actually has dripped off the leek is in conformity with one's intention. But water remaining on the leek in no way has fallen under the person's approval. This is indicated by the facts of the matter, the results of the person's actual deed.

The net result of this brief review is that the conceptual shank of the tractate Makhshirin is shown to be formed of five successive layers of generative principles, in sequence:

1. Dry produce is insusceptible, a notion which begins in the plain meaning of Lev. 11:34, 37.

2. Wet produce is susceptible only when *intentionally* wet down, a view expressed in gross terms by Abba Yosé as cited by Joshua.

3. Then follow the refinements of the meaning and effects of *intention*, beginning in 'Aqiba's and Tarfon's dispute, in which the secondary matter of what is tangential to one's primary motive is investigated.

4. This yields the contrary views, assuredly belonging to second-century masters, that what is essential imparts susceptibility and what is peripheral to one's primary purpose does not; and that both what is essential and what is peripheral impart susceptibility to uncleanness. (A corollary to this matter is the refinement that what is wet down under constraint is not deemed wet down by deliberation.)

5. The disputes on the interpretation of intention—Is it solely defined by what one actually does or modified also by what one has wanted to do as well as by what one has done?—belong to Yosé and Judah and his son Yosé.

So we see that the paramount theme of the tractate is the determination of the capacity of the eligible liquids to impart susceptibility to uncleanness. The operative criterion, whether or not the liquids are applied intentionally, obviously is going to emerge in every pericope pertinent to the theme.

If we now summarize the central and generative theme of our tractate, we may state matters as follows.

First, liquids are capable of imparting susceptibility to uncleanness only if they are useful to men, e.g., drawn with approval, or otherwise subject to human deliberation and intention. The contrary view is that all liquids without distinction impart susceptibility to uncleanness.

Second, liquids capable of imparting susceptibility to uncleanness do so only if they serve a person's purpose, are deliberately applied to produce, or otherwise irrigate something through human deliberation and intention. The contrary view is that however something is wet down, once it is wet, it falls within the rule of Lev. 11:34, 38 and is subject to uncleanness. With these simple statements in mind, we understand why the tractate takes the shape that it has, and not some other. We know why it asks the questions it does. When we wish to describe what we have seen in our examination of the trees, the groves, and the whole forest, this is what we find to report.

The exegesis of the tractate and the explanation of the methods of exegesis, from individual units to the structure of the tractate as a whole, are now complete. The logically consequent question is why someone should have made up such a tractate, what sort of group will have received it, and, especially, why at just this time— the middle of the second century—will just these issues have appeared to be so urgent and compelling. There are methods for reflecting on these questions and proposing answers to them.[1] But they no longer remain within the narrow limits of the exegesis of

---

[1] My *Method and Meaning in Ancient Judaism, Method . . . Second Series,* and *Method . . . Third Series* (I: Missoula, 1979; II and III: Chico, CA, 1980: Scholars Press for Brown Judaic Studies) carries this matter forward.

the formal and conceptual traits of a single tractate. These other methods draw us toward the structure of a whole division, and, as is clear, of the complete document—not to mention the Israelite intellectual and mythic world in which that document comes to full expression and closure. Having reached the limits of our literary-exegetical methods and fully worked them out in the context of a single, suitable tractate, I have nothing more to say.

But in the future I shall, and I hope others will too. For the approach to the interpretation of a highly formalized and public document such as Mishnah surely is to be adapted for the study of the bulk of the rabbinical literature, most of which shares, in general, the literary traits of Mishnah. When we open the pages of the two Talmuds, of the diverse types of compilations of biblical exegesis called *midrashim,* the Jewish prayerbook, the Siddur, even some of the Targumim, as well as many other documents of ancient Judaism, the first thing we see is the collective, anonymous, formulaic, and highly formalized character of the rabbis' language. The second thing we notice is the hand of the redactors, the people who put together these highly formalized materials into larger conglomerates, even into chapters and tractates. Then as soon as we see these first two traits, we realize that we have to ask in a fresh way those same questions of form, meaning, and context that we raised in explaining Mishnah in this book: What did the person who phrased matters in this way want to tell us? Where do we locate the exegetical fulcrum of his unit of thought? What is the generative problematic behind the document as a whole and its individual parts? How is the document organized? Does the principle or organization reveal something deeper about the intentions of the document's framers? These questions, which we have pursued from the smallest to the largest units of a single tractate, have to be addressed to all of the tractates of Mishnah, to the immense literature created in response to Mishnah as the Talmuds, the *midrashim,* and the rest of the enormous corpus of writings, all of them unsigned, all of them the work of many individuals who insisted on speaking as a group, none of them prepared to admit that he has a single thought "of his own."

One minor question remains. After we have patiently and painstakingly taken up a tractate of Mishnah, pericope by pericope, chapter by chapter, and, finally, the entire tractate, we ought to ask ourselves whether we can now complete that labor of exegesis carried nearly to its conclusion by dealing with *Mishnah as a whole.*

We are able to define a pericope and show how it works. We have the knowledge to locate its exegetical fulcrum. We know how to spell out the logical requirements of its language. So we state the meaning imputed to that language by the people who used it, who phrased their question and their answer in just this way and not some other.

We also are able to define a "chapter." We know how to locate the larger principles behind the arrangement of materials in one group and not in some other.

Finally, we are in a position to specify both how we uncover the generative problematic of a whole tractate and how it accounts for the exegetical treatment of a tractate's topic: one set of problems instead of some other set of problems.

But has all of this new intellectual power given us the capacity to answer the simple question, So if *this* is Mishnah, then *what* is Mishnah? For the net effect of all this work is to make the definition of Mishnah exceedingly difficult.

That is not to suggest Mishnah is unique. If it were unique, we should be unable to study it. For we learn through using what we already know. We build knowledge and understanding by using analogies and contrasts that our mind and imagination provide. What is unique also is unknowable, because it lies beyond the power of analogy and contrast.

Yet what analogy is useful? Mishnah is not a philosophical treatise. What philosopher of metaphysics talks about damp barley and the muzzle of an ox?

Mishnah is not a law-code. Who ever heard of a law code so useless in deciding the concrete law, so repetitious in its structure of problems, and so uninterested in concrete times and places, as this one?

Mishnah is not a school book, for the same reason it is not a law-code or a philosophical treatise. For to whom will someone have wanted to teach these sorts of things? And for what purpose will people have wanted to learn them?

Mishnah is *like* a philosophical treatise, because it takes up a profound issue of interpretation of what it means to be human and of what we are supposed to do. Mishnah is *like* a law-code, because, after all, it does make descriptive-normative statements that tell me the consequences of what I do. Mishnah is *like* a school-book (a textbook, such as this book) because it organizes and teaches knowledge in a systematic and obviously purposive way. It is like all those things, but is not those things.

What we have accomplished is a fresh approach to the interpretation of *a* Mishnah-tractate. What we have not accomplished is to explain what *Mishnah* is. When we ask that question,[2] so different from the questions of this book as to be deemed wholly other and utterly unrelated to what we have done, then we shall hope to have concluded the work that has occupied us here. It is right to end with the question that leads us out of the orbit of this book and its range of discourse: If *this* is Mishnah, then *what* is Mishnah?

---

[2] I do raise it in my *Judaism: The Evidence of the Mishnah* (The University of Chicago Press, 1981).

Glossary

Glossary

'Am ha'ares   In sayings attributed to second-century sages in Mishnah, an *'am ha'ares* (boor, landsman) is one who does not tithe all of his or her food meticulously and does not preserve a state of cultic cleanness when eating ordinary—not consecrated—food. These sources are mainly in Mishnah-Tosefta Demai. See Richard S. Sarason, *A History of the Mishnaic Law of Agriculture*. Part Three. *A Study of Tractate Demai*. Part One (Leiden, 1979: E. J. Brill).

Apocopation   Defined on p. 24.

Apodosis   The predicate of a sentence; the then-clause.

'Aqiba   Mishnaic authority who flourished at the turn of the second century. He is supposed to have been the principal teacher of Judah, Meir, Simeon, and other authorities of the middle of the second century, that is, of the period after the Second War against Rome ("Bar Kokhba's war"), 132-135. In the present tractate, his basic idea is what presents the problems on which the succeeding generations of sages are at work. The picture of 'Aqiba as the thinker who laid forth much of Mishnah's work therefore is accurate, so far as this tractate is concerned.

Attribution   The placing of a saying in the mouth of a named authority. A saying thus is attributed to the person to whose name it is attached by the form, 'WMR, says. Thus *X says* is an attribution.

Clean/unclean   These are translations, for convenience' sake, of THWR, TM'. The meaning is inferred from context. One who is clean/THWR may (1) go to the Temple or (2) eat his cultically clean food at home in a state of personal cultic cleanness. The terms have nothing to do with hygienic cleanness and are solely of a cultic venue.

Collective document   A document lacking the name of a single author and the traits that would indicate that only one person is responsible for the style and even the substance expressed in said document. A collective document is one that avoids indications of individual authorship or authority.

197

Confluence of theme and form	When a given problem, principle, or conception is expressed in a distinctive formal or formulary pattern, which then changes when a new theme, problem, or principle comes to hand, we have a confluence — a flowing together — of theme and form, that is, of what is said and of the formal traits of expression. An intermediate unit of tradition is a set of small units of tradition sharing a single theme and a single formal pattern.
Conglomerate	A group of two or more small units of thought (pericopes/pericopae). Synonym for intermediate unit of tradition.
Connectives	Defined above, at M. 5:10, p. 72. It is the notion that given substances are deemed to form a single object for purposes of measuring volume or for transferring and receiving uncleanness.
Drawn water	Mishnah distinguishes between flowing water and drawn water. Water flowing in its natural condition is not susceptible to uncleanness and has the power to remove an object or a person from the status of uncleanness. Drawn water — that is, water that has been subjected to human intention and deed — is susceptible to uncleanness and is not able to remove an object from the status of uncleanness.
Eleazar	Several sages bear the names Eleazar or Eliezer, variously, but an Eleazar/Eliezer lacking a father's name usually is Eliezer b. Shammu'a, a sage of the period after Bar Kokhba's war.
Eleazar b. 'Azariah	An authority who flourished at the turn of the second century.
Eliezer	In the setting of sayings assigned to an Eliezer and Joshua, the sage under discussion is always Eliezer b. Hyrcanus, who flourished in the last quarter of the first century and is supposed to have been a student of Yohanan ben Zakkai. See my *Eliezer ben Hyrcanus. The Tradition and the Man* (Leiden, 1973: E. J. Brill), I-II.
Eliezer b. Jacob	An authority of the mid second century.
Exegesis/ exegetical	An exegesis is an interpretation of the meaning of a phrase or sentence, an effort to draw out and make explicit what the person who said the sentence wished to say.
Exegetical fulcrum	When we approach a given unit of tradition, we look for the main problem, around which the other difficulties requiring explanation tend to revolve. When we have found what is the heart of the matter, we should be able to solve all the secondary or subsidiary problems of the pericope and so to state what we believe to be the principal point. This I call the exegetical fulcrum — the point, once found, on which to rest so as to move the world.
Ex opere operato	Something that happens all by itself, automatically, without regard to context or circumstance.
Father of Uncleanness	A principal source of uncleanness, for example, a corpse, a menstruating woman, a *Zab*, a *Zabah* (see Leviticus 15:1ff.).
Form	A recurring particle of speech that bears no meaning of itself but imparts meaning to a syntactic construction. A form is exemplified by the particle, 'WMR, which has no concrete meaning but serves only as an attributive.

Formal pattern	The arrangement of words in a single and recurring syntactical pattern, without regard to the meaning of what is expressed, indeed, in avoidance of paying attention to the specificities of meaning. Formal patterns are specified above, pp. 23-25.
Generative problematic	The fundamental question addressed to a given theme or topic that brings into being the specific problems investigated by a given tractate of the Misnah. Defined in context above, pp. 166-167.
Halakhah	A normative statement of how people should behave and of how things truly are. A "law."
Hillel	An authority believed to have lived toward the turn of the first century of the Common Era. See my *Rabbinic Traditions about the Pharisees before 70* (Leiden, 1971: E. J. Brill) I-III.
House of Hillel	Collectivity of authorities supposed to have been the disciples of Hillel. Sayings in the name of the House of Hillel and of the contrapuntal group, the House of Shammai, are collected and interpreted in my *Rabbinic Traditions* II. Many such sayings in fact deal with problems or disputes on principles vivid in the middle of the second century, so the names of the Houses of Hillel and Shammai clearly serve pseudepigraphic purposes. See my *Purities* XVII, *Makhshirin*, pp. 202-222 for discussion of why it is highly likely that the names of the Houses in the present tractate in fact mask the persons of mid-second-century authorities, especially Judah, Meir, Simeon, and the like.
House of Shammai	See above.
Houses, the	See above.
Hypothetical-exegetical reconstruction, etc.	This phrase refers to a method of guessing at the way in which people reached conclusions about the deeper meaning of Scriptural laws, or the secondary or even tertiary meanings to be imputed to them. The *exegetical* part refers simply to interpretation of Scripture. The reconstruction is my own, hence totally *hypothetical*. The mode of thought is very simple. As I have shown in many instances (I refer to my *Method and Meaning in Ancient Judaism. Second Series*, Mishnaic philosophers take for granted that something is either like something else and therefore follows the rules governing that other thing, or it is not like something else, and therefore follows exactly the opposite of the rules governing that other thing. That is what is meant by *analogical* (=like) or *contrastive* (=unlike). By that simple principle we are able to move from Scripture's simple assertions to "facts" imputed or adduced by exegetes at a remove of three, four, or even five stages in reconstructing analogies and opposites. Concrete examples are offered in the reference given above.
Intermediate unit of tradition	A "chapter," defined above, pp. 137-140.
Ipsissima verba	The words actually spoken by a person to whom a saying is attributed; something really said, exactly as the person said it.

"It is [is not] under the law, If water be put"	Formulary allusion to Lev. 11:37-38. Equivalent to saying, It is [is not] susceptible to uncleanness, or, with reference to water, It has [does not have] the power to impart susceptibility to uncleanness.
Joshua	Joshua ben Hananiah, an authority of the last quarter of the first century, associated with Eliezaer b. Hyrcanus and occasionally represented as the master of 'Aqiba.
Judah	Judah b. Ilai, a principal authority of the period after the Second War against Rome, flourished in the second third of the second century. Many of his rulings reveal a clear-cut position that what a person has done defines what that person wanted to do, so that deed is definitive of antecedent intention.
Judah the Patriarch	Generally called simply, "Rabbi," Judah the Patriarch, who flourished at the end of the second and beginning of the third century, is generally credited with having promulgated the redaction and legal authority of the Mishnah. He plays only a small role within the document, though he is cited somewhat more often in Tosefta.
Lemma	A brief saying.
Log, quarter-*log*	A liquid-measure.
Meir	Meir, commonly associated in disputes with Judah, Simeon, and Yosé, is assumed to have flourished in the second third of the second century. In the present tractate he takes up the opposite of Judah's position in the interpretation of the consequences of 'Aqiba's fundamental position, see above, pp. 186-190.
Mishnah	Mishnah is a code of laws, made up by Jewish sages who flourished from before the two great wars against Rome, 66-73 and 132-135, to about two generations thereafter, thus from about 20 to about 200 of the Common Era (= "A.D."). This code of laws covers how Israelite life will be organized in accord with the sanctity of Israel, the Jewish people, the Land of Israel, the Temple and cult of Israel in Jerusalem. The basic idea of Mishnah is that when all things are orderly and well-regulated, each in its place in accord with its own logic, then Israel is at that moment of sanctification of which the priestly code's Creation-myth speaks at Gen. 2:4: *The heavens and the earth were finished and all their host.* Then *God blessed . . . and sanctified. . . .* Mishnah is divided into six divisions: Seeds, or agricultural law, on how crops are to be grown in accord with biblical taboos and how crops are to be taxed and tithed in accord with God's wishes for the poor and the priests; Appointed Times, on how the life of the cult and the village is to be carried on on special, holy days; Women, on how to regulate the transfer of a woman and accompanying property from the father to the husband in a marriage, what is required of a man and a woman when they are married, and how a marriage is dissolved and property disposed of; Damages, on the civil law and government of the Israelite community; Holy Things, on the conduct of the cult on ordinary, everyday occasions and on the maintenance of the Temple buildings; and Purities, on sources of cultic uncleanness, things susceptible to cultic uncleanness, and modes of purification from cultic uncleanness. Each of these six divisions is

divided into tractates, or subdivisions, of which there are sixty-three in all. Mishnah is accompanied, early in its history after it is closed and finished, by a collection of supplements, called Tosefta. Tosefta is organized exactly as is Mishnah and follows its topical outline, down to the individual division of the tractates into chapters, and, normally though not always, even the topical program of chapters. So without Mishnah, Tosefta's supplements mean little. Indeed, Tosefta contains three types of materials, two of them dependent on Mishnah. The first type cites and then simply glosses Mishnah. The second type does not cite Mishnah verbatim but depends upon Mishnah, which is clarified in Tosefta's linguistically autonomous, but conceptually dependent, saying. The third type is relevant to Mishnah's theme but is essentially autonomous of Mishnah. The first two types fill up approximately two-thirds or more of Tosefta.

Pericope	A complete unit of thought, requiring no further information or articulation to spell out its main point; the smallest whole "unit of tradition." Plural: pericopae or pericopes.
Protasis	The if-clause of a sentence; the subject, fully articulated.
Rabbi	See Judah the Patriarch.
Redaction	The work of drawing together completed pericopae into larger groups, ultimately giving essentially final formulation to the chapters and the tractate as a whole; the act of closure.
Shammai	See Hillel.
Shank of a chapter/tractate	The main body of coherent materials of a given chapter or tractate; the mass of related units of tradition/pericopae that form the bulk in volume and the center in conception of a larger unit. The shank of a chapter will be the units of the chapter that bear the burden of expressing the main points therein. The shank of a tractate is the largest conglomerate of materials central to the principal idea or conception of the tractate as a whole.
Sifra	A post-Mishnaic critique of Mishnah's pericopae relevant to the Book of Leviticus, which also serves as a systematic compilation of exegeses of the Book of Leviticus. Sifra repeatedly makes the point that what Mishnah says on topics important to the Book of Leviticus is well founded not on the basis of reason but on the foundation of Scriptural exegesis alone. It therefore takes up a highly critical position on the Mishnah's failure to associate nearly the whole of its conceptions and laws with particular Scriptural exegesis.
Sifré	A parallel commentary on Numbers and Deuteronomy.
Simeon	See Judah, Meir.
Simeon b. Eleazar	An unimportant authority of the middle third of the second century.
Simple declarative sentence	A sentence consisting of a subject and a predicate, or a subject-verb-complement. The subject serves as subject of the verb, the verb then continues the subject and refers to the complement; or the predicate is tightly joined to the subject. All this is in contrast to the apocopated sentence and is defined, in context, above, p. 24f.
Slops	Dirty water, which also is assumed to be unclean. See above, s.v. *clean*.

Superscription	The opening statement of a unit of tradition, when it stands by itself and not as part of a long declarative sentence or an attributed saying, is called a superscription. It serves as the topic sentence of a dispute, or as the opening statement of an undisputed pericope.
Tarfon	An authority of the last third of the first century, often associated in disputes with 'Aqiba, serving as a foil for the latter's genius.
Tosefta	See Mishnah.
Tractate	See Mishnah.
Triplet	A set of three rules that use precisely the same formulary pattern to express precisely the same idea, often in a more complicated way as the repetition proceeds. A triplet should be distinguished from a set of three pericopae in the same formal pattern, e.g., apocopation, and dealing with the same theme, saying pretty much the same thing about that theme. The principal distinction is that the formal traits of a triplet are repeated in the language in which each of the three stichs of the triplet is expressed, so the form is internal, not merely external.
Urine, gentile	Urine of gentiles is a source of uncleanness, that of Israelites is cultically clean.
Usha	See Yavneh.
Yavneh/Usha	Yavneh is a town on the south coast of the Land of Israel, and Usha is a town in Galilee, not far from present-day Haifa. To Yavneh came many of those who survived the destruction of the second Temple in 70, and, there, are supposed to have organized some sort of school or institution. When we speak of "Yavneans," we mean people who flourished in the period after 70. Usha is supposed to have been an equivalent center after the Second War against Rome, and consequently, people who are supposed to have flourished in the period after 140, and the age in which they lived, are called Ushans, and Usha, respectively. These terms are for convenience' sake only. They refer to groups of authorities whose sayings commonly are juxtaposed or joined. Thus we find sayings of Joshua, Eliezer, Tarfon, Gamaliel, 'Aqiba, Yosé the Galilean, commonly drawn together within the limits of a given pericope, but not associated with such names as Meir, Judah, Yosé, and the like ('Aqiba is an occasional exception to this rule). We call "Yavneans" therefore authorities who appear with one another, but never, or hardly ever, with "Ushans." These latter include Simeon, Meir, Yosé, Judah, various Eleazars and Eliezers, Simeon b. Gamaliel, and so on. They then occur with one another, but rarely, or hardly ever, with "Yavneans."
Yosé	See above: Judah, Meir.
Yosé b. R. Judah	The son of Judah, Yosé reworks his father's principles, above, p. 188.
Zab, Zabah	Leviticus 15:1ff. refers to a man or a woman who suffer a genital flux, the woman in a time outside of her regular menstrual period, and these persons are unclean, as specified, for having suffered that flux or unusual genital excretion.

Abbreviations and Bibliography

Abbreviations and Bibliography

Ah.	'Ahilot
Albeck	H. Albeck, *Seder tohorot* (Jerusalem and Tel Aviv, 1958)
Ar.	'Arakhin
A.Z.	'Abodah Zarah
B.	Bavli, Babylonian Talmud
B.B.	Baba' Batra'
B.M.	Baba' Mesi'a'
B.Q.	Baba' Qamma'
Ber.	Berakhot
Bert.	Obadiah of Bertinoro, 1450-1516. Mishnah-commentary, ed. Romm.
Bes.	Besah
Bik.	Bikkurim
C	H. Loewe, *The Mishnah of the Palestinian Talmud (Hammishnah 'al pi ketab-yad Cambridge)* (Jerusalem, 1967)
Dan.	Daniel
Danby	Herbert Danby. *The Mishnah* (London, 1933)
Dem.	Dema'i
Deut.	Deuteronomy
Ed.	'Eduyyot
EG	*Hiddushé Eliyyahu MiGreiditz.* From Mishnah ed. Romm (Vilna, 1887)
Erub.	'Erubin
Git.	Gittin
GRA	Elijah ben Solomon Zalman ("Elijah Gaon" or "Vilna Gaon"), 1720-1797. From Mishnah, ed. Romm (Vilna, 1887), for M. and from standard text of Tosefta Seder Tohorot in Babylonian Talmud, for T.
Hag.	Hagigah
Hai	*Hai Gaon, Perush 'al seder tohorot* (Berlin, 1857), reprint 1970.

205

Hal.

Hallah

HN

Hazon Nahum, Eleazar Nahum. From reprint of Mishnah, ed. Romm

Hoffmann

David Hoffmann, *Mischnajot*. VI. *Ordnung Toharot. Punktiert, ins Deutsche übersetzt, und erklärt* (Third edition: Basel, 1969). From M. Negaim 3:7: John Cohn. From Niddah: Moses Auerbach.

Hor.

Horayot

Hul.

Hullin

Jastrow

Marcus Jastrow, *A Dictionary of the Targumim*, etc. (Reprint: N.Y., 1950)

K

George Beer, *Faksimile-Ausgabe des Mischna-codex Kaufmann A 50* (Reprint: Jerusalem, 1968)

Katsh

Abraham I. Katsh, *Ginze Mishnah. One Hundred and Fifty-Nine Fragments from the Cairo Geniza in the Saltykov-Shchedrin Library in Leningrad* (Jerusalem, 1970), Plates 148-154.

Kel.

Kelim

Ker.

Keritot

Kil.

Kila'yim

KM

Kesef Mishneh. Joseph Karo. Commentary to Maimonides, *Mishneh Torah.* Published in Venice 1574-5. Text used: Standard version of Maimonides, *Mishneh Torah.*

Lev.

Leviticus

Lieberman, *TR*

Saul Lieberman, *Tosefeth Rishonim. A Commentary. Based on Manuscripts of the Tosefta and Works of the Rishonim and Midrashim and Rare Editions.* III. *Kelim-Niddah.* IV. *Mikwaoth-Uktzin* (Jerusalem, 1939). Used: IV, pp. 106-119

Lieberman, *YK*

Saul Lieberman[n], *HaYerushalmi Kifshuto* (Jerusalem, 1934) Part I, Vol. 1

M.

Babylonian Talmud Codex Munich (95). (Reprint: Jerusalem, 1971)

M.

Mishnah

MA

Mishnah Aharonah. Ephraim Isaac of Premysla. Published in 1882. From reprint of Mishnah, ed. Romm.

Ma.

Ma'aserot

Maharam

Meir ben Barukh of Rothenberg (1215-1293). See Sens.

Maimonides, Ed. *Constantinople*

Mishneh torah leharambam. Defus Qušta' [A.M.] *269* [= A.D. 1509]. (Repr. Jerusalem, n.d.)

Maimonides, *Mishnah-Commentary*

Mishnah 'im perush Rabbenu Moshe ben Maimon. Trans. Joseph David Qappah. VI. *Seder Tohorot* (Jerusalem, 1967)

Maimonides, *Uncleanness of Foodstuffs*

The Code of Maimonides. Book Ten. The Book of Cleanness, trans. Herbert Danby (New Haven, 1954), pp. 331-394. Checked against *Mishneh Torah*, ed. Romm.

Mak.

Makhshirin

Me.

Me'ilah

Men.

Menahot

Miq.	Miqva'ot
ML	*Mishneh Lammalekh.* Commentary to Maimonides, Mishneh Torah. Judah Rosannes 1657-1727. For source, see KM
M.Q.	Mo'ed Qaṭan
M.S.	Ma'aser Sheni
MS	Mele'khet Shelomo. Shelomo bar Joshua Adeni, 1567-1625. From reprint of Mishnah, ed. Romm.
N	*Mishnah 'im perush HaRambam. Defus rishon Napoli [5]252* (1492) (Jerusalem, 1970)
Naz.	Nazir
Nid.	Niddah
Num.	Numbers
Oh.	Ohalot
P	*Shishah sidré mishnah. Ketab yad Parma DeRossi 138* (Jerusalem, 1970)
Pa	*Mishnah ketab yad Paris. Paris 328-329* (Jerusalem, 1973)
Par.	Parah
PB	*Mishnah Codex Parma "B" De Rossi 497. Seder Tohoroth.* Introduction by M. Bar Asher (Jerusalem, 1971)
Pes.	Pesaḥim
Purities	J. Neusner, *A History of the Mishnaic Law of Purities* (Leiden, 1974-1977) I-XXII.
Rabad	Abraham ben David. Supercommentary to Maimonides, *Mishneh Torah*
Rabad, *Sifra*	Abraham ben David. Commentary to *Sifra.* From ed. Weiss
R.H.	Rosh Hashshanah
Rosh	Asher b. Yeḥiel, *Commentary to Makhshirin.* For source, see Sens.
San.	Sanhedrin
Segal	M. H. Segal, *Makshirin. Translated into English with Notes,* in I. Epstein, ed., *The Babylonian Talmud. Seder Tohoroth* (London, 1948: The Soncino Press), pp. 463-497
Sens	Samson ben Abraham of Sens, ca. 1150-1230. From reprint of *Mishnah Seder Tohorot* in Babylonian Talmud, ed. Romm. (Vilna, 1887)
Shab.	Shabbat
Sheb.	Shebi'it
Shebu.	Shebu'ot
Sot.	Soṭah
Suk.	Sukkah
T	*Sidré Mishnah. Neziqin, Qodashim, Tohorot. Ketav yad Yerushalayim, 1336. Ketab yad beniqud lefi massoret Teman.* (Reprint: Jerusalem, 1970). Introduction by S. Morag
T.	Tosefta
Ta.	Ta'anit

Tem.   Temurah

Ter.   Terumot

Toh.   Tohorot

Tos. Reng.   Karl Heinrich Rengstorf, ed., *Rabbinische Texte. Erste Reihe. Die Tosefta. Text. Übersetzung. Erklärung. Herausgegeben von Gerhard Kittel and Karl Heinrich Rengstorf. Band 6. Seder Tohorot. Text, Übersetzung, Erklärung.* 3. *Tohorot-Uksin,* edited by Gerhard Lisowsky, Gunter Mayer, Karl Heinrich Rengstorf, and Emanuel Schereschewsky. (Stuttgart, 1953-1967) T. Mak. is the work of Gerhard Lisowsky.

Tos. Zuck.   *Tosephta. Based on the Erfurt and Vienna Codices,* with parallels and variants, by M. S. Zuckermandel (Repr. Jerusalem, 1963).

TR   See Lieberman, *TR*

T.Y.   Ṭebul Yom

TYT   *Tosafot Yom Tob.* Yom Tob Lipmann Heller, 1579-1654. From reprint of Mishnah, ed. Romm.

Uqs.   'Uqsin

V   *Seder tohorot ʿim perush . . . Moshe bar Maimon. Nidpas ʿal yedé Daniel Bomberg bishenat 5282* [= 1522]. *Venezia.* (Venice, 1522. Reprint: Jerusalem, 1971).

Y.   Yerushalmi. Palestinian Talmud

Y.T.   Yom Tob

Yad.   Yadayim

Yeb.   Yebamot

Zab.   Zabim

Zeb.   Zebaḥim

Indexes

General Index

Abba Yosé, intention, use of liquids, 143, 188-89
Abba Yosé Holi Qofri of Tibe'on, intention, use of liquids, 101, 123, 181, 187
Albeck, H., intention, use of liquids, 104, 129-31; secondary use of water, 44, 47-48; steam as connector, 71; water susceptible to uncleanness, 39
'Aqiba, intention, use of liquids, 114-15, 189; liquids imparting uncleanness, defined, 86-88, 161-62, 185; secondary use of water, 61, 67-68, 153-54, 156-57, 183-84, 187-89
Asher b. Yehiel, intention, use of liquids, 98, 104; secondary use of water, 69; water susceptible to uncleanness, 41

Danby, Herbert, incapacity to impart uncleanness, 75; mixing liquids, 33, 37

Eleazar, secondary use of water, 55, 57
Eleazar b. 'Azariah, liquids imparting uncleanness, 82-84
Eliezer, intention, use of water, 113-14; liquids imparting uncleanness, defined, 82
Eliezer b. Jacob, incapacity to impart uncleanness, 78
Elijah ben Solomon Zalman, intention, use of liquids, 99, 110-11, 128, 131, 133; secondary use of water, 47, 54, 68; water susceptible to uncleanness, 40

Heller, Yom Tob Lipmann, incapacity to impart uncleanness, 78
Hillel, House of, intention, use of liquids, 101-106, 108-16, 118, 122-31, 142-44, 181; secondary use of water, 54-57, 67, 152-53, 156, 183
History of ideas, 4-6, 9-16

Incapacity to impart uncleanness, 73-79
Intention, use of liquids, 98-119, 121-34, 181, 187-90

Jastrow, Marcus, secondary use of water, 66
Joshua, intention, use of liquids, 101, 105-106, 114, 123-31, 143, 181, 187, 189
Judah, incapacity to impart uncleanness, 76, 78; intention, use of liquids, 113-15, 134, 190; mixing liquids, 34-36, 38; secondary use of water, 45-48, 149, 152, 182-83; water susceptible to uncleanness, 39-42, 182

Liquids imparting uncleanness, defined, 79-88, 161-62, 185
Literature or linguistics, analysis of, 4-6, 10-13, 15, 18, 20, 23

Maimonides, incapacity to impart uncleanness, 76-77; intention, use of liquids, 98, 101, 109-10, 118, 123, 126-27, 131-33; liquids imparting uncleanness, 80-81, 84-85; mixing liquids, 30-31;

211

Index to Biblical
and Talmudic References